UNIVERSITY OF CAMBRIDGE
ORIENTAL PUBLICATIONS

NO. 17

STUDIA SEMITICA

VOLUME II

UNIVERSITY OF CAMBRIDGE ORIENTAL PUBLICATIONS PUBLISHED FOR THE FACULTY OF ORIENTAL STUDIES

1 *Averroes' Commentary on Plato's Republic*, edited and translated by E. I. J. ROSENTHAL

2 *FitzGerald's 'Salaman and Absal'*, edited by A. J. ARBERRY

3 *Ihara Saikaku: The Japanese Family Storehouse*, translated and edited by G. W. SARGENT

4 *The Avestan Hymn to Mithra*, edited and translated by ILYA GERSHEVITCH

5 *The Fuṣūl al-Madanī of al-Fārābī*, edited and translated by D. M. DUNLOP

6 *Dun Karm, Poet of Malta*, texts chosen and translated by A. J. ARBERRY; introduction, notes and glossary by P. GRECH

7 *The Political Writings of Ogyū Sorai*, by J. R. MCEWAN

8 *Financial Administration under the T'ang Dynasty*, by D. C. TWITCHETT

9 *Neolithic Cattle-Keepers of South India: a Study of the Deccan Ashmounds*, by F. R. ALLCHIN

10 *The Japanese Enlightenment: a Study of the Writings of Fukuzawa Yukichi*, by CARMEN BLACKER

11 *Records of Han Administration*, vol. I, *Historical Assessment*, by MICHAEL LOEWE

12 *Records of Han Administration*, vol. II, *Documents*, by MICHAEL LOEWE

13 *The Language of Indrajit of Orchā*, by R. S. MCGREGOR

14 *Japan's First General Election, 1890*, by R. H. P. MASON

15 *A Collection of Tales from Uji*, by D. E. MILLS

ALSO PUBLISHED FOR THE FACULTY

Archaeological Studies in Szechwan, by T.-K. CHENG

CAMBRIDGE ORIENTAL SERIES

1 *Modern Arabic Poetry: an Anthology*, by A. J. ARBERRY

2 *Essays and Studies presented to Stanley Arthur Cook*, edited by D. WINTON THOMAS

3 *Khotanese Buddhist Texts*, by H. W. BAILEY

4 *The Battles of Coxinga*, by DONALD KEENE

6 *Studies in Caucasian History*, by V. MINORSKY

(This series was first published by Taylor's Foreign Press and then by Vallentine, Mitchell & Co. There was no number 5.)

ERWIN I. J. ROSENTHAL

STUDIA SEMITICA

VOLUME II

ISLAMIC THEMES

CAMBRIDGE
AT THE UNIVERSITY PRESS
1971

Published by the Syndics of the Cambridge University Press
Bentley House, 200 Euston Road, London N.W.1
American Branch: 32 East 57th Street, New York, N.Y.10022

Library of Congress Catalogue Card Number: 70-116836
Standard Book Number: 521 07959 4

Printed by offset in Great Britain
by Alden & Mowbray Ltd at the Alden Press, Oxford

CONTENTS

INTRODUCTION *page* vii

PART I · POLITICAL PHILOSOPHY IN MEDIEVAL ISLAM

1 Ibn Khaldūn: a North African Muslim thinker of the fourteenth century 3
(*Bulletin of the John Rylands Library*, vol.24, no.2, October 1940, pp.307–20)

2 Some aspects of Islamic political thought 17
(*Islamic Culture*, vol.XXII, no.1, January 1948, pp.1–17)

3 The place of politics in the philosophy of Ibn Bajja 35
(*Islamic Culture*, vol.XXV, jubilee number, part I, 1951, pp.187–211)

4 The place of politics in the philosophy of Ibn Rushd 60
(*Bulletin, School of Oriental and African Studies*, vol.XV, no.2, 1953, pp.246–78)

5 The place of politics in the philosophy of Al-Farabi 93
(*Islamic Culture*, vol.XXIX, no.3, July 1955, pp.157–78)

6 Ibn Jaldūn's attitude to the *falāsifa* 115
(*Al-Andalus*, vol.XX, 1, 1955, pp.75–85)

7 The concept of *eudaimonia* in medieval Islamic and Jewish philosophy 127
(*Storia della Filosofia Antica e Medievale*, Firenze, 1960 (Atti del XII Congresso Internazionale di Filosofia, 1958), pp.145–52)

8 Some observations on the philosophical theory of prophecy in Islam 135
(*Mélanges . . . . Henri Massé*, ed. Ali-Akar Siassi. Teheran University, 1963, pp.343–52)

PART II · RELIGION AND POLITICS IN MODERN ISLAM

9 The role of Islam in the modern national State 146
(*The Year Book of World Affairs*, Stevens & Sons Ltd., London, 1962, pp.98–121)

10 Some reflections on the separation of religion and politics in modern Islam 171
(*Islamic Studies* (Karachi), vol.III, no.3, September 1964, pp.249–84)

11 Politics in Islam 207
(*The Muslim World*, vol. LVII, no. 1, 1967, pp. 3–10)

APPENDIX OF ADDITIONAL NOTES 215

INDEX 217

Acknowledgements are due to the editors and publishers of the works listed above for permission to reproduce the papers in this volume.

INTRODUCTION

The collection here offered contains the majority of my contributions to periodicals, *Festschriften*, memorial volumes, and papers read at international congresses. They cover a period of more than thirty-five years and are the result of research in two adjacent, inter-related fields of study: Judaism and Islam. The studies are here distributed over two volumes for the convenience of those readers who are more interested in only one of the branches of Semitic studies. But owing to the languages employed in the various texts upon which the studies are based, as well as to the subject matter, some of the studies included as chapters in volume I could just as well be put as chapters in volume II or vice versa. For the subjects treated are, in fact, closely interconnected both in language and subject matter.

Thus, Arabic language and grammar and lexicography are of great importance for the exegesis of the Hebrew Bible. For the science of Biblical exegesis among the Jews in the Middle Ages and later was decisively influenced under Islam by Arab grammar and lexicography (cf. my *Judaism and Islam*, London and New York, 1961, part two, for a general account), although Hebrew grammatical and interpretative canons go back to the Tannaim and Massoretes. Yet, the decisive development of the literal interpretation of the Hebrew Scriptures to a fine art and a sharp weapon in their defence and for the preservation of a living Judaism began with Saadya Gaon (882–942) whose Arabic Bible translation became authoritative and whose linguistic attainment and commentaries made possible the flowering of Bible study in East and West during the later Middle Ages. For this reason chapters 4 and 5 of volume I are included in that volume: Saadya's literary activity on behalf of Judaism was necessitated as much by the defence of Rabbinic Judaism against Jewish heretics and rationalists as against Muslim and Christian attack. Philosophical Bible exegesis also begins with him under the impact of *Kalām* and reached its peak in the context of medieval Jewish religious philosophy greatly influenced by Islamic philosophy which transmitted and at the same time transformed Greek and Hellenistic philosophy. Chapters 11 and 12 of volume I belong as much, therefore, to volume II ('Islamic Themes'); but since they are concerned with Judaism in the first place they are included in 'Jewish Themes'.

On the other hand, important works of Islamic philosophy are extant—sometimes solely—in Hebrew translations. In the case of Averroes, the Arabic originals of his commentaries on Plato's *Republic* and on Aristotle's *Nicomachean Ethics* have so far not been discovered. Without their Hebrew versions the work of Averroes, the Muslim religious philosopher and the commentator of Aristotle in particular, could not be understood and appreciated. Since his *Commentary on Plato's 'Republic'* forms an integral part of his thought—together with those on Aristotle's *Corpus* and with his extant philosophical–theological writings—volume II, chapter 4, partly based on it, belongs to 'Islamic Themes'.

In passing it may be noted that volume II, chapter 3 is an extension of my earlier study 'Politische Gedanken bei Ibn Bâǧǧa' (in *Monatsschrift für Geschichte und Wissenschaft des Judentums*, 1937) which, in the absence or through inaccessibility of the Arabic originals, was based on their Hebrew translations and is not included in the present collection. The Hebrew translations of some of Alfārābī's political writings are also not without value for a better understanding of his thought.

So far, we have mainly touched on the linguistic connection between the two volumes. Of greater significance is undoubtedly their thematic interrelatedness. Jewish philosophy within the limits of normative Judaism begins much earlier, with Philo of Alexandria who already clearly recognized the fundamental problem posed—by untrammelled rational inquiry—to a religion centred in a law for which divine revelation is claimed and which is thereby perfect, immutable and permanently valid and obligatory. In that it is far superior to and divided from the *nómos*, the man-made law of Greek philosophy. In the Middle Ages no less the confrontation between revelation and reason principally took the form of the contrast between divine and human law in both Islam and Judaism. The occasion for its emergence in Judaism was—apart from Saadya and a few other Jewish thinkers in the Muslim East—the living contact of Jewish thinkers with Islamic philosophy in Muslim Spain. The common ground between Jewish and Islamic philosophy and between both and Greek–Hellenistic philosophy was the concept of law and its basis in justice, the foremost virtue in state and society. It was this concept which secured to Greek–Hellenistic philosophy an entry into Islam and Judaism.

The study of the political philosophy of Plato and Aristotle enabled the *falāsifa*—on the basis of the religious and political unity of Islam as faith and a way of life—to see more clearly the political character and significance of the *Sharī'a* of Islam and, in turn, enabled the Jewish religious philosophers—

despite the absence of an independent Jewish polity—to see, with the help of these *falāsifa*, the political significance of the Torah. The *falāsifa* had the difficult task to reconcile not only the demands of the *Sharīʿa* with a very different political reality, but also with the metaphysics of Aristotle and with the political philosophy as expressed in his *Nicomachean Ethics* and even more in Plato's *Republic* and *Laws*. To some extent, Messianism with its promise of a restored, ideally just and perfect Jewish polity took for the Jewish philosophers the place of the actual and ideal Islamic state of the *falāsifa*. (We are not concerned with the theory of the *khilāfa* as part of the *Sharīʿa* in this context, but rather with the *Sharīʿa* and Torah in relation and contrast to the *nómos* of Plato and Aristotle.) As is clear from volume II, chapters 3–5, there is neither uniformity of attitude among these three Muslim philosophers nor absence of ambiguity or inconsistency in their utterances. But despite the brilliantly argued plea for the primacy of philosophic truth and the subordination of religion to philosophy in the case of Alfārābī and Averroes I still hold to my basic position—at any rate with regard to Averroes—while in the case of Alfārābī a fresh attempt must be made since we now have a critical edition of his *K. al-milla al-fāḍila*. Briefly this position is that I am convinced, from my reading of the relevant texts and from the standpoint of Islam, that rationalism with its sovereignty of human reason is not reconcilable with Muslim (or Jewish) faith in the Middle Ages. I would term the position of, say, Averroes and Maimonides, intellectualism. The difference between rationalism and intellectualism in the Middle Ages is that the latter starts from the sovereignty of God and the primacy of revelation and his law. Rationalism does not restrict free, independent rational speculation and does not exempt the prophetic nature and activity of Moses and Muḥammad respectively from the psychological theory of prophecy and from the other prophets. Certain religious doctrines must be accepted by all believers, elite and masses alike. Hence, the ideal religious state and its law—*Sharīʿa* or Torah—are superior to and not identical with the ideal *pólis* and its *nómos*. A closer study of Alfārābī's *k. al-milla* and a comparison of it with his other political writings *may* result in a modification of my views. In my *Political thought in medieval Islam* (p. 163) I left open a decision whether Alfārābī understood the concept of the future life in the traditional Muslim or in the esoteric, philosophical sense. At present I still doubt the correctness of applying esotericism to the interpretation of religious philosophers who were, to my mind, Muslims or Jews first and disciples of Plato and Aristotle and their successors in Hellenistic philosophy second, certainly in political philosophy. It all depends on whether the *Sharīʿa* was accepted as superior to the *nómos* or identified with it as only equal. As long as those living under the *Sharīʿa* or the Torah hold that only divine law guarantees man the Highest Good as the aim of politics in the shape of well-being in this world and happiness in the next it seems difficult to maintain the primacy of philosophic truth which is accessible to the metaphysician exclusively. For religion and philosophy teach the same truth, only by different means. It is true that the love of God as the realization of man's Highest Good is the highest stage in the quest for happiness, above and beyond the knowledge of God (cf. volume I, chapter 13), but this is still within intellectualism, to my mind, and, although the *amor Dei intellectualis* is clearly reserved for the intellectual elite and out of reach of the masses, all believers can reach their respective stages of happiness through obedience to the divine law: the Jew by fulfilling the commandments (*miṣwōth*), and the Muslim by observing the *Sharīʿa*. Averroes did not for nothing reproach Plato that he neglected the third estate.

Thus, in a very real sense, the philosophical interpretation of Scripture is only a part of the paramount demand on all believers to acquire *ʿilm*, knowledge (which includes philosophy for the intellectual elite), and at the same time to live the commandments of religion (*ʿamal*), that is, intellectual understanding and ethical behaviour.

Thus political philosophy in medieval Islam and Judaism is only a special application and extension of Scriptural exegesis which also lies at the root of volume II, chapters 9–11, posing the question of the nature of Islam and its place in a modern national state.

In volume I, chapters 3 and 6–9 are extensions of Jewish Biblical exegesis into the question of Jewish–Christian relations centred in Biblical exegesis, or at least starting from it. Chapters 3, 6 and 7 deal with a special aspect of this Jewish exegesis in that they trace its presence in the English Bible culminating in the Authorized Version (the King James Version) and its impact on sixteenth-century Christian Hebraists. *Hebraica Veritas* was their battle-cry, and in their attempt to establish it and to secure through it the Word of God and the Reformation they made good use of Jewish exegesis. Since the concept of *Hebraica Veritas* is closely linked with the principal question at issue between Christians and Jews, namely, who was the *Verus Israel*, the adherents of the Old or the New Covenant, these chapters are part of the wider complex of the 'dialogue' between the Church (both Catholic and Protestant) and the Synagogue. As such, it begins with the Church fathers, as is well known. But it reached new heights in the later Middle Ages, thanks to the refinement of Biblical exegesis, chiefly characterized by the plain meaning of Scripture on which the Jews took their stand against a militant Church trying to convert them to the Christian faith. This 'dialogue' is not confined to the commentary literature (with which chapters 3 and 6–8 are chiefly concerned), but extends to religious disputations forced by the Church on the Jews and is never free from polemic and apologetic. Hence, we cannot expect a real dialogue which can only take place on the basis of the equality of both partners. These disputations, together with polemical writings by Jews, including an attack upon the New Testament, are adduced—in addition to medieval Jewish Bible commentaries and views of religious philosophers—in chapter 9, a contribution to a composite work *Kirche und Synagoge*. The subtitle of this work—'A Handbook on the history of Christians and Jews'—reflects its concern with Christian–Jewish relations from New Testament times to 1930. The story of these relations is amply documented with source material in translation.

My chapter is called '*Jüdische Antwort*' because the Jews were throughout on the defensive and wrote in the first place an 'answer to the Christians' (chapter 8) in defence of Judaism and in order to fortify and encourage the Jews to remain loyal to their ancestral faith, the continuing valid truth of which they staunchly maintained. The Christians naturally insisted on having the only true faith and, largely with the help of Jewish converts to Christianity, hoped to convince the Jews by challenging them to answer specific questions. The questioners at these disputations supported their contention that Jesus was the Messiah promised in the Old Testament with arguments taken from the haggadic (i.e. non-preceptive) part of Talmud and Midrash. The Jews not only denied these claims, taking their stand on the non-obligatory character of stories as opposed to the obligatory part in form of laws and regulations, but tried—though in vain—to bring the discussion round to the nature of God. For they denied the doctrine of the Trinity and with it the divine nature of Jesus Christ. For the Jews, the messianic prophecies in the Old Testament were not fulfilled during the Second Commonwealth—in the lifetime of Jesus—but the Messiah was still to come. Nor would they agree that the New Covenant had superseded and annulled the Old: the Torah was God's perfect revelation through Moses and retained its validity and obligatory character to the end of time.

These basic differences in attitudes and the consequent understanding of the Bible—for the Jews Holy Writ, the perfect, complete and eternally valid revelation of God, for the Christians the Old Testament as an integral part of Holy Writ, incomplete, but completed and fulfilled in the New Testament through the life and death of Jesus Christ—are treated at length. It is to be noted that the Jewish answer is neither an academic exercise nor a purely literary activity of the learned. It has its place in the daily struggle for Jewish survival, its *Sitz im Leben*, of which it is the literary expression. This is made clear in volume I, chapter 8, illustrated from certain literary expressions. '*Jüdische Antwort*' places this literary war in the context of the social and economic life of medieval Jewry no less than in that of the relentless missionary activity of the Church which reached its climax in the so-called religious disputations forced on an unwilling Jewry at bay. In fact, these disputations were little less than trials of people accused of blindness and obstinacy. The Jewish spiritual leaders were summoned before a tribunal consisting of the highest dignitaries of Church and State who employed Jewish converts to Christianity in their intimidating attempt—in the form of question and answer—at convincing the leaders of the truth of the Christian interpretation of the messianic prophecies of the Old Testament so that they would have to abandon their (Jewish) interpretation, acknowledge the Christian truth and draw the logical and moral consequences: conversion of their own person together with the Jewish masses whom they led and represented. It is not without significance that the Church chose this unequal contest at least partly as a means—hoped to be effective and successful—to combat and eradicate judaizing tendencies among its heretical adherents.

Apart from the theological 'dialogue' political and economic pressure became stronger and more dangerous. The necessary, but odious Jewish occupations of moneylending and taxfarming, combined with uncertainty of the right of domicile, the threat of expulsion and repeated exactions of heavy taxes and special payments for the privilege to exist and earn a living, made the Jewish position ever more precarious. Church and State combined in harassing the Jews who aroused the hostility of the Christian masses with the result that conversions to Christianity increased with increasing pressure and had a demoralizing effect which cramped the mental and physical powers of those called upon to answer Christian attack and argument.

Naturally, this state of affairs is more hinted at than openly reflected in the vast commentary literature which was obviously determined by the Biblical texts which the Jews had to interpret in defence against Christian claims that the promised Messiah had already come in the person of Jesus, son of God, whose advent had superseded and annulled the Law of Moses. The medieval Jewish commentators had recourse to the plain meaning of Scripture with the help of grammatical accuracy and historical argument. The religious philosophers, particularly Saadya, Maimonides and Albo, one of the Jewish leaders at Tortosa, whose views are adduced in extensive quotations, mainly relied on logic in their exposition of the simple, absolute unity of God making full use of philosophical arguments borrowed from Aristotle. The argument from history is also employed, alongside with that from personal experience. The anti-anthropomorphism is naturally very much to the fore in the refutation of the divine–human nature of Jesus Christ, and Maimonides in particular is at pains to demonstrate the untenability of the doctrine of the Trinity or Tri-unity with the help of his distinction between God's essence and his attributes which are attributes of action, not of essence. (In this connection the rigorous exercise of censorship by the Christian authorities deserves mention since we can often only discover the true, full meaning of his views, and those of the Bible commentators, thanks to the chance survival of uncensored manuscripts.)

As far as the religious disputations at Paris, Barcelona and Tortosa are concerned, reliable evaluation of their arguments is somewhat hampered by the paucity of full Hebrew reports. This applies in particular to Tortosa of which disputation we have a Hebrew report only of the first five of sixty-nine sessions, but a full Latin protocol. The theological argument apart, we learn a good deal about large-scale conversions of Jews after the several sessions, about the state of mind—anxiety and uncertainty—and the difficult physical condition of the Jewish learned 'participants'.

Of the polemical writings a treatise by Efodi demands special attention since it is directed against the New Testament and shows an understanding of Christian doctrines, especially of the Trinity and of the Transubstantiation, much more profound than anything Jews have written before and for a long time after him. This work deserves detailed examination. Lastly, Isaac Troki's treatise is briefly discussed which does not advance beyond Efodi's, but is important since it reflects the attitude of protestantism at the end of the sixteenth century (which is, however, no different from that of the Catholic Church). It was widely read and overshadowed Efodi's tract written almost 200 years earlier before the invention of printing. Moreover, Efodi is still in the direct line of polemicists who had to face up to the fact that even their personal friends forswore the faith of their fathers. The point was made before that the Christian 'questions' were put by Jewish converts to the dominant religion in the majority of cases which embittered the Jewish defenders and sharpened the polemic between Jews and Christians in the late Middle Ages.

It was thought advisable to give this rather fuller summary of volume I, chapter 9, because it is written and republished in German as part of a German publication which is directly concerned with a real dialogue on equal terms in the wider context of the self-critical examination of Christian–Jewish relations in the new Germany after the disastrous Hitler regime.

Today, when a real dialogue is being attempted, the arguments put forward by medieval Jews having to face the combined might of the Church and State in adverse circumstances are still worth consideration. For they demonstrate the theological irreconcilability of the Jewish truth and the Christian truth. Yet, at a time when organized religion—be it Judaism, Christianity or Islam—is fighting for its very life it *may* be possible to come together on the ethical plane, eschewing doctrinal differences. For today, as in the Middle Ages, in the Reformation and since, logic is not always the best guide and persuader where faith and 'ideology' are concerned.

This lesson is also clear from volume I, chapter 14, since the New Jewish Learning (*Wissenschaft des Judentums*)—exemplified in Ismar Elbogen—arose in a 'liberal' age against the background of the Enlightenment and the French Revolution at first in support of the emancipation of the Jews and their civic equality. It applied to the sources of Judaism the literary and historical criticism of modern Europe and presented Judaism as a rational faith in our time. In this necessary task the *Wissenschaft des Judentums* could not always free itself from polemic and apologetic because it has its *Sitz im Leben*: the equality of Jewish citizens of a national secular State whose majority are Christians, be they believers or not. Whether it has succeeded to supply the essential intellectual affirmation of faith (other than orthodox, traditional Judaism) is still an open question.

Islam is today faced with the same problem: the acute crisis of Faith. The secularization of Islam is as serious a danger to its meaningful survival as a force in the modern national States of Muslims which have arisen from the end of the First World War onwards, as is that of Judaism and of Christianity. This serious problem is at the root of the three last chapters of volume II, the last of which was originally intended by the editor of *The Muslim World* as an introduction to a special issue of the journal (hence, its brevity).

All the studies are here reprinted in a facsimile of their original form, and their original pagination is included at the foot of pages, in brackets, to enable the reader to follow up cross references within individual chapters (continuous pagination for each of the volumes precedes this original pagination). Owing to the technical process of production only misprints could be corrected and it was not possible to make the transliteration of Hebrew and Arabic uniform throughout both volumes. But there should be at least uniformity in the individual chapters. A few additions, mostly of a bibliographical nature, have been printed in an appendix at the end of each volume: reference to an additional note in the appendix is indicated in text or footnotes by the use of a dagger symbol.

It is my pleasant duty to thank the Publications Committee of the Faculty of Oriental Studies, Cambridge University, and in particular, its chairman, Mr E. B. Ceadel, for agreeing to republish the twenty-five studies in book form. I should also like to thank those concerned with the production of these two volumes for their care and understanding help.

E.I.J.R.

Pembroke College, Cambridge
August 1969

PART I

POLITICAL PHILOSOPHY IN MEDIEVAL ISLAM

I

IBN KHALDŪN: A NORTH AFRICAN MUSLIM THINKER OF THE FOURTEENTH CENTURY

IBN KHALDŪN (1332-1406) was an exceptional man, and writer, and cannot easily be fitted into the Mediæval order of things. The last decade has seen a number of studies devoted to the description of this fascinating personality. All these attempts at assigning Ibn Khaldūn his exact position within the intellectual development, his place among the world's thinkers, have focussed attention upon a particular aspect of his teaching according to the particular approach and interests of the various writers.

It may therefore not be out of place if we attempt, in a brief essay, to map out the characteristic ideas which Ibn Khaldūn develops in the Introduction (*muqaddima*) to his Universal History (*kitâb al-ʿibar*). We may be permitted to refer the reader to our earlier study on *Ibn Khaldūn's Gedanken Ueber den Staat* [1] for a detailed discussion, with extensive quotations, of what is given in the following pages. We begin by asserting again that Ibn Khaldūn was a Muslim, and must be seen against the background of Mediæval Islam if we are to understand his teaching.[2] For, if we tear him away from his spiritual background, we cut loose his roots and are apt to lose ourselves in an historically dubious and unjustifiable modernisation by attaching to him labels taken from modern economics and sociology. It

[1] *Beiheft 25 der Historischen Zeitschrift*, R. Oldenbourg (München/Berlin, 1932). To the Bibliography given there must be added: G. Bouthoul, *Ibn-Khaldoun, sa philosophie sociale* (Paris, 1930).†

[2] Cp. Professor H. A. R. Gibb's critical long review of my monograph in *The Bulletin of the School of Oriental Studies*, 1933, under the title: "The Islamic Background of Ibn Khaldūn's Political Theory."

cannot, however, be denied that there are to be found in his *muqaddima* striking parallels with the teachings of representative European thinkers from the eighteenth century onwards. But we must beware of seeing in Ibn Khaldūn an actual precursor of these thinkers and their systems as a whole, be they Vico, Comte, Hegel, Marx or Spengler. These parallels, on the other hand, are no mere coincidence. They testify to the premature birth of modern scientific inquiry into the human *group* rather than into the individual, and as such they are highly significant for the history of the human mind. But we must not forget that in the fourteenth century they are erratic, and not an organic growth of the modern age. Their emergence was possible in a time of transition, when the Mediæval order gave way, gradually, to a new grouping of political, economic and spiritual forces. They are the result of a method unparalleled in these days and commonly attributed to the age of the Renaissance: empiric observation by an impartial intellect. If a comparison must be made, we can still think of no closer parallel in matters political than Macchiavelli, though even so the differences between the two thinkers are considerable.[1] Yet, there is in Ibn Khaldūn many a characteristic feature of the Renaissance: his quest for empirical truth, his political activity often so reminiscent of the Condottiere, his humanistic conception of culture and civilisation. With such like traits he reaches out from his Islamic root and environment. Islam, for him, is the choicest fruit of a God-guided and Godward-directed human effort to give a community a lasting spiritual content, a complete answer to all the problems of life. At least in theory, it furnishes the complete answer to his empirical inquiry into the organisation of the human race.

But he was not only a Muslim judge, he was also a statesman and a scholar. Gifted with shrewd insight into the world as it is, he constructed a theory of the origin, growth and development of human society organised in a state invested with power and authority. This theory is seemingly unorthodox, even irreligious, and certainly not at one with the rules for political organisation

[1] I cannot repeat here what I have discussed at length in my above-mentioned monograph.

laid down by the *Shari'a*, the revealed " Canon Law " of Islam, nor with the Ideal State of the *Falasifa* after the model of Plato's *Politeia*.† Thus, though starting from Islamic States of his own experience, he transcends the confines of Islam and tries to establish general principles and rules which should be applicable to every human group. The Islamic State, based on the ideal *Shari'a*, is outside his inquiry. Its principles and rules are described by Al-Mawardi, often quoted by Ibn Khaldūn whenever he describes Islamic institutions like the Chalifate, Imamate, and other offices of State.[1] As a realist and empiricist, he looks at the political order of his day and tries to discover its underlying principles which he, then, extends to any and every state founded by man and maintained by human law. He thus arrived at creating a New Science, that of History, which comprises human society as a whole and its achievement in culture and civilization which he terms *'Umrân*. This is the great, new object of his searching inquiry.

It is of no serious consequence that Ibn Khaldūn bases his theory of human civilisation exclusively on the history of the Arabs, and in particular on that part of it which he helped to shape himself, North Africa. He uses other material only as far as his vast knowledge of every available Arabic source offered him. If we only realised that the differences between Islam, Christianity and Judaism in the Middle Ages are much more of a theological nature than that they vitally affected the common outlook on a life, starting from, centring in and leading to God, we should not see in Ibn Khaldūn's neglect of the history of Christian Europe such a serious defect. (Needless to say, that geographical factors, political situation and characteristics of the respective populations play an important part in these differences.) True, he generalises exclusively on information supplied by the Islamic world he lives in. But his frank criticism of Arab faults and defects, chiefly in the sphere of Empire building and maintaining, should be sufficient proof that the admittedly limited material enabled a man who was trained in Greek philosophy,

[1] Cp. on Al-Mawardi the careful, instructive study by Professor H. A. R. Gibb in *Islamic Culture*, Vol. XI, 3, 1937, under the title " Al-Mawardi's Theory of the Khilafah."

Muslim traditional sciences, and the practical art of government, to arrive at his conclusions concerning the unalterable laws which underlie the course of events. Moreover, the political reality which was the object of his inquiry as a phenomenon of human nature was not more or differently affected by Christianity than by Islam. The State as it is, not as it ought to be, was the object of his searching inquiry. And his own observations of this institution supplied him with the laws and principles he formulated. He was neither a cynic nor a romantic, neither an activist nor a fatalist: he was a realist. And futile and cumbersome as dabbling in politics must have appeared to the scholar in him, he could not help trying his hand at the game. But an ardent desire to get at the laws of political calculation and intrigue, of administration and strategy rather than personal vanity and lust for power seem to have prompted him. He was first and foremost a scholar. Only so can we understand that though a successful ambassador, a negotiator of skill and ability, a statesman at the heart of the political administration, a capable general, he was not interested in reform. His self-appointed task was to find out empirically the laws underlying that process which is called history. As a scholar he diagnosed. He was neither a healer nor a reformer. There is no reason to style him a fatalist *qua* Muslim. He discovered that the laws governing human society organised into political entities are as unalterable as those of human nature. He saw his task in establishing these laws, and by his success he became the first thinker to include the whole of society in a scientific inquiry. At the same time, he subjected the organisation of society, the State, to a hitherto unknown investigation, as he did not start from any presuppositions of a religious or moral order. For he assigned to the State a life of its own, independent of any external laws. It follows its own laws like any other natural phenomenon. That he was a Muslim did not affect his formulations, though the scene of his disinterested observations was naturally the Islamic Empire. Being intensely interested in the origin and progress of human society, he looked for and found its laws. What puzzles and often misleads his readers into doubting his " orthodoxy " is that he arrived at his views of the independence and self-sufficiency of the political order, the State, quite apart from the *Sharīʿa.* The State has its laws in itself. To found and maintain a State can be quite independent of any religious foundation and contents. The natural requirements of human life necessitate association and organisation backed by force and authority. This is not to say that a religious State does not exist, still less that a religious State is not vastly superior to a human creation. It is nothing but a statement of fact—not touching the higher existence of a religious State—based exclusively on experience. It does not pronounce upon the qualities, merits or demerits of the secular as against the religious State. Valuation is quite alien to Ibn Khaldūn. But he leaves no doubt that the Islamic State (for him identical with the religious State) is superior to the political State, as the former has man's happiness in the future world at heart whilst the latter cares only for his material well-being in this world. Herein he agrees with the Muslim (and Jewish) philosophers, but it is outside his interests, which are centred on the real State, founded on force and power and maintained by laws agreed upon by the " citizens " of the State and backed by an authority vested in a ruler who relies on his army to guarantee order and security within and protection against enemies from without. But whenever he discusses Islamic institutions he sides with unimpeachable orthodox tradition. This can be gathered nowhere better than from his attack—completely in the vein of Al-Ǵazzālī—on philosophy by stressing the futility and obvious shortcomings of metaphysics as against the superior revealed truth of Islam, the certainty of faith as against the fallacious probability of human reason and its inadequacy to explain things out of human reach. Moreover, he was by nature an empiricist, and thus averse to speculation. Besides, he was not primarily interested in the individual soul and its perfection and happiness ; his main interest centred round the group, the community of individuals organised in the State. As a Muslim he naturally realises the impact of Islam on individual and collective life alike, and he avers more than once in unequivocal terms (strikingly reminiscent of Macchiavelli) the absolute necessity of religion for a really united and effective State. But it is the State he has in mind, not the revealed truth of Islam.

How does he build up his theory, and how does he conceive of society?

Sound observation of the successive North African dynasties which he served taught him two things before all: First, human groups organised in a State are natural phenomena like human beings and like them pass through the stages of birth, growth, decline and death. Secondly, the various stages of such an organic life follow each other after an appointed order with clock-like regularity. Law, the law of cause and effect, not arbitrariness, rules individual and group life alike. This law derives from human nature, and is unalterable. Human nature demands association and organisation in a political State, as we remarked before. The State is like a living organism, and its life proceeds in cycles. Authority in the State results from a powerful family founding a dynasty. State and dynasty are, however, not identical, for dynasty may give way to dynasty without upsetting the fabric of the State. The State is the frame within which human activity can unfold itself in building that culture and civilisation to describe which is Ibn Khaldūn's aim in writing his History. He is—at least in theory and in his *muqaddima*, yet strangely enough not in the actual historical narrative—not satisfied with the old method of the chronicler to furnish data and confine his task to narrating the actual events. His purpose is to make events intelligible by establishing their cause and by relating them to the driving forces of human endeavour and achievement, and taking into account climatic and geographical factors. For the first time, thus, he discovers *one* leading principle, one guiding central idea in the process, decreed by nature, of associating men into political groups guaranteeing their lives and releasing their faculties for material civilisation and more permanent spiritual values, forming what we are accustomed to term culture. This driving force he sees in the *'Aṣabiyya*, the common bond uniting members of one family, one tribe, one nation, and driving them to corporate action on behalf of the community thus bound. It is the only politically creative factor, bestowing authority upon the chosen leader of a group and giving him the necessary support for action through his kinsmen imbued with the same ideal. To conceive of such a force was possible only for an Arab, proud of his noble descent, who traced his ancestors in Yemen back to the times of Muhammad, whom they helped and served. But *'Aṣabiyya* is more than a blood tie, though this is its nucleus in the beginning. It soon incorporates a common ideal, such as, e.g., the idea of *Djihâd*, Holy War, and Islam, in particular, has transformed and often supplanted it through its call to propagate and spread the true faith by sword and persuasion. We are not concerned here with the curious rivalry, and at the same time complementary nature of religion and *'Aṣabiyya.* This belongs to a special study such as I have given in my monograph referred to at the outset. Suffice it to say that the two spiritual forces are complementary rather than exclusive of each other. That Ibn Khaldūn stresses the one rather than the other is due to his standpoint at the time. If he discusses a political institution within Islam he naturally speaks of an *'Aṣabiyya* coloured with religious enthusiasm, and sees often *'Aṣabiyya* as the united response to the religious call. But he is not blind to two facts: First, that in a State based on revelation, *'Aṣabiyya,* though indispensable, is subordinated to the religious ideal which it helps to realise itself and which cannot realise itself without it. Secondly, he knows that *'Aṣabiyya* can very well bring into existence a purely political State based on power and conquest with the sole purpose of establishing dominion and domination. But he would not be a Muslim if he did not realise that sheer power is not sufficient to maintain and develop dominion, and that one single *'Aṣabiyya* is not capable of constant regeneration to be powerful enough to rally sufficient force round the holders of power and authority. It is here that religion steps in and gives the original *'Aṣabiyya* its creative contents and sustaining impulse. But on psychological grounds he saw that *'Aṣabiyya*, an active, fighting ideal gives way, though only gradually, to obedience. And prolonged obedience is often detrimental to manliness and active courage. This question of individual will-power and striking force is bound up with the second factor which Ibn Khaldūn discovered as making history: the contrast between the free, self-relying life in the country (both desert and arable lands) and the peaceful protected life in towns. The Arab and soldier in him made him insist on the natural superiority—as far as manly qualities are concerned—of the life of *bâdiya* or *badâwa*, the rural mode, over against the sedentary town life with its more refined manners and corresponding callings of artisans and merchants. It is wrong to make Ibn Khaldūn despise the civilised life (*ḥadâra*). He is far from deploring a natural process which stands under the unalterable law of human nature. Nor does he see in the necessary transition from the *badâwa* to the *ḥadâra* a deterioration and distortion. It is for him as necessary as the change from night to day. It carries with it all the potentialities of human progress and cultural advance, and follows logically from man's desire to satisfy his higher ambitions of an intellectual and æsthetic order after the necessities of life have been guaranteed. This inherent urge in human nature for the true and beautiful cannot be kept back. It makes a clear advance over the food-gathering and food-producing stage of the more primitive, animal type of man. But the advance is only possible after the sure foundations of an agricultural community have been laid and developed. He may have considered the tribal community with the *sheikh* as the *primus inter pares* as the Golden Age, but he was realist enough not to mourn the loss of this first stage of human association which had, of necessity, to give way to the second stage: the founding of a State with a capital and a ruling dynasty.

The transition from the *sheikh* to the founder and first ruler of a dynasty with their following is the result of the psychological urge for improved conditions. Again, of necessity it soon gives way to the establishment of absolute rule of a sovereign, since the founder emancipates himself from his associates in matters of political leadership and administration. At this stage only can we speak of a State in the strict sense, i.e. after sovereignty has been established and all authority is vested in the hands of one man.

Before following up the political process, it is to be noted that the distinction drawn between *badâwa* and *ḥadâra* is of far-reaching importance. *Badâwa*, to emphasise it once more, comprises the various stages of a life representative of desert-dwellers, nomads, cattle breeders and cultivators of the soil, whereas *ḥadâra* denotes urban life and civilisation. Yet, these descriptions are only approximate, as they are actually almost untranslatable terms, like *'Aṣabiyya.* For it marks the decisive dividing line in the progress of human organisation and advance. As this organisation is subjected to the natural law of generation and decay, the development is a natural and necessary one; no valuation can enter, for each stage represents a necessary step in a development, and is in itself as good as the next stage, not morally, of course, but justified by its necessity. Man passes through a process in the course of which he loses qualities which are excellent in themselves but must not be valued in the absolute, but rather seen in relation to the respective stage of that society of which man is a member. Therefore, if the characteristics of the first stage in the laborious process of human civilisation are manly courage, fierce independence, and ever-vigilant watch over freedom of action and self-protection and self-reliance, which get lost in the change-over to fenced-in towns, where a particular class, the soldiers, undertake the function of protection of all citizens, this is a natural process which cannot be reversed. In exchange, man develops other qualities: no longer forced to defend himself against enemies in the open country his abilities for making peaceful instruments are released. He becomes a craftsman and artisan, or a trader and merchant and contributes towards raising the standard of living as well as the ways of dwelling and clothing. The arts and sciences receive a great stimulus from the court and those near it, and hand in hand with the material civilisation there develops a culture worthy of the name. And yet, just as the *bâdiya*-life carried the germs of destruction in itself, so civilisation and culture breed their own decline in the natural development to luxury and ease and in their train moral laxity and depravity, until decay sets in, ending in a dissolution of the formerly healthy society which gradually becomes corrupted and hurries to its extinction.

Ibn Khaldūn states these facts, arrived at by impartial inquiry, and by doing so he has fulfilled but one part of his set task: to describe the process of history as an ever-returning cycle the necessity of which is prescribed by nature, wherefore we have to accept it. But he goes deeper than this by asking for the reasons of this eternal movement. Generally speaking, he finds the answer in human nature with its manifold desires and aspirations. From his own experience of history in the making he generalises and perhaps unifies and simplifies a little too much, prompted by a truly scholarly motive: the quest for an underlying law to which all phenomena of the historical process can be related by logical deduction. But there is an irrational factor as well, the acting of which often upsets and offsets the logical cycle. And it is this element which Ibn Khaldūn overlooked as most over-systematising thinkers are apt to do. But the real significance of his reasoning lies not so much in that he found a guiding principle in the working of the human mind subject to the law of causality nor that he discovered, in the *'Aṣabiyya*, one central driving force for the existence, growth and decline of the State. Rather it lies in his fundamental perception of the interrelation between the various factors which in their sum make up human life organised in society. We must repeat that he thought in terms of politics, that he reviewed all spheres of life in relation to the State. Political thought there has always been in Islam, but it either started from the *Sharī'a*, and the problem was how to harmonise the existing State with the explicit regulations of the *Sharī'a*, or it started from Plato and tried to harmonise the actual State with the ideal State of perfect reason, losing itself in speculation. Moreover, in the minds of most Muslim thinkers both trends of thought interacted upon each other. Ibn Khaldūn, however, for the first time started from a hitherto unknown quantity: the human society. His problem was: how did society, as the aggregate of individuals, form itself into a political organisation, and how did it develop? The individual interested him only in so far as it formed part of that politically organised society. Human nature required, as the Greeks taught, political organisation. Ibn Khaldūn repeats Aristotle's Platonic dictum as his predecessors had done. He finds that association alone is not sufficient, that constraint must be put on man and his selfish wishes in the form of law. He says very little of this law in practice, as this was done for him by the interpreters of the *Sharī'a*. Law is a necessary part of the political fabric, and only as such a factor does it enter Ibn Khaldūn's thought. But he is much more explicit about the two essential factors of a working State: Economy and Army, the two pillars of the political power. It is important enough that he formulated laws of political economy—as we would say in our modern terminology—that he saw the connexion between supply and demand and, consequently, the cost of goods, that he distinguished between things necessary for the bare maintenance of life, things which were useful beyond the necessary and, lastly, things which were luxuries, going beyond the useful and serving pleasures, both material and spiritual. But what is of greater significance still is that he saw a logical, necessary connexion between these three categories in progressive development which overturns and leads downward to ruin. And not only did he see connexion and development by stages within one and the same sphere, but he discovered interrelation between one and another. He perceived that the economic sphere cannot without serious consequences for the machinery of society be looked upon as segregated from finance, army, spiritual culture. They are all interconnected, and only if they are in perfect equilibrium on the basis of a mutual give-and-take is the State at its best and functions normally and effectively. He views all these factors, economic, legal, financial, religious and cultural under the political aspect. How must all these factors be brought into line with the requirements of the State? His empiric nature made him see the effect which a disturbance in one sphere had on the other spheres of life, and he discovered the law of causality at the root of this mutual influence. This is something quite new and revolutionary and, indeed, far advancing into the modern age. Nowhere can this be seen better than in his plea for sound finance, moderate taxation and free economy. Dealing with a State built on force through conquest and maintained by military power, the financial position held the key to the balance of the political life. The State passed through five phases (conquest, building up of dynasty, reaching and maintaining the peak, decline and fall) within four generations of the ruling dynasty. Within these phases the economic life expands with the expansion and consolidation of the dynasty. The human urge to comfort and ease has a stimulating effect on the economic life. The more that goods are produced, the more that refined works of art are created the greater become the demands of the possessing classes. Increasing luxury makes increased demands on the treasury, and the result is higher taxes and customs charges. With a growing population, the necessities get cheaper and cheaper, the turnover has to make up for the dwindling gain and profit. The prices for luxury articles go up but increased taxation takes away the profit, with the result that agriculturists, artisans and merchants alike become weary of their toil, lose interest in their work, so that the treasury cannot count on regular, let alone increased returns.[1] As the State at this stage has to rely on mercenaries, the question of their pay preoccupies the governing classes to the exclusion of almost everything else, apart from their wish for an easy, good life. The monarch very often takes the disastrous step of taking an active part in the national economy by trying to set up a monopoly in agriculture and/or trade and commerce, thus ousting the less moneyed natural workers in these occupations until he ruins them and himself as well in the end. The State without adequate protection, for lack of funds to pay the mercenary army, then falls an easy prey to outward attack and/or revolt from within.

True, this is a deduction from actual conditions in Ibn Khaldūn's own day where States changed hands continually. On this account his conclusions may be limited to his own time, and not necessarily applicable to political development generally. But more significant is the undoubtedly new and correct perception of the causal interdependence of economy, finance and political power, to the exclusion of chance and personal initiative. Examples could be multiplied from other activities within the State which are of peculiar interest to the psychologist, economist, military strategist or the student of law and political science. They all bear out the one result: that here in the fourteenth century a North African thinker advanced, through his own experience in his own land and in Muslim Spain, a complete

[1] This is a résumé of Ibn Khaldūn's exposition. A more detailed, documented account is given in my monograph in the Chapter *Staat und Wirtschaft*. The economist must judge for himself the correctness of these views.

theory of human civilisation and culture progressing in a politically organised society. Neither the ideal State of a divinely inspired law-giver nor of philosophic speculation is the object of his science. It is the State built on conquest and force, inspired by the corporate will of a group (*'Aṣabiyya*). But will for what? Will for power and domination. Many a reader and critic of Ibn Khaldūn has stopped at that point and labelled him a materialist. But to take such a view would be one-sided, as it does not take into account that the spiritual environment of Ibn Khaldūn is the highly developed Islamic civilisation. This alone explains the large room Islamic institutions occupy in his analysis of the social-political organism, as well as the indisputable fact that human nature must be curbed by values outside it which transcend custom and habit, the great influence of which Ibn Khaldūn realised and took into account. If we bear this in mind, we may be able to clarify the apparent confusion which exists between *'Aṣabiyya* and Religion. As a student of reality, Ibn Khaldūn saw that either can exist without the other. But he also saw that a lasting political order is unthinkable without the co-operation of the two. Only if *'Aṣabiyya* is transformed by religious zeal and higher aim into a spiritual, formative ideal, only then enduring results of a character far exceeding sheer force and lust for power will be achieved. On the other hand, no religious ideal will see its realisation without that corporate will and enthusiasm behind it. It needs always a party to realise in actual life the message of an ideal. No wonder, therefore, that Ibn Khaldūn clung to Islam as the superior State, as the ideal society of man striving for dominion and power, not for their own sake but in order to enforce the ideal of human perfection and happiness in this world and in the world to come. He, thus, not only repeated what Muslim thinkers (and for that matter Jewish as well) from Alfārābī to Averroes had stated before him, viz.: that the State based on human law cares for the citizen's earthly welfare only, whereas the State based on the revealed (superior) law, the *Sharī'a* (or *Torah*), ensures earthly and other-worldly bliss. He was honestly convinced of this as the result not so much of rational speculation as rather of his own experience. It would, however, be likewise wrong to label him an idealist. For he was too much of a political observer to overlook the realities of human relations. And it is gratifying to see how this scholar who conceived of the historical process and man's eternal struggle within it in the form of a cycle, by his own empiric quest was led back to the starting-point of the unquestioning faithful Muslim (and for that matter every Mediæval thinker): that only the religious ideal is capable of inspiring man to create permanent values which survive dynastic and national-political boundaries.†

2

SOME ASPECTS OF ISLAMIC POLITICAL THOUGHT

ISLAM as a way of life expresses itself in the *Shari'a*, the revealed law based upon the *Qur'ān*, the *Sunnah* of the Prophet Muḥammad and the *Ḥadith*, the body of authentic traditions. The authoritative interpretation of the *Shari'a* is contained in the *Fiqh*, arrived at by the *Ijmā'*, consensus of the jurists as the authoritative representatives of the *Jamā'a*, the Muslim community.

An independent political theory cannot, therefore, be expected in Islam. But constitutional law forms a necessary part of every exposition of *Fiqh*. This constitutional law presupposes the existence of the state within which the earthly life of the *Jamā'a* runs its course, in preparation for the other world, for the life to come. In the Muslim state supreme authority, temporal as well as spiritual, is vested in the Khalīfa, the vicegerent of the Prophet of *Allah*.

As far as the Islamic state is concerned, the jurists never ask themselves the question whether a state must be, nor how it originates. It is, and its function is to guarantee the maintenance of pure Islam, the application of its Law, the *Shari'a*, and the defence of orthodoxy against heresy. Rights and duties of the caliph are clearly defined and laid down by the *Ijmā'* of the jurists of Sunnitic Islam. With schism raising its head soon after the death of Muḥammad, who made no provision for his successor as the Commander of the Faithful, the problem of lawful succession to the *Khilāfah* was very pressing and serious. Apart from strictly theological divisions and controversies, it was principally the theory and practice of the *Khilāfah* which divided orthodox from heterodox Islam with its many sects.

For the purpose of this paper, we must confine ourselves to a brief consideration of the theory of the *Khilāfah* in orthodox Islam. We follow, as the representative exposition, what Al-Māwardī laid down in his *Al-Aḥkām as-Sulṭāniyah*, (*Ordinances of Government*)* a treatise devoted to

* Edited by Enger, Bonn, 1853. *See* also French translation by Count Leon Ostrorog, Paris, 1901 with a general introduction to Islamic Political Law.

constitutional and administrative law. Prof. Gibb* has made it abundantly clear that this work is anything but an academic exposition of the theory of Government according to the *Sharī'a*. It is rather an attempt at vindicating the orthodox position in the light of contemporary events and at re-asserting the claim of the caliph to spiritual and temporal overlordship against Sunnite no less than Shī'ite conquerors and rulers of Muslim territories within his realm. The authority of Muslim law had to be upheld against princes and generals who, by brute force, had established their own authority over parts of the Abbasid Empire. An orthodox Muslim could not submit to an authority other than that conferred by the *Jamā'a* upon the lawful caliph. And yet, he could not deny that in reality neither the caliph nor even the *Jamā'a* were at times unable to assert this authority which was alone recognised by law. Nor, could he overlook the *de facto* authority and effective power and control of these rulers. If, however, the conquerors acknowledged the supreme authority of the Abbasid Caliph in matters spiritual and temporal by mentioning his name in prayer and by entering into a contract with him, their rule was legalised inasmuch as it rested upon delegated authority. Thus, the unity of the community of the Faithful was preserved. The legal fiction was maintained, that the Caliph ruled supreme and no conflict of loyalties plagued the *Jamā'a* since the men, who would otherwise be usurpers and rebels, were clothed with the mantle of legality.

Yet, it was not only authority established upon force and conquest that challenged the orthodox political theory of the God-ordained *Khilāfa*. As is well known, under the influence of Greek and Hellenistic philosophy, Reason claimed the right to inquire into the laws of Politics. The philosophers wanted to know, by independent rational inquiry, why should there be a state and what was its purpose. Whilst they did not deny that the Islamic state was the outcome of Revelation, they averred at the same time that Reason necessitated it just as much. Likewise, they admitted that the *Khalīfah* ought to administer the state in such a way that the purpose of the Law would be fulfilled, *i.e.*, to improve the Faithful by watching over their right conduct so that they, in turn, helped, as moral beings, to maintain the state and that they prepared themselves in the moral state for the world to come. Yet, the *Falāsifa* insisted not only on perfection in morals but demanded perfection in knowledge and understanding as well. This threefold perfection was to them the indispensable condition for the *imitatio Dei* as the ultimate goal of the individual person.

Al-Māwardī's statement that the institution of *Imām—Imāmah* equals *Khilāfa—is* required by revealed law (*Shar'*) not, as some profess, by Reason (*'aql*) is clearly directed against the *Mu'tazila* but no doubt also against the *Falāsifa* generally. The basis for his claim is to be found in

* *See* his succinct analysis of Al-Māwardī's doctrine in his article *Al-Māwardī's Theory of the Khilāfa* published in *Islamic Culture*, XI, 3 (1937), which I have used. The reader might wish to consult Al-Māwardī's other treatise on morals, his *k. Adab ad-Dunyā wad-Din*, edid. O. Rescher.

three passages in the *Qur'ān* (*Sura* II, 28 ; IV, 62 and XXXVIII, 25). The last-named is specially significant in that the *Khalīfah* is not only to judge truthfully but that David is chosen and not Moses. This may suggest that David here stands for the highest temporal authority : the *Khalīfah*, as the successor of the Prophet, is, at the same time also the successor of David as king and judge. He is *to defend the Faith and to administer this world.* Al-Māwardī goes on to stress the superiority of the Revealed Law over Reason. For, Reason demands government against lawlessness and anarchy and the wise guards himself against strife and discord being guided by his own reason. But Revealed Law has bestowed temporal authority upon him to whom it has delegated spiritual power. *We are therefore obliged to obey those Imāms who rule over us.*

Properly-qualified persons elect from among the properly-qualified candidates the one who is most suitable to fill the vacancy created by the death or the disqualification of the reigning caliph. One of these conditions enjoins knowledge of the relevant qualities which *Fiqh* has laid down for the caliph. This was probably in actual fact even more often absent than *'adalah* in the elector.

Of the seven qualifications a candidate must possess the first is *'adalah* and the second is knowledge (*'ilm*) which enables him to make independent decisions and pass judgments on points of Law (*ijtihād*). This was, in practice, left to the *mujtahids*, the professional jurists, and to the *muqallids*, their successors. Moreover, the caliph must possess physical health and must be capable of discharging his duties which comprise governing his subjects and directing the affairs of state in person. Besides, he must have courage and determination to protect the territory of Islam and to wage the holy War (*jihād*). Finally, he must be a descendant of the *Quraish*.*

The election is completed by a contract, voluntarily entered into, without force or constraint.

If there are two equally-qualified candidates the electors choose according to the exigencies of the times. At the time of external danger and of political upheaval, preference is given to the courageous one ; if the times are quiet they prefer the learned candidate who is capable of putting down heresy and of upholding the Faith.

Once elected the caliph has to safeguard Islam in conformity with the *Ijma'* of the *Jamā'a*. He must see that justice is being done. He must restrain the strong and protect the weak. He must nominate the right persons for the offices of the state, must take a personal interest in the administration. Though he can delegate authority the responsibility is ultimately his.

* *Cp.* Ibn Khaldūn's treatment in his *Muqaddima*, (Beyrut, 1879), pp. 168/71 which is based on Al-Māwardī's exposition but elaborates greatly on the last condition. *See* also my *Ibn Khaldūn's Gedanken über den Staat. Ein Beitrag zur Geschichte der mittelalterlichen Staatslehre.* (*Beiheft*, 25, *of the Historische Zeitschrift*), 1932, Munchen/Berlin., esp. chapter on *State and Law*, pp. 648.

It is clear from the foregoing that, according to the orthodox view, the spiritual and temporal powers are united in the person of the caliph. His chief task is to create the conditions necessary for the full working of the *Shari'a* which aims at the willing submission of the entire Muslim community as well as of the individual to the supreme will of Allah Whom to serve means right-doing.

This ideal was rarely attained. Yet, this should not detract from its intrinsic value as a fully-developed Theocracy. And even if it only lived on as a fiction it is precisely this fiction which has saved Islam from the ruinous struggle between Papacy and State in the west and from disintegration with the extinction of the caliphate.

II

Siyāsa, government, in the orthodox view is conditioned by the *Shari'a* and the 'Defender of the Faith' has to be guided by the moral obligations of the *Shari'a* in his execution of the duties of government. But *siyāsa* can also be understood in a secular sense as political government and administration executed by a ruler who, be he Muslim or not, is actuated by the will for power. He claims authority as the man who holds power in his hands. His problem is *how* to govern. The Persians have given much attention to this question and have treated of it in the so-called "Mirrors for princes and magistrates." It is only natural that Muslim writers should have taken up this literary form. One of them is relevant to our purpose. He is Ibn aṭ-Ṭiqṭaqa who wrote in 1302 a book for him *who governs the people and directs the affairs*. The treatise is dedicated to the ruler of Mossul after whom it is called *k. al-Fakhrī*.* It was the intention of the author neither to discourse on the origin of the royal dignity and its essence nor on its division into religious and secular authority, nor was he concerned with what is in agreement with the requirements of the Revealed Law and what is not, but rather to treat of *the principles of government and rules of conduct* (*ādāb*) *from which one derives advantage in happenings and events, in the government of the subjects, in the protection of the kingdom and in the improvement of morals and conduct.* It goes without saying that the *Khilāfa*, conditioned by the *Shari'a*, is outside the purview of Ibn aṭ-Ṭiqṭaqa. He is concerned with the kingdom (*mulk*), its ruler and his subjects. But even so, the tasks of both kinds of institutions are, on the whole, the same: political and moral concerns, with this difference that the *malik* is not called upon to defend the Faith—this is the duty and the privilege of the *Khalīfah*—whose sovereignty the *Amir* of Mossul, theoretically at least, recognises nor does he look upon

* Edited by Ahlwardt and more recently anew by H. Derenbourg, Paris. Ibn Miskawaih does not contain anything new beyond Ibn aṭ-Ṭiqṭaqa. His ethical treatise *k. Tahdhib al-Akhlāq* contains some interesting remarks on social obligations of the individual which have a 'political' colouring.

the inhabitants of the kingdom as the community of the Faithful. They represent for him the king's subjects rather than the servants of Allah. He likens the relationship between the ruler and the subjects to that between the physician and the patients rather than between the despot and the slaves. The successful government—both from the point of view of political success in terms of power and influence and from that of the improvement of morals—depends on the character and ability of the ruler. All his actions must be directed by the best interests of the state. He must possess intelligence (*'aql*) *through which empires are governed* ; justice (*'adl*) to ensure prosperity and sound finances as well as the good conduct of men ; knowledge enabling him to converse with the scholars—a social accomplishment and a means to attract to his court savants and poets rather than a political qualification. Ibn aṭ-Ṭiqṭaqa also mentions *the fear of God as a quality which is the root of all good and the key to every blessing, for if the king fears Allah the servants of Allah have confidence in him.* Here we see clearly the political importance and usefulness of religion, an idea greatly expanded in Ibn K͟haldūn* and strongly reminiscent of Machiavelli. Next we would mention *Fear and Respect through which the order of the kingdom is preserved and guarded against the ambition of the subjects.* The prince must also be versed in the art of government (*siyāsa*) which is *the capital of the king. On it he relies in order to maintain (sound) finances, to preserve morals, to prevent evil, to subjugate wrong-doers and to forestall injustice which leads to civil war and rebellion.*

The man so gifted has the duty to protect the country, to ensure the fortification of the frontiers and the security of the roads. In return, he is entitled to the obedience of his subjects. Strict justice and impartiality, the protection of the weak and humble against injustice as well as the assistance equally of those near to and far away from him—all these are essential duties of the good ruler.

The qualities required of a successful ruler form the subject of the first part of the *k. al-Fak͟hrī.* The second and main part of the author's *History of Dynasties* describes the reign and administration of caliphs, sulṭans, emirs, governors and wazirs and there are but few signs of originality. But now and again a lively interest in politics can be detected. The principles laid down for good and successful government are, no doubt, at least partially derived from observation of actual historical events and of the reaction of rulers to them. These rulers are being judged by their success or failure to meet contingencies. Their political ability is the author's primary concern. And yet, the *S͟harī'a* with the *K͟hilāfa* as the institution to implement it, was a living reality for Ibn aṭ-Ṭiqṭaqa no less than for any and every Muslim. Its superiority over man-made *mulk* was self-evident. But it was an ideal far removed from political reality. And it is just this political reality with which he is concerned.

* *See* my *Ibn K͟haldūn's Gedanken, etc., loc. cit.* chapter *State and Religion*, p. 50 *ff.* Beyrut edition, pp. 137/9 ; 176/8 ; 180/1 ; 190 ; and *State and Law*, Beyrut, 165/6 ; 109/11.

It is immaterial whether the ethical trend of his political thought is due to his Islamic environment and to his Muslim faith or rather to the influence of the philosophers: the Power-State and its successful government form the object of his study, the subject of his advice to rulers and the content of his treatise. His intention was to supply rulers with a guide for the business of government. To probe into the foundations of the state, its origin and development was outside his interest.

That the *Falāsifa* touch on this side of Political Philosophy is equally due not so much to a genuine interest as to the fact that their Greek masters Plato and Aristotle are vitally concerned about these matters. It is more by way of transmission of Platonic thought in particular and in commenting upon it than by way of an independent inquiry that this topic is dealt with in Muslim philosophy of east and west. It was, in fact, left to Ibn Khaldūn to evolve a political philosophy properly so called within the framework of a philosophy of History.

III

The *Falāsifa* occupy a peculiar position in the realm of Political Thought. This position might be delineated as intermediary between the theological-juristic treatment of the State on the basis of the Divinely Revealed Law and the historical-political approach as the result of the study of the actual State built upon Power. It cannot, however, be stressed too emphatically that, from whatever angle the writers approach the problem of government, they are all Muslims and they are all convinced of the superiority of the Ideal Islamic State as envisaged and demanded by the *Sharīʿa* over all other states, even over Plato's Ideal State, his *Republic*. As educated Muslims they are all trained in the science of *Fiqh* and the other disciplines of Islamic culture. Some were practising judges, professional jurists. This is of importance in the case of the philosophers in particular since they are—though primarily interested in the individual soul and its perfection—at least in their political conceptions guided by the central idea of Law on the one hand and of the individual as a citizen of a state founded on and guided and directed by Law on the other. This Law—be it revealed or laid down by the wise—has universal validity and absolute authority. With the notable exception of two of the western *Falāsifa*, Ibn Bājja and Ibn Ṭufail, highest perfection of the individual is possible only in the state. Just as Plato's philosopher attains happiness only in the Ideal *Politeia* so Averroes'—and before Alfārābī's—adept of the speculative sciences gains ultimate perfection and happiness only in the perfectly led and administered Ideal State which is ruled over by the philosopher-king who is identical with the Lawgiver and *Imām*.

It is not possible to deal with the most important *Falāsifa* extensively in this short survey. We must confine ourselves to Ibn Rushd, the disciple of Alfārābī and Ibn Bājja. Alfārābī, 'the second teacher,' was influenced by *Politeia* and *Nomoi* and as a result wrote two political treatises, *Madina Fāḍila* and *k. al-Siyāsāt*, also called *k. al-Mabādī*. Averroes states in the beginning of his *Paraphrase* of Plato's *Politeia* that he had not come across Aristotle's *Politics* and had consequently to comment on the *Politeia* as the second, practical part to the first theoretical part of the foremost of all arts, Politics.[2] The theoretical part is contained in Aristotle's *Nicomachian Ethics*.[3] Both stand in the same relationship to each other as do in Medicine the *Book of Health and Illness* to that of *Maintenance of Health and Removal of Illness*. The principles of the practical science of Politics are Will and Choice, its subjects are the things of the will dependent on our action. In his *Commentary* on the *Nicomachian Ethics*, Averroes defines Virtue as the purpose of Politics (*Hahanhagah ham-Mēdīniṭ*). The highest Good, peculiar to man is—according to another of Averroes' statements—the activity of the rational soul demanded by Virtue. This is, however, possible in the perfect state only. He makes it quite clear—as he likewise does in the *Paraphrase*—that highest intellectual perfection is possible only in the Ideal State. Man is, therefore, a part of the State, he cannot live without it and he must contribute his share to its maintenance and functioning in his own interest as well as in that of the citizens as a whole. To be a citizen is part of the purpose of man. This undoubtedly goes beyond the commonly-made assertion that man is a *zōon politikon*. For, whilst all the *Falāsifa* agree that man cannot exist by himself—he needs help and support to obtain food, clothing and dwelling—this only means that man must join with others and form a society built upon the principle of mutual help to obtain the necessities of life. However, it does not explain the necessity of the state. Man's faculties are manifold, so are his needs. In order to provide for all, leadership and organisation are necessary so that everyone does that for which he is best fitted by nature. Averroes accepts Plato's plea for one activity for each person. If the state is to fulfil its purpose of guaranteeing man's welfare and happiness, it must provide facilities for the development of man's faculties, the material as well as the spiritual ones. Man is gifted with Reason and his aim is to reach happiness with the help of his reasoning faculty. If the state were nothing but the provider of the material needs of man and the protector of life and property against the superior force of the stronger, then man would never reach his goal. This goal

---

1. See my *Maimonides Conception of State and Society* in *Moses Maimonides*, ed. I. Epstein, London, 1935, where this point is dealt with and also the indebtedness of Averroes to Alfārābī. Further, *cp.* my *Politische Gedanken bei Ibn Bājja* (*MGWJ*, 1937, Festschrift for Prof. E. Mittwoch) where Averroes' attitude to Ibn Bājja is fully discussed.

2. See my *Averroes' Paraphrase on Plato's "Politeia," JRAS*, Oct., 1934. Quotations from the *Paraphrase* in the subsequent pages are based upon the text which is now being finally prepared for publication from seven Hebrew MSS.

3. I have used the Bodleian MS. (Mich, 277). The quotations are to be found on pp. 23b, 30a.

is, according to Aristotle, the perception of all existing things in a state of blissful contemplation, or according to the *Falāsifa* a stage higher even than the perception of God. We cannot here enter into a discussion of the various stages of that perception until, especially among the Jewish thinkers, this knowledge of God is extended to the Love of God expressed in a never-ending striving to become like God as much as is humanly possible through the conscious imitation of His ways. We are here exclusively concerned with the bearing which this striving for personal happiness of the rational soul has on the state. It is clearly not sufficient that there exists any kind of state. For, the success or failure of man's striving to attain his goal depends—at least in the view of Averroes—entirely upon the right kind of state. The perfect state as envisaged in the *Sharīʿa* has—philosophically speaking—its equivalent in the Ideal state of Plato. Both are conditioned by a universally binding, valid and authoritative Ideal Law. The state which Plato wants to establish is built on the Law which the philosophers, the wise, have devised. Averroes, as a skilled jurist and a keen observer of the Islamic states of his time, stresses the extreme difficulty of such an undertaking. He underlines it, moreover, by emphasising how it is indispensable for the king to possess perfect intelligence and the full knowledge contained in the speculative sciences. The ideal ruler is—to repeat it—not only wise in that his intellect is perfect, is ever ready to concentrate upon perceiving the *intelligibilia*. He is also the Lawgiver. Now, we find in *Maimonides* the equation between philosopher and prophet, based upon Alfārābī. He is a prophet whose intellect and imagination have both received the full force of the emanation of the *Active* Intellect. If that emanation is confined to the intellect alone the result is a Lawgiver. Averroes is doubtful whether the ideal ruler must possess the gift of prophecy. He assigns this matter of serious deliberation a place in the first part of Political Science. That he was familiar with Alfārābī's theory of prophecy is evident. His equation of the philosopher-king with the Lawgiver and *Imām* is literally taken over from Alfārābī as we know from the latter's *k. Taḥsil as-Saʿādah.*[1] All depends therefore on the correct interpretation of *Imām* which the Hebrew translator of Averroes' *Paraphrase* renders by *kohen*. The Hebrew text is corrupt. But its meaning can be gathered from Alfārābī's just referred to *k. Taḥsil as-Saʿādah.*[2] *Imām is he whom one follows as chief.* In its technical sense, we know it denotes the leader in the communal prayer behind whom one prays. The question arises whether Averroes has substituted prophet by *Imām* whilst modifying Alfārābī's conception of prophecy ? Does he consequently imply that Plato's philosopher-king is—translated into Islamic terminology and adapted to Islamic conditions—identical with the *Khalīfah* one of whose principal

1. Edition, Hyderabad, 1345 A.H., p. 43.

2. Dr. Paul Kraus has, at the time, ingeniously recognised the original Arabic version, since confirmed by the Alfārābī passage (*see* previous note).

functions is to act as *Imām* in the Friday-prayer ? If this were so, Averroes would still be within the orthodox political conception even though he stresses the intellectual and ethical qualifications of the ideal ruler and passes over in silence any religious duties of the head of state. Moreover, in his discussion of the aim and purpose of man—without which he considers education for citizenship to be futile and useless—Averroes reviews the various opinions held on this subject. As behoves a Muslim he first states the aim to be the will of God as postulated by the religious laws in force in his own time. But, he goes on to declare that the perception of this divine will is possible through prophecy only. The will of God demands a twofold effort on the part of man. First comes the acquisition of *abstract knowledge alone like the knowledge of God commanded by our Law* and then action required by Ethics. He avers that both postulates, *i.e.*, that of religious law and that of philosophy, are identical in character and purpose.

If we had to define the common ground between Islam and Platonic political philosophy which alone enabled the *Falāsifa*, especially Averroes —to insist on this identity of purpose, we would call this basis nomocracy. And this in spite of the emphasis Averroes lays on the monarchy (kingship) as the ideal constitution, followed closely by aristocracy. The former is conditioned by Islamic history which forms the background of Averroes' experience and supplies him with examples for his illustrations to Plato's ideas and arguments. The latter is due to the fact that the *Paraphrase* is an interpretation of Plato's *Politeia*, supplemented by the *Nomoi*, and by Aristotle's *Nicomachia*. The two last-named works were commented upon by Alfārābī already.

Whilst thus the ideal state in the orthodox view is a theocracy, the emphasis of the *Falāsifa* shifts to the *Nomos* and their ideal state is a nomocracy. It is, indeed, the central place of law in Islam as well as in Greek political philosophy as understood by the *Falāsifa* which has made possible the reception of Aristotelian and Platonic ideas in Muslim philosophical thought. The connexion between political leadership and law is very close. In his *Commentary* on the *Nicomachia* Averroes stresses that the *mudabbir* is concerned about Virtue to the exclusion almost of everything else. It is the leader's desire and will to make the citizens *good, excellent and submissively bent under the laws*. In another passage he discusses the functions of the *absolute ruler* who is in the first place *the guardian of equity. And when he guards equity he guards justice. Political equity is identical with legal equity*. This last-mentioned comment shows the close affinity of Politics and Law in the thought of Averroes. Plato no less than Aristotle was his teacher whose theories could not fail to strike home with a professional Muslim jurist. Another remark in this *Commentary* illustrates this : *Political equity is partly* (of the realm of) *natural law partly* (of that of) *human law*.*

* *Loc. cit.*, pp. 38a, 98a, b.

Next to moral leadership, wisdom as a 'political' virtue is linked to the realm of law. Averroes interprets Plato's wise *polis* which possesses knowledge and wisdom as a state whose *wise citizens thoroughly understand all the laws and statutes.* This equals good government and good counsel for which knowledge of the speculative sciences is required. Thus, he says : *Good government and good counsel are undoubtedly a kind of knowledge, only we cannot say that this city-state possesses good government and good counsel on account of wisdom in the practical arts such as agriculture, carpentry and others. If this be so, then it possesses wisdom only in that knowledge which we will set forth* (*i.e.,* theoretical knowledge of the speculative sciences). *It is evident that this wisdom can only be achieved through knowledge of the human aim since this government tends in that direction. It is likewise evident that we understand the human aim only through the speculative sciences. Thus, this city-state is necessarily....wise in two* (kinds of) *knowledge simultaneously, i.e., practical and theoretical knowledge. Consequently, this wisdom will be found in the smallest part of the city-state among the philosophers. The reason is that these* (philosophical) *natures do exist much less frequently than the other natures, the artisans. It is obvious that this wisdom fittingly persists in the leaders of the city-state who rule over it. If this be so, then the leaders of the city-state are necessarily the wise.* The qualification of knowledge (*'ilm*) which the *khalīfah* must possess is thus interpreted in the Platonic sense. Likewise, Averroes has no difficulty to square the law of the *Shari'a* with the law as laid down by the philosophers in the ideal *Republic.* He distinguishes between general laws of a normative character and particular laws which the citizens can easily derive from the general (and authoritative, valid) laws. Such *partial laws and good moral instructions like to honour one's parents, to keep silence before adults* the citizens will, no doubt, evolve themselves. *It is therefore not appropriate to lay down laws for such like partial matters because once the general laws are laid down and firmly established the citizens will, by their own initiative, proceed towards making those partial laws. For, everybody will only be moved in the direction nature and education move him, if good then good if bad then bad. He, however, who seeks to promulgate these partial laws without having* (*first*) *laid down the general laws—as happens to many lawgivers—resembles* (*the physician*) *who heals sick persons who, because of their excessive desires, cannot receive any benefit from the remedies with which they are treated.*

Averroes' continual adaptation of Platonic views to Muslim conceptions and Islamic conditions can equally be seen from his comment on Plato's statement about the temples, prayers and sacrifices. He replaces—naturally—the gods by *The Most High and what He commanded through prophecy as if Plato were thinking those were divine matters and should therefore be respected as such in the State.* Averroes further puts the laws *which entrench in the souls humility and glorification of God be He exalted* on a level with all the other laws and injunctions. In his *Commentary* on the *Nicomachia* he expressly states that these regulations for prayer and sacrifices vary with every nation, religion, time and place.

When Plato distinguishes between instruction by persuasion and by coercion, Averroes draws a parallel with the *Shari'a* which enjoins persuasion and war as the two ways leading to God. In general, it is worth noting that Averroes is primarily interested in the practical problems raised by Plato and he concentrates on the concrete application to existing states and to current political situations rather than on the philosophical discussion of abstract ideas. Needless to say that he abandons the dialoguic form of Platonic argumentation, that he replaces Greek poetry by pre-Islamic poetry and that he fully shares the orthodox condemnation of them as harmful. And yet, they are harmful and dangerous from the point of view of the state and citizenship—just like in the *Politeia*—and not from the point of view of Revealed Religion and theological dogma. He is interested in the philosopher as the ideal ruler, the perfect example of the good citizen rather than as a metaphysicist.

He shows considerable historical understanding when he takes Galen severely to task for censoring Plato who thinks that a thousand guardians are sufficient and who assigns a certain circumference to the *polis*. He rejoins that Plato wrote for his own time and drew his conclusions on the basis of then prevailing conditions. He would, so Averroes reasons, certainly have revised his views if he had lived at the time of the *Oikoumene*.

The discussion of the imperfect states and of bad constitutions offers Averroes an opportunity to criticise contemporary political institutions and economic and social conditions. Such bad conditions point to the correctness of Plato's views about the guardians, *e.g.*, that they should have no property nor possessions of any kind. Or, when he states: *Equity and true belief which are the business of Justice are nothing else than what we said before concerning the government of this city-state. That is that it is fitting for every citizen to adhere to one civic activity. And this is the activity for which he is prepared by nature. Now, this is the equity which bestows upon the city-state salvation and perpetuity as long as there is present in it continuity. If this is so....then equity exists in this city-state in that every one of its citizens does only that for which he is singled out by nature. This is civic justice just as perversion* (of justice) *in states which is the cause of iniquity is nothing else but that every one of its citizens is trained in more than one thing.* In this connexion Averroes stresses the excellence of Plato's *Republic* and its superiority over the states of his own time in which evils afflict their citizens. He also agrees with Plato in training women like men for *one* occupation and deplores that women in Muslim states are destined for procreation only the more so since they are twice as numerous and would be very useful if engaged in one of the occupations necessary for the existence and preservation of the state. Deeply conscious of the foundation of the just state upon a General Law, Averroes' repeated insistence upon this point of one civic occupation for every citizen, man and woman alike, may be taken as evidence for his admiration for Plato's law of the state. Muslim tradition of the *Khilāfa* and the discrepancy between it and the existing *mulk* in his own day must have sharpened his mind specially to appreciate Plato's plea for justice and equity based upon law in the Ideal State.

Here is clearly that common ground which guided the *Falāsifa* in their approach to Greek and Hellenistic political philosophy.

As for Averroes in particular, man interested him as a citizen with duties towards the state. The good citizen serves the community by willingly discharging the allotted duty to the best of his natural ability which is fostered by education. The state ruled by a moral law aiming as it does at the moral perfection of the citizen must afford man the best opportunity for the attainment of his legitimate goal: highest intellectual perfection in the form of the perception of God. Repeatedly, in his *Paraphrase* no less than in his *Commentary* on the *Nicomachia*, Averroes insists on man being of necessity a citizen. He stresses, against Ibn Bājja, that it would be impossible for man to live without the state.[1] He deprecates the solitary life both from the individual and from the group angle. Just as man cannot attain perfection by segregating himself from the community even in the imperfect state, so can social life not flourish without every citizen sharing in the common tasks of producing the necessities and amenities of life and without contributing to the defence and protection of the state as organised society. It is true, Averroes does not deny that it is impossible to attain perfection in an imperfect state, but he denies—equally emphatically—that it is possible even for the metaphysicist to attain perfection outside a political organisation. He has, thus,—as I have stated elsewhere[2]—taken up the main trend of Alfārābī's political thought in deliberate opposition to Ibn Bājja and Ibn Ṭufail who not only maintain that man can rise in a solitary life to the dwindling heights of mystical contemplation of the Divine, but even advocate his segregation. This is a line of thought indicated in Alfārābī under *ṣūfi* influence and developed by the *Ikhwān aṣ-Ṣafā*. The *Pure Brethren* are, in turn, greatly indebted to Alfārābī's interpretation of Plato's political ideas and devote a whole chapter of their *Encyclopedia* to the Law and the Lawgiver which they seem to have lifted bodily from Alfārābī's *Madina Fāḍila* (ch. 28). Alfārābī refers to the elect who live in an imperfect community as *strangers*. Ibn Bājja defines, in his *Hanhagat ham-Mitbōdēd* these strangers as men far removed from their surroundings spiritually although they are physically present in the state.[3] Ibn Ṭufail goes a step further and draws the logical conclusion of picturing his hero as a kind of Robinson Crusoe turned speculative mystic. It is to be noted that Ibn Bājja despite his considerable borrowing of Platonic thought and imagery, has divested this material of its political connotation and

1. *Cp.* my *Politische Gedanken bei Ibn Bājja, loc. cit.* pp. 153/68.

2. *Ibid.*, p. 164f.

3. *Ibid.*

relevance. His interest is a purely speculative one. He concentrates on the individual soul seeking union with the Divine through union first with the Active Intellect. Qualities of the ruler, constitutional forms, duties of ruler and ruled are not subjects for his inquiring mind. We find no place allotted to the Law, its educative function and its political relevance. Lacking this central position it does—for Ibn Bājja—not provide the basis and background for man who strives to attain his destiny.[1] The speculative sciences—demanded by the Law according to a notable passage in Averroes' *Paraphrase*—help man in the wise city-state to reach his goal, *i.e.*, to perceive God through self-perception. This is precisely the view of Ibn Bājja who declares that knowledge gained through the speculative sciences leads the striving intellect nearer to God Whose most beloved creature he is. The ideal philosopher must be guided, however, by those laws and statutes which govern the ideal state without, however, being obliged to live in such a political community. And it is merely to illustrate by analogy that Ibn Bājja mentions the perfect state and some of its characteristic features. Averroes, as has been remarked before, will not admit that man can reach perfection and happiness in solitude and he refutes Ibn Bājja's claim that whilst it is easier even for the philosopher to reach his goal in a political organisation, especially in the perfect state after the model of the *Politeia*, this intellectual seeker can achieve happiness in isolation. Ibn Bājja ignores the state when he credits the metaphysicist with striving in constant intellectual endeavour to approximate God implying, however, that the mass of ordinary intellects needs the state in order to realise their intellectual nature. He has not only introduced the west to the mystic trend in Muslim philosophy, he has also undoubtedly sharpened the critical eye of Averroes to perceive clearly the dangers of solitary life and to understand and repeat with obvious approval the insistence of Aristotle—in the wake of his teacher Plato—that man is a *zōon politikon* and has, as an intellectual person, definite obligations towards the political community.[2]

IV

State and society as phenomena in their own right, subject to laws of their own have only slowly been recognised in a world bound by an all-embracing Law to which every manifestation of the human mind was subjected. It would certainly be tempting to see a deliberate and conscious development from the theological-juristic conception of the Muslim state over the reception (and characteristic adaptation) of Platonic-Aristotelian

1. *Ibid.*, pp. 159f; 162, 164/5; 167.
2. *See* my *Averroes Paraphrase*, etc., *loc. cit.*

thought-categories *via* Ibn aṭ-Ṭiqṭaqa's unsystematic attempt at historical-political realism to the grandiose political theory of the systematic philosopher of history Ibn Khaldūn. But the time has not yet come to pronounce with any reasonable degree of probability on such a straight line of development in political thought however attractive it may appear to a western mind. The idea must, therefore, be left to further detailed investigation which has to be applied to the whole literature under review and which must never lose sight of the all-important fact that we deal with Muslims for whom Islam offers the ideal solution.

That Ibn Khaldūn has appropriated the whole theological, juridical, philosophical and historical material which fourteenth century Islam offered is an undisputed fact. How far his sovereign grasp of this weighty tradition can account for his own system is another matter.*

It is his original approach to history and to human culture that sets him apart. This approach is new in conception no less than in method and cannot be explained as either a systematic *Summa* of traditional Islamic doctrine and teaching or as a new attempt to blend Hellenistic science and philosophy with Islamic civilisation. That both have left their indelible mark on his mind and writings goes without saying. That he has emerged as an empiric individual thinker is partly at least due to his training in Aristotelian thinking seen through the eyes of *the* Commentator Averroes. That he could train his observing eye on the historical process as a whole, that he could discover an underlying law in the political and social organism, that he could see the group as well as the individual as a distinct factor in social and political life, all this is unquestionably the result of his strong Arab consciousness and of his intimate knowledge of the political and cultural history of Islam from its foundation to his own day. That he took an active part in moulding history in North Africa as general, judge, diplomatist and scholarly historian and philosopher has given him that valuable experience of the living forces at work in the human group as distinct from the aspirations of the individual soul which enabled him to probe deeply—with rare independence and absence of prejudice—into the causes and motives of political life. What strikes the eye of the average observer of the historical process as a composite and very complicated phenomenon which he registers in more or less accurate description,—usually with an axe to grind,—Ibn Khaldūn subjects to the dissecting knife of the impersonal scientist. His aim is to lay bare the various constituent elements which make up human life in group-association. He discovered that the state has a life of its own which is governed by unalterable laws like the human organism. The state has its origin in necessity, it grows out of the free association of like-minded people who are bound together by one common bond, it develops by a determined

* For a full account *see* my *Ibn Khaldūn's Gedanken*, etc., *loc. cit.* and also my article in the *Bulletin of the John Rylands Library*, XXIV, 2, Oct., 1940, under the title : *Ibn Khaldūn : A North African Muslim Thinker of the Fourteenth Century.*†

effort of the acknowledged leader who gradually changes into an absolute monarch, reaches its climax, inevitably declines and decays. The peak-period of the state is characterised by a flourishing economic life, a high standard of education, by refined manners, a prosperous, yet dignified mode of living, by great cultural achievements in art and science, and all classes of citizens work harmoniously together for the common good, driven by a common determination. The decline sets in with a slackening of effort on the part of the ruling monarch and his dynasty which rapidly affects all the classes of the population. The inevitable result is a growing corruption and demoralisation. The ruler tends to intervene actively in the economic life of the state, creating monopolies which are detrimental to those engaged in this branch of trade and commerce. Taxes are raised and in consequence the artisans and traders lose interest and the economic life declines. Laxity in morals destroys the foundations of family and group life, discord grows and disunity takes the place of a common bond and endeavour. In short, the life of the state proceeds in cycles. Like natural organisms states rise, grow and develop, decline and fall in an eternally repetitive regular cycle. It is characteristic of Ibn Khaldūn's detached approach to the historical process that he does not put any valuation on the results of his critical inquiry. History—for him—is not to be understood as the progressive deployment of the best in human nature, both intellectually and ethically, with inevitable retrogression at times, but showing an upward trend, consciously fostered by religio-ethical teaching. Ibn Khaldūn does not even put the question of progress, he says nothing about successive dynasties which are building upon foundations laid by their predecessors. No doubt, every new dynasty which comes to power by conquest, revolution or intrigue or also by the driving force of a religious ideal as was the case with the Almoravids and Almohads, inherits the material civilisation prevailing in the time of its predecessor in power. He is not interested in moral judgments, it is quite immaterial to him whether the moral and cultural achievements are higher or lower than under a previous dynasty. What matters is that it is the same driving force—*'aṣabiyya*—that prompts a new dynasty to wrest power from another disintegrating ruling family and to establish its own authority instead. The achievements of its reign depend upon the character of that *'aṣabiyya*. If its contents is sheer will to power alone, reinforced by the united élan of the clan, it will spend its force and precipitate the inevitable turning of the cycle. If it is—on the other hand—strengthened and often gradually supplanted by the religious ideal—as is the case with Muslims generally—the natural process of growth, peak, decay and fall is spread over a longer period. But the five phases of the state run their course during four generations of a dynasty. Where religion as an active influence comes in life is certainly fuller, the achievements are more considerable. The scholar has, for the first time in history, chosen as the field of his penetrating study human society as a whole, the political scientist has made an equally fruitful discovery, *viz.*, the causal interdependence of the contributing factors in the closely-woven fabric of the state. As a Muslim and a student of Greek philosophy at the same time the paramount importance of Law for the maintenance of social life, for the security of individual life and for the protection of property is evident for him. But he sees Law not in the form of the *Sharī'a*—admittedly the ideal constitution of the perfect Islamic state—it is for him one of several important factors in the state and in its natural development. He realised, for the first time in history, the principal importance of a stable economy, not only in itself but in relation to a well-balanced budget and to an efficient, loyal army. Sound finance and disciplined army are the two pillars of the Power-State. A free economy without monopolies dominated by the ruler is equally essential to the security and prosperity of the state. All these factors must be in a state of equilibrium if the stability of the state is to be ensured. The least disturbance of one of them has serious repercussions upon the others. This is, in fact, the important original contribution which Ibn Khaldūn has made to the understanding of history in general and to the history of political theory in particular. Unlike the ideal state of the *Sharī'a* or of the *Falāsifa* as the disciples of the Greek philosophers Ibn Khaldūn's state is the actual state, the State in the Flesh, not in the Spirit. Ibn Khaldūn studies the history of Islam, its institutions and especially its many states of his time. He boldly drew general conclusions from his impartial study and crystallised his own experience into a novel theory about *'umrān*, the sum-total of human achievement in history. Although Islamic society provided him with the material for his observations and deductions he considered his conclusions to be applicable to every state. He makes allowance for the innate urge to power in strong individuals but he does not allow—we think—sufficient scope for the *imponderables* in human nature generally and in the group-mind in particular and its manifestations in religious and political movements. He could not make this allowance if his New Science was to provide a sure basis for the understanding of the historical process, especially in its political aspect. The law of absolute causality brooks no rivals, neither in the form of the absolute will of the Creator-God Who rules the Universe, nor in the shape of the arbitrary whim of the despot who is animated by the lust for power. And yet, it must not be forgotten that as a devout Muslim he saw in Islam the most perfect system of life. But this did not blind him to the reality of political life. As a shrewd observer of the state as it was—not as it ought to be—he would assign Religion only a place of utmost importance, no doubt—alongside with other powerful factors which together determine and make up the life of human society. The ethical teachings of Religion, its command to study and apply the Law in order to enable man to come near to God through knowledge of Him exerted an incomparably strong influence on the spiritual nature of man. Moral and intellectual perfection are unthinkable without this religious knowledge. But at the same time Ibn Khaldūn fears that its appeal to faith and obedience may be detrimental to the active participation of man as a citizen in the affairs of the political community. It is this aspect which is uppermost in the mind of Ibn Khaldūn as a political thinker who would not allow the ideal to obscure the lessons of history.

3

THE PLACE OF POLITICS IN THE PHILOSOPHY OF IBN BAJJA

THE posthumous publication of the *k. tadbir-ul-mutawahhid* of Abu Bakr b. al-Sa'igh b. Bajja (Avempace) in its entirety by the lamented distinguished Spanish Arabist Asin Palacios in 1946 affords a welcome opportunity for a fresh study of one aspect of the philosophical writings of this Muslim thinker of the west : his part in the transmission of Platonic ideas as they affect Political Thought in Islam. We are indebted to the scholarship of Professor Asin not only for the edition with an annotated Spanish translation of this treatise[1] which was hitherto known only from Hebrew extracts incorporated by Moses Narboni in his Commentary on Ibn Tufail's *Hayy b. Yaqzan*, apart from the edition with an English translation of the first part of the Arabic original by Dunlop in 1945.[2] Asin has in addition edited other works by Ibn Bajja : his *k. fi-l-nabat* and, of immediate interest for our problem, his *risalat fi-l-wada'* and *k. ittisal-ul-'aql bi-l-insan.* These two last named treatises are also extant in manuscript in Hebrew translations, and these enable us to restore the Arabic text in the few places where it is illegible through damage.[3] The Hebrew is moreover useful

1. Published under the title : *El Regimen del Solitario*, Madrid-Granada, with Introduction and a Summary of the contents. The editions of the other texts mentioned are also provided with introductions and summaries which are very useful in view of the difficulty of Ibn Bajja's style and diction. We were unfortunately unable to consult Prof. Asin's article "*El filosofo zaragozano Avempace*" which he published in *Revista de Aragon*, 1901.

2. In *Journal of the Royal Asiatic Society*, 1945, pp. 61-81. That the chapters headed *al-qaul fi-l-suwari-l-ruhaniyya* form an integral part of the *k. tadbiru-l-mutawahhid* is clear not only from their contents—Dunlop mentions himself that the Hebrew version contains considerably more material—but also from external evidence. For Ibn Bajja refers in his *k. ittisalu-l-'aql bi-l-insan* repeatedly to his *tadbir*, *e.g.*, p. 12, line 12 and last line ; p. 13, line 8 explicitly thus : وقد تلخص ما يخص هذه الصور الروحانية المتوسطة فى كتاب المتوحد and again on p. 21, lines 10 f. A similar instance may be quoted from the *risalatu-l-wada'* where we find a heading *fi-l-lidda* on p. 31 of Asin's text. Thus, quite a number of separate headings listed in the Catalogues of the Bodleian Library-Oxford and of the former Royal Prussian State Library-Berlin are most likely only chapter headings and not separate treatises. This is clear from their shortness. I am, moreover, indebted to Dr. Beeston, Keeper of Oriental Books at the Bodleian Library, for supplying me with a list of headings of Ms. Poc. 206. He also stressed that this MS. was "strictly speaking *not* a collection of treatises by Avempace, but rather an anthology of extracts from his works."

3. The treatises were published by Prof. Asin with a Spanish translation, Introduction, Summary of contents and copious, learned notes in *Al Andalus* : *Tratado de Avempace sobre la union del intelecto con el hombre–fi-ittisali-l-'aqli-bi-l-insan*, 1942, VII and *La Carta de Adios de Avempace* risalatu-l-wada', 1943, VIII. I.
The *lacunae* can be restored from the Hebrew version of the *risalatu-l-wada'*, preserved in *MS. Hebreu* 959 of the Bibliotheque Nationale, Paris under the title *Iggeret hap-Petira*. *E.g.* Asin, p. 19 last line ("for the most part illegible") can be reconstructed from f. 87b, line 7. ; Asin, 30, 5th last line from f. 91a, line 6. The Hebrew is more explicit than its original in a passage where Ibn Bajja quotes Aristotle as having refuted an opinion of Plato's; the Hebrew adds "*in the Book De Anima*" (Asin 17, 10 -f. 88b, 16. *See* also *n.* 25, *below*).

for the understanding of the difficult text as being a faithful and intelligent rendering. Ibn Bajja's successors Ibn Tufail and Ibn Rushd have both testified to the often sketchy, obscure and ambiguous nature of his writings[4] which seem to have been handed down to us by one of his disciples.

Thus, it is the complete original text of the *tadbir* which adds considerably to our knowledge and better understanding and appreciation of his thought. It may, therefore, not be out of place to re-examine the place of *Politics* in his philosophy in the light of the new and more complete material now available and to this task the following pages are devoted. It can be stated at the outset that this renewed study confirms, in every important point the conclusions drawn in our first attempt in 1937,[5] which was used in a previous article published in this Journal in 1948. However, we are able to add more details and thus give not only a fuller account of the *tadbir* and the light it throws on statements in the other treatises used for our inquiry, but also illustrate the importance of Plato's ideas for the shaping of Muslim thought on *Politics*.

In view of the prominence which this problem of the reception of Platonic philosophy by the Muslims has rightly gained in recent years, a few general observations must precede a discussion of the place Ibn Bajja occupies as one of the chief actors in this fascinating chapter of cultural relationships in the Middle Ages. Platonic ideas have found their way among the Muslims in various ways, as is well known : directly from Plato's Academy and its later off-shoots, indirectly through Aristotle and his Peripatetics and later the Alexandrian school. Though doubts have been expressed whether Alfarabi, the all-influential 'Second Teacher', has accepted the so-called *Theology of Aristotle* as genuine, the fact remains that he devoted a special treatise, *The Book of agreement between the ideas of the two philosophers, the Divine Plato and Aristotle*, to the task of harmonizing in neo-platonic fashion the views of both.[6] It is as yet an open question whether the original works of Plato (and Aristotle),

---

4. *See* L. Gauthier, *Hayy ben Yaqdhan*, Beyrouth, 1936, Arabic text, p. 12 for Ibn Tufail's statement. Ibn Rushd mentions towards the end of his treatise *On the possibility of the union* (of the human with the Active Intellect) Ibn Bajja's *tadbir*. *See* also next note.

5. *Politische Gedanken bei Ibn Bagga* in : *Monatsschrift f. d. Geschichte u. Wissenschaft d. Judentums* (*MGWJ*), 1937, 3. This article will be quoted henceforth as *PG*. Ibn Bajja is briefly dealt with in our article published in *Islamic Culture, XXII*, 1, entitled *Some Aspects of Islamic Political Thought* referred to henceforth as *SAIPT*. It is unavoidable that some repetitions, especially from *PG*, will occur. This may be excused the more since the publication of *MGWJ* ceased with the liquidation of German Jewry by the Nazis. The reader is asked to consult especially the notes in *PG*. The present article is concerned solely with the thought of Ibn Bajja and his relationship to Alfarabi whereas Ibn Rushd must remain outside its scope. Nor can relevant references to Ibn Rushd in *PG* and *SAIPT* be repeated. It is hoped to deal with Ibn Rushd's dependence on and attitude to Ibn Bajja in a separate article. Asin's notes also deal fully with Ibn Rushd's comments upon Ibn Bajja, especially those contained in the *risalatu-l-wada*! Munk and especially Steinschneider in his *Alfarabi* and in his *Hebr. Uebersetzungen* etc. (§ 206 and *passim*) contain valuable material. †

6. *See* our *Maimonides' Conception of State and Society* published in the Jubilee Volume *Moses Maimonides* by Dr. I. Epstein, London, The Soncino Press, 1935, p. 193 and *SAIPT*, p. 6f. *See* also : F. Dieterici, *Alfarabi's philosophische Abhandlungen*, Introduction and Arabic text, especially, p. 5.

or Alexandrine Summaries and Commentaries only found their way into the study of the Falasifa. Texts like the recently published *De Platonis Philosophia* of Alfarabi[7] and fragments from Galen's Summary of Plato's *Republic*[8] as well as the forthcoming publication of Alfarabi's Summary of Plato's *Laws* and of Galen's Paraphrase on his *Timaoos* will help towards a solution of this question. That Ibn Rushd used Galen's Paraphrase for his own on the *Politeia* is clear from his polemics against Galen.[9] But it would be premature to decide such a complicated matter in advance of a close scrutiny of the texts available and of expert application of Classical linguistic and literary criticism. The significance of the new material lies in the fact that it confirms the vital importance of Galen as an intermediary in philosophy no less than in medicine, and of Alfarabi as the leading Muslim philosopher and dispenser of Greek philosophy. For to him is due the spread of Platonic ideas among the Falasifa and the Jewish mediaeval philosophers. The special interest and value of his Summary of the philosophy of Plato lie in the emphasis which it places on Plato as a political philosopher which is strikingly evident from the summaries the author gives of such Dialogues as *Politikos, Phaidon, Republic, Laws, Crito* and *Apology*,[10] and from the way in which he links their contents to the overriding question of human happiness and perfection which he treats fully in his own independent political treatises, the *madina fadila*, the *k. al-siyasat al-madaniya* and the *k. tahsil-ul-sa'ada.*

One further point may be made : we must not overlook the danger of generalisation and over-simplification, a danger vastly increased by the peculiar ways which the diffusion of Greek philosophy took among the Falasifa. Yet, a careful reading of Ibn Bajja, on the basis of Alfarabi and in retrospect from Ibn Rushd tends to confirm our introductory remarks to a lecture delivered during the Maimonides' octocentenary celebrations of the University of Cambridge :[11] " if one were to say that Aristotle was the unquestioned authority in the field of Logic, Physics and Metaphysics whereas Plato is to be looked upon as the master in the field of Ethics and Politics, it would perhaps simplify matters too much, but it comes near the truth." This may be challenged for Ethics seeing that Aristotle's *Nicomachian Ethics* was commented upon by Alfarabi, cited by Ibn Bajja and once more commented upon by Ibn Rushd, and remembering that the division into Ethics and Politics as

---

7. Published by Fr. Rosenthal & R. Walzer as Vol. 2 of *Plato Arabus*. *See* also the critical study on it by L. Strauss : *Farabi's Plato* in : *Ginzberg Jubilee Volume*, New York, 1945.

8. *See* R. Walzer, *Galen on Jews and Christians*. This study contains references to and quotations from the extant fragments of Galen's *Summary*. Whether Walzer is right in assuming that Ibn Rushd's *Paraphrase* on the *Republic* is based on this *Summary* is not easy to decide. It is of interest also for Ibn Bajja who quotes Plato and refers to his *Republic* in the *risalatu-l-wada'* and specially in his *k. tadbiru-l-mutawahhid*.

9. *See* SAIPT, p. 11.

10. *See De Platonis Philosophia* §§ 18, 23, 24, 25, 27. This ' political ' interpretation of Plato's philosophy may have been in Alfarabi's Greek source—translated into Arabic—or may represent an adaptation to Islamic conceptions.

11. *See* n. 6, *above*.

the theoretical and practical parts respectively of the foremost art goes back to Aristotle. Yet, a perusal of Ibn Rushd's Commentary on the *Nicomachian Ethics* alone justifies the assumption that Aristotle's theoretical part was interpreted in the light of Plato's practical one. It will, of course, have to be shown how Platonic notions accepted, though even modified, by Aristotle, were emphasized by the Falasifa.[12]

II

In the light of these observations it is evident that the plea we entered in our earlier study *Politische Gedanken bei Ibn Bajja*[13] for a com-

12. R. Walzer in his article on *Arabic Transmission of Greek Thought To Mediaeval Europe* (*Bulletin of the John Rylands Library* XXIX, 1, July 1945) asserts. " Al-Farabi—and Averroes after him—followed Aristotle in Logic, Physics, Psychology, Metaphysica and Ethics, although slightly changing Peripatetic Metaphysics by adding Neoplatonic elements. But in Politics—possibly following some Greek predecessor in Alexandria—he deliberately chose Plato as his guide.. " We are inclined to think that this statement needs qualification with regard to Ethics as we stated in the text. On the question of Platonism in Islam *see* also the article by S. Pines in *Islamic Culture* XI, 1937. Ibn Bajja is of great importance for this problem for he is the link between Alfarabi and Ibn Rushd and the frequent references to him by Ibn Rushd, mostly polemical, in his Commentaries on Aristotle's logical writings and especially on his *De Anima* should be collected and related to this whole complex of the reception of Greek ideas. This can, however, only be undertaken on the basis of Ibn Bajja's own Book *On the Soul* alone extant in bulk in the Berlin MS. Whether he owes anything to Ibn Bajja in his attack on Galen's logical writings should also be examined. For Ibn Bajja's own work and its proper understanding and estimate it will be necessary to ascertain how far his doctrine of *Spiritual Forms* goes back to Plato's *Ideas*, directly or through Alexander of Aphrodisias whose treatise *On the Spiritual Forms* he quotes in his *k. ittisal*, p. 18. 3. *See* also next note.

13. *PG* (*see n.* 5), 153-7, with *ns.* 1-15. The following additions concerning his own writings and references to those of others may be made : of his own writings he quotes in the *tadbir* his *Commentary on the Seventh* (Book) *of De Auditu* (Asin, 17. 7 and *see* his *n.* 25 on p. 48 of his translation), also 33. 10). To works by Aristotle must be added : *Rhetoric* (*tadbir*, 25. 2) ; *Metaphysics* (*ibid.*, 61.16); *De Sensu et Sensibili* (esp. Book II, *ibid.* 25.17 *et passim*) ; *Analytica Post.* (*ibid.*, 9.16) ; *Hermeneutica* (*k. ittisal*, 26). Once Ibn Bajja refers, in his *risalatu-l-wada'* to the *Nicomachia, Book XI.* Asin questions the correctness of this reference since the *Nicomachia* contains only 10 Books. But the Arabs added to these the two books of the *Magna Moralia* as Books XI and XII of the *Nicomachia* (*see* Steinschneider, *Hebr. Uebers.*, 215). Asin's references to the *Eudemian Ethics* are misleading since this book was not known among the Arabs as far as we know.†

As for Plato, we have to add references to the *Republic* (*tadbir* 49, last line where the Fifth Book is mentioned ; *risalatu-l-wada,'* 25.10 together with the *Phaidon*). In *PG, n.* 11 we stated *Kriton* for Hebrew *qaron* (in an *addendum*, p. 168 *Phaidon*, following Steinschneider) and the *Laws*. The Hebrew text f. 89a, 6th line from bottom has : *besepher han-Nimusim ubesepher qaron.* Were it not for the reference to ' *the fifth of the siyasa Flatun*, which we just quoted we could interpret *fi-l-siyasati* in the *risala* as *Laws* since they are counted as a complement to the *Republic* from Alfarabi onwards (*see De Platonis Philosophia*, § 27). But they are correctly termed *nawamis* and there can be no doubt that the Hebrew translator is in the wrong.

As for Alfarabi, there is a reference in the *k. ittisal*, 9 to his *k. fi-l-wahdati* which Asin cannot identify.

Hippocrates is mentioned in the *tadbir* (p. 17) and Galen repeatedly not always in approval. The reference to his *Book of the Preservation of Health* is certain (p. 12.1). It is followed by كما وضعت في صناعة الطب which Dunlop translates (p. 78): " as I have laid down in the *Art of Medicine.*" Asin seems to have understood it with the verb in the passive—but then it should be *wudi'a*—unless we emend to *wada'ahu*, in which case it would still refer to Galen. Indeed, Galen wrote a treatise called *k. fi-l-sina'ati-l-tibbyya* according to Bergstraesser (*Abhandlungen f. d. Kunde d. Morgenlandes* 46, p. 41). On the other hand, the possibility cannot be ruled out that Ibn Bajja refers to his own writings on matters medical of which several are listed both in MS. Poc. 206 of the Bodleian and in MS. Nr. 5060 of Berlin. Some of these bear indeed identical titles with those listed by Hunain as having been translated by him or his school into Arabic (*see* Bergstraesser).

Here is a fruitful field of research ,not only in connection with Ibn Bajja. *See* also P. Kraus-R. Walzer, *Galeni Compendium Timaei Platonis* (to be published any moment as vol. I of the *Plato Arabus*). Introduction pp. 9 ff. where the learned editors discuss the question of Galen's interpretation. It appears to have been a mixture of Peripatetic and Neo-platonic canons. If, as Walzer believes, Galen's *Summaries* were the

prehensive treatment of this Muslim philosopher and for a considered appraisal of his significance can only be repeated with even greater emphasis since the more important of his works are available in the original in Prof. Asin's excellent annotated editions.[14] For our part, we must confine ourselves to that section of his work which has some bearing upon *Politics*. As explained in *Politische Gedanken* and summarized in our article in this Journal[15] Ibn Bajja is passionately interested in and concerned about the happiness and perfection of the individual soul. Politics enter into his philosophic inquiry only in so far as they affect—positively or, more often, negatively—the attainment of this goal. State and Society interest him not as such, their origin and development, their aim and object only in so far as they can help to understand and further the life of the individual striving for perfection. References to government, constitutions, classes, economy, arts and crafts, war, administration of justice, the political and social implications of the art of medicine have their place in his scheme more often than not as illustrations and analogies. They do not interest him as phenomena in their own right. When Plato studies the individual citizen with his virtues and vices he does so in order to find an answer to the questions : what is justice ? What is the best government ? How do we arrive at the Ideal State ? Not so Ibn Bajja who only asks : what is the ultimate aim of the truly human individual and how can this philosopher attain his aim ? Whilst he is convinced that a perfect state is desirable since it would provide the ideal background for his philosopher he knows that man has to live in an imperfect state. Far from acknowledging any obligation on the part of the philosopher towards the State in which he lives, in compliance with Plato's demand that the philosopher should rule the perfect state in justice, his problem is rather to find an answer to the question whether man needs the state in order to attain his goal. He is concerned lest the imperfect State hinder or even prevent the individual from attaining his object and he asks himself whether it is possible for the philosophic man to sever his connexion with his community with whom he has after all nothing in common. That man has a right, perhaps even a duty to isolate himself appears to be taken for granted by him. The question is, therefore, narrowed down to this : must the *mutawahhid*, the philosophic soul who segregates himself from society, be and remain a part of the state ? This leads to the further

---

texts which provided the Falasifa with the knowledge of Plato's philosophy, the latter's harmonizing tendencies could be explained. We know, however, from Ibn Bajja that he was aware of fundamental differences between Plato and Aristotle (*see PG*, n. 11 and *k. ittisal*, p. 20.60 on Plato's *Ideas* rejected by Aristotle).

A further urgent task waiting to be undertaken concerns the exact relationship of Ibn Bajja to Ghazzali and Sufism. *See* also *n.* 19, *below*. Ibn Sina does not seem to have been known to Ibn Bajja, yet this needs confirmation.

14. These editions greatly facilitate such an undertaking. They contain a wealth of useful information and a first discussion of the principal problems raised by the difficult material. They must serve as a basis for a fuller investigation.†

15. *SAIPT*, p. 12f.

question : how can one be a part of a whole—and only so can one be perfect—and at the same time live apart from one's fellow men, at least in mind, though one may be within society with one's body, like a stranger ?[16]

In all this concentration on the happiness and perfection of the individual who aims as a spiritual being at the union with the (active) intellect which elevates him to a state of perfect bliss, Ibn Bajja uses Platonic conceptions, images and analogies.[17] These are either taken from Plato's own writings—mentioned by name or unacknowledged but verifiable—or from Galen's Summaries or are borrowed from Alfarabi, especially from his *k. al-siyasat al-madaniya*, *k. tahsil al-sa'ada* or *k. fi ara'i ahli-l-madinati-l-fadilati*, though without acknowledgment.[18]

III

It is against this general background—rather sketchily and incompletely drawn—that we have to analyse the references to political matters in the three treatises under discussion. It appears from a comparison of such statements that Ibn Bajja started from an ideal position in the *risalat-ul-wada'* represented by the Ideal or excellent State (*al-madinat-ul-fadila*) which is contrasted with the non-excellent, imperfect states as regards virtues and the nature of man, basing himself on Plato's *Republic* as depicted by Alfarabi in his afore-mentioned 'political' treatises. In the *tadbir* the emphasis is laid on the *mutawahhid* and his conduct in face of the difficulties which the imperfect states create, be they simple or composite, with the ideal state as the pattern reminiscent of the discussion in Book IX of the *Republic*. The central theme is the philosopher's blessedness, his progress from the lowest to the highest *Spiritual Forms*—Plato's Ideas—the vision of which leads him to union with the Intellect to which topic the third treatise, *k. ittisal-ul-'aqli bi-l-insan*, with frequent reference to the two other treatises is devoted. A proviso must, however, be added, *i.e.*, if the order of writing is as we are inclined to assume on the basis of our reading of the treatises and the manner and development of their argument. We are led to this view by the just mentioned shifting of emphasis which falls on now one

16. This is fully discussed in the *tadbir* and will engage our attention later on in this article in connection with Alfarabi. *See* also, PG, 160 ff. and esp. 165.

17. *E.g.* the simile of the Cave; comparisons with the arts and crafts like medicine, navigation, weaving, shoemaking ; the example of Socrates. *See* also throughout this article references to Plato in the text as well as in the notes.

18. His dependence on Alfarabi deserves special attention. Asin often cites parallels from Alfarabi's treatises. But it will have to be ascertained whether in some cases Ibn Bajja made an independent approach to Aristotle rather than using Alfarabi's Commentaries on Aristotle's logical and physical studies. To quote only one instance : do Ibn Bajja's examples taken from the animals on p. 55.7 ff. of the *tadbir*—when he describes the composite nature of man's actions, partly animal, partly human—go back to Aristotle (*see* Asin's *notes* on p. 93 of his translation) or rather to Alfarabi's *k. tahsilu-l-sa'ada*, 28.6 ff. (Hyderabad 1345) ? That Ibn Bajja does not mention Abu Nasr's specific works is rather significant. For an exception *see n.* 13, *above* and *PG*, *n.* 11. Yet, parallels can be found in large numbers, quite apart from terminology. *See* later on in text and *notes*.

now another of the elements constituting in their combination the ' way of life ' of the speculative philosopher in search of ultimate perfection and blessedness. There is, moreover, significance in the fact that the *risalat-ul-wada*ʿ never mentions the *k. tadbir-ul-mutawahhid* in which *Spiritual Forms* are fully expounded, nor does it refer to the *k. ul-ittisal-ul-ʿaql bi-l-insan* although it treats itself of *ʿaql.* Further evidence for our view may be found in the omission of any reference to the *tadbir* when Ibn Bajja attacks Ghazzali in his *risalat-ul-wada*ʿ for seeing the ultimate aim of man in the delight (*iltidhadh*) experienced in speculative contemplation when he lived in isolation.[19] Yet, we would not press either of these two points too far. Suffice it to point out that whilst Ibn Bajja is at one with the other Falasifa in postulating union with the Intellect as the ultimate aim of man as a rational being, he ignores the political relevance of the Divine Law (*shariʿa*) and its educative value for man as a citizen. His exclusive concern for individual spirituality and the consequent neglect of the obligations of citizenship account for the relegation of Politics proper to a secondary position in his system, as was stressed earlier in this article and on previous occasions. This makes it the more difficult to present his ' political philosophy ' in a coherent form and as something complete in itself possessing a value of its own. Yet, by the use of political terms and arguments—though mainly, to repeat, by way of illustration and analogy—he has followed a line of thought which sets him apart from his predecessors Alfarabi and Ibn Sina no less than from his successors of whom Ibn Tufail continued his ' way ' to a logical conclusion whereas Ibn Rushd in strong opposition to his a—political, not to say anti—social individualism returned to the main line of Platonic *Politics* in direct succession of Alfarabi and Ibn Sina.[20]

IV

Alfarabi, as is well known, tried to harmonize Platonic conceptions with Islamic demands as laid down in the *Shariʿa* : hence his discussion of the duties of the ruler (*raʿis*) in whom qualities of the philosopher-king blend with those of the *khalifa* as described by Al-Mawardi.[21] This in

---

19. *risalatu-l-wada*ʿ (Asin) : 22.15 ff.

Ibn Tufail, p. 10, *loc. cit.*, criticises Ibn Bajja for his misrepresentation of the meaning of *iltidhadh* as understood by the Sufis. Asin deals with this point in his Introduction both to the *risalatu-l-wada*ʿ and to the *k. ittisal* defending Ghazzali against Ibn Bajja's strictures. It is Asin's view that the only difference between the two thinkers in relation to the ultimate aim is that for Ibn Bajja intellectual preparation through study of the speculative and generally secular sciences is indispensable.

Note the term *al-mudun al-kibar* which may be modelled upon Alfarabi's *al-'umam al-kibar* (*cp. k. al, siyasat*,40).

Ibn Bajja takes Ghazzali to task again in the *tadbir*, 27.9 ff. (*see* also Asin's *ns.* 52-4 to his translation, p. 59 f.) and mentions the Sufis again on p. 46. 10 f. (p. 82 of translation, with n. 102). Ibn Bajja devotes much space to a discussion of pleasure or delight, based on Aristotle's *Nicomachian Ethics* (esp. Book VII ch. iv and Book I, ch. viii, 10-13) and on Plato's *Republic* 580-2 and esp. 586.

20. *See PG*, 165 and *SAIPT*, 13.

21. *See SAIPT*, 2 f. and *Maimonides' Conception, etc.*, *loc. cit.*, 198. ; also Alfarabi, *mad. fad.*, 59-61 and *tahsil*, 41-43, esp. 43.18 f.

itself would not have made out of the Greek ideal ruler the Islamic counterpart but for Alfarabi's important stipulation that the prophetic quality must be possessed by the philosopher-statesman who is to be the ideal Islamic ruler. This he discusses in connection with the central subject of his philosophy and that of all subsequent Muslim and Jewish thinkers in his wake : human perfection and happiness, or better, blessedness.[22]

Ibn Bajja accepts Alfarabi's definition of the ultimate aim of man as the attainment of intellectual perfection which must be preceded by moral perfection. But he concentrates on the government of the human self of the individual speculative philosopher—to repeat once more—and not on the ideal philosopher-king who is also lawgiver and prophet, nor on the best government of the State over which this most perfect philosopher-king rules. Now, it is worth noting that in the *risalat-ul-wada*' human perfection and blessedness is made the subject of inquiry within the framework of the State and is considered possible of realization in the ideal or perfect State in the first place but also not impossible in the imperfect states. Yet, in order to attain his highest perfection man must live in Society which is politically organized in the State. There is interaction between man's perfection and that of the State. This naturally implies that highest perfection is attainable only in the perfect State, in the *madina fadila*. The ruler of the Ideal State is therefore called *ra'is*,[23] and we may add, *ra'is* in the meaning Alfarabi gives this term in his *k. fi ara'i ahli-l-madinati-l-fadilati*.[24] Ibn Bajja assigns to the real ruler the task of " *alloting to him over whom he rules such tasks the execution of which ensures the subject* (*mar'us*) *will reach the goal destined for him through these actions—and no other goal.*" The proper relationship between ruler and ruled is thus that " *between master and pupil.*" The regent (*mudabbir*) of the other imperfect states. . . . — compared to the horseman who exercises rule over the bridle—is *ra'is* only in a figurative sense insofar as he resembles the king in certain respects.[24a]

---

22. *See Maimonides', etc., loc. cit.*, 196 f. and *SAIPT*, 6-8.

23. *risala* (Asin) : 30.19-27.

Cp. Alfarabi, *k. al-tanbih ala tahsil sabil al-sa'ada* of which only its Latin translation was available to us in the edition of Salman (*Recherches de Théologie Ancienne et Médiaevale*, XII, 1940) 39 : " *rectores* (*i.e., al-mudabbirun*) *enim solummodo constituunt cives bonos per ea quibus exercitant eos in bonis actionibus, quales vero actiones sunt honeste.*"

Cp. also *k. al-siyasat*, 51, 4 ff.

24. *mad. fad.*, 57 and 59 ; *k. al-siyasat*, 54 ; *cp.* also *ibid.*, 48 f.

24a. *Cp.* Alfarabi, *k. al-siyasat*, 48 on *ra'is* and *mar'us* and particularly 69, 14 ff on these two kinds of men in democracies. On the Heads in other states *see ibid.*, 58 end, 59 beg. ; 59.9 ff. 61.13 ff (in a timocracy) ; 65, 4 ff. (tyranny). *See* also *PG*, *n.* 22.

Such a comparison will illustrate the fundamental difference in approach, attitude and interest that separates Ibn Bajja from Alfarabi despite the striking parallels in expression. Ibn Bajja uses Alfarabi to state concisely how the attainment of the goal—which is for him the same as for Alfarabi—depends on leadership in the perfect and imperfect states. Alfarabi goes into considerable detail about the varying nature of *sa'ada* in the different States and how that affects the leaders, their nature and their actions in the state.

Cp. also Aristotle, *Nic. Ethics*, *Book* I, *ch.* I, 4 f.

At the same time, it is possible for man to confine himself to the virtues in the other non-perfect states with real benefit accruing from them.[25] The virtuous men " *are like the guardians in the state who are at the head of the people and through them the affairs of the state are being perfected for through the ethical virtues there exist in it social relations on account of which the state becomes perfect.*[26] He continues the discussion of human faculties under the aspect of the master-servant relationship and in contrast with the animals which share some virtues with man, entirely in keeping with Alfarabi's exposition,[27] in the larger context of man's destiny. Thus, the arts of " *medicine, navigation, agriculture, rhetoric and generalship are evidently all subordinate faculties. For, generalship is only* (directed) *towards the welfare of the state so that it may perform the task for which it was prepared. Rhetoric is intended to furnish persuasion by which philosophy is illumined. For, were philosophy non-existent, rhetoric would be useless and vain.*[28] It is interesting to compare Alfarabi's summary of Plato's *Gorgias* in his *Plato's Philosophy* with this negative assessment by Ibn Bajja. The strong expressions used rather suggest that Ibn Bajja was more fully acquainted with Plato's adverse views on Rhetoric. For Plato the orator was a serious rival of the statesman.[29] The political significance and danger do not determine Ibn Bajja's views, though.

Since these arts serve another purpose they cannot be the final goal. This is no other than the Intellect which exists in man in a way quite different from other faculties. He becomes, indeed, a divine being and comes as near to God as possible through it. Ibn Bajja then explains the nature of this Intellect by Plato's famous simile of the Sun as seen with the naked eye or through reflexion in the water. If its essence can be contemplated and perceived it is like seeing the Sun without intermediary. Otherwise, we perceive the Intellect through the *Intelligibilia* in greater or lesser proximity. " *It is clear that this goal is intended for us in our nature. But this is possible only in political association.* (For) *men were fashioned opposite to each other in their stations so that through them the State*

---

25. *risala* ; 33..9 f.

The Hebrew version reads *she'ar, i.e.* Arabic *sa'ir* for Asin's *siyar* and we are inclined to follow the Hebrew.

26. *risala* ; 34.19-26.

Cp. also *n.* 24a, *above.*

27. *See k. tahsil al-sa'ada*, 28.6 ff.

28. *risala* : 35.3-6.

Cp. also Alfarabi on the arts and crafts in the state as means to the human end, *e.g.*, *mad. fad.*, 65, 15 ff. Agriculture is mentioned in k. al-siyasat, 49.2 and 59.12 *e.g.*, Generalship *k. tahsil*, 25, 18 f. and 32, 9 f.

Rhetoric defined in his *Ihsa al-'ulum* (ed. Gonzales Palencia, Madrid 1932, p. 25) as the art of persuasion The same term is used in Ibn Bajja (*iqna'*) in the same sense. In his summary of the *Gorgias* which, according to Alfarabi means *al-Khidma*, *service*, (*see* on this curious translation *DePlatonis Philosophia*, *loc. cit.*, XVII), the negative character of Rhetoric is stressed, since its employment in reflecting over the *existing Things* does not give us —Plato makes this clear—this knowledge (*See ibid.*, text p. 8). Ibn Bajja's *hikma*, philosophy, is identical with *'ilmu-l-nazari fi-l-maujudat* of this passage. *Cp. Nic. Eth.*, *Book* VI, *ch.* VI, 1-3 *See* also *Tadbir* (Asin), 57, 2 ff.

29. *See Gorgias*, 466 C ; 520 B and generally Ernest Barker, *Greek Political Theory*, 1947, pp. 133 ff. and 199 on quadrivium and trivium respectively. This book is an excellent guide to Plato's political thought.

should be perfected in order that this purpose be achieved.[30] Here Ibn Bajja is still in full agreement with Alfarabi and the other Falasifa that political association is necessary so that man can achieve his purpose. Variety of natural disposition compels men to associate in a state in order to assure themselves of intellectual perfection through the perfection of the state. This contrasts strongly with the position Ibn Bajja adopts later in his *k. tadbiru-l-mutawahhid.* But at this stage we note already his exclusively metaphysical motivation of political association. Mutual help in acquiring food, shelter and clothing, mutual protection and defence of life and property, regulated by Law, do not for him furnish the reasons for the origin and development of the State as for all the other Falasifa. It is only logical that Ibn Bajja should now proceed to an explanation of how the union with the Intellect can be effected. There are two methods for this possibility : one natural, the other supernatural or divine. The natural one is attained by science by man's own spontaneous (and unaided) effort. The divine way originates in God's help through his messengers and prophets who spread that knowledge which is God's most precious gift to man. Quranic verses are cited to prove that this science, this knowledge is postulated by the *Shari'a.* God wishes man to draw near to Him. This is possible only by a knowledge of His essence. It is for this reason that God created the Intellect, His dearest creation and creature. Through its possession man has become a created being dearest to God. Only through knowledge can man draw near to God, therefore knowledge leads to God and ignorance removes man from Him.[31]

Ibn Bajja illustrates the special character of the truly human man by comparisons with the animal world. This applies in particular to the meaning and value of Delight or Pleasure (*iltidhadh*).[32] " *The political human contact for mutual help such as contact for instruction and perception is the intellectual encounter. The divine encounter is for the necessity of this kind of science.*"[33] This, then, is the ultimate aim.

No doubt, the religious fervour apparent from the elated description of the Divine element in man, the Intellect, is genuine. The space allotted to this description is considerably larger than that given over

---

30. *risala* : 37 . 7-16.

Cp. also Alfarabi, *mad. fad.*, 54. In the *k. ittisal* Ibn Bajja uses the same simile to emphasize the difference between the *su 'ada* and the *jumhur* (20.3f) and later on makes again the distinction between clear, direct vision and vision through reflection. *See* Plato, *Republic* VII, 514-516 C and ns. 35, 37 and 41, *below.*

Alfarabi uses the same analogy of direct or intermediate vision of the sun in his discussion of the Active Intellect in the *k. al-siyasat,* 7 and, to illustrate the difference between imagination and perception, 55.8 ff.

31. *risala*: 3 8. 24-39. 14.

Note that self-perception is the noblest form of knowledge leading to the most exalted stage of the perception of the intellect. Asin refers in a note to the observation of I. Goldziher in : ZA XXII that this *Hadith* is spurious and of neo-platonic origin. Ibn Bajja chose it deliberately, no doubt.

32. *Cp. n.* 19, *above.*

Suffice it to emphasize the need for a comparative study of the meaning of *iltidhadh* in Sufi teaching.

33. *risala,* 39-24-40.3.

to the description of the natural way, the way of secular study based upon man's own reasoning exclusively. Yet, striking as this treatment is it is only one phase—and we repeat our suggestion that it is the first phase—in a development that centres in and ends with the union of the human with the Divine Intellect which, though strictly an intellectual, cogitative process is not so far distant from Ghazzali's religious way.[34] Whilst the *risala* maintains the participation of the seeker after this union in the political community the *k. ittisal* shows no trace of any connection with a State. In this respect it reflects the culmination which Ibn Bajja's thinking reached in the later chapters of the *k. tadbiru-l-mutawahhid*. In this work its author has shaken off the strong influence which Alfarabi's political-mindedness has exerted upon him in the *risala*. But he has not freed himself from his literary dependence upon his master.

V

Alfarabi defines the science of *Politics* as the science dealing with the things through which the people living in states in political association attain happiness, every one of them according to his natural disposition.[35] It follows from that that Alfarabi will never countenance an individual's segregation and isolation from the community in order to attain highest perfection by himself. No, he needs the assistance of many men.[36]

We will now consider in detail how Ibn Bajja—by contrast—solves the problem which he sets his *mutawahhid* in relation to the State, in the first place the imperfect states. It is obvious that the perfect state is ruled with justice and love and thus enables its citizens to reach their goal, the happiness of the philosopher who through practice of the speculative sciences experiences the bliss of union with the Active Intellect after the perception of the highest spiritual forms. "*Speculative knowledge* (*al-nazar*)," says Ibn Bajja in his *k. ittisal*, . . . *is the future life and it is the utmost happiness* (*or, blessedness*), *unique to man*."[37] Obviously,

---

34. This is, at least, the opinion of Prof. Asin Palacios. *See* his introduction to the *k. ittisal*.

35. Alfarabi, *k. tahsil al-sa'ada*, 16.4-8.
and *Cp.* also p. 15 about النظر الالهى

From the *Book of the Agreement, etc.* (Dieterici, *Alfarabi's* philosophische Abhandlungen, p. 5 of text) this passage is relevant: والبرهانيات موكولة الى اصحاب الاذهان الصافية والعقول المستقيمة والسياسيات موكولة الى ذوى الاراء السديده والشرعيات موكولة الى ذوى الالهامات الروحانية واهم هذه كلها الشرعيات

The stress laid on the *Shari'a* is a notable feature, entirely absent in Ibn Bajja.

36. Alfarabi, *k. tahsil*, 14 : 6-9 and 12-14.

Man must co-operate with others, therefore, he is called الحيوان الانسى والحيوان المدنى
Cp. also *mad. fad.*, 54, 1-10.

37. *k. ittisal* 17.25 f. and Alfarabi, *k. tahsil*, 15.14 ff.

There are three grades of ascent to this union : the first, natural one, is achieved by the exercise of the practical arts, the second through speculative knowledge—this grade is compared to seeing the sun in water, *i. e.* reflection, not actual seeing (*see above*)—and the third is the grade of the blessed ones (*al-su'ada*) who see a thing in itself, *i.e.*, the real thing in its essense. *See, ibid.*, p. 18 f. †

the Ideal State alone can be the scene of this progressive ascent of man true to his unique destiny. The problem of Ibn Bajja was, therefore, to find a way for such a man to attain his goal under unfavourable conditions such as prevail in the existing states which lack true and right opinions and consequently are not administered like the Ideal State. He found the answer in the isolation of the individual. It is his *tadbir*, self-government, Ibn Bajja wants to set out in this treatise.[38]

He begins with a definition of the term *tadbir*, distinguishing between its general connotation and particular application—he has not studied and commented upon Aristotle's and Alfarabi's logical writings in vain. Its proper application is to city states (*mudun*) and to the household (*al-manzil*). Yet, *the term "government of the household" is only rarely employed* and *then in a homonymous and restricted sense.*'[39] By contrast, the term is then applied to God and His absolute rule over the world, the noblest of all, which is only called *tadbir* because of the alleged similarity it bears with the creation of the world.[40] It is interesting to observe that Ibn Bajja distinguishes between the philosophers (*al-falasifa*) and the mass of common people, the *vulgus* (*al-jumhur*). The former use this term (and, we may add, all terms) in its "*pure association,*" *i.e.*, homonymously whilst the latter use it in an "ambiguous," *i.e.*, equivocal sense.[41]

" *Plato*, says Ibn Bajja, "*explained in the* '*Republic*'[42] *the nature of the government of states and what the meaning of right therein is and wherefrom error reaches it....and he pronounced on merit, ignorance or vice.*[43]

See Alfarabi, *k. tahsil*, 15, 14 ff for another kind of progressive intellectual endeavour towards perfection and *Philos. Abhdlg loc. cit.* p.31 about knowledge of God and the philosopher's *Imitatio Dei* (*al-tashabbuhu bi-l-khaliq*). *Cp.* Plato, *Theaetetus*, 176B: "*to become like God so far as this is possible ; and to become like God is to become righteous and holy and wise.*" *See* also 176 C.

38. *tadbir* (Asin) : 29.10 f.

39. *tadbir* (Asin) : 4.13 ff.

Dunlop reads for يردف in Asin's text يروف and notes : "so MS. apparently. Perhaps روقه" (p. 64). Consequently he translates differently. We follow Asin.

40. *tadbir* (Asin) : 4.15-5.1.

Cp. with this Alfarabi's statement (*A's philos. Abhdlg.* 5) : البارئ جل جلاله مدبر جميع العالم

41. *tadbir* : 5.3 ff. الجمهور بتشكيك الفلاسفة باشتراك This distinction between the philosophers and the mass of the people is, as is well known, common to the Falasifa and some Jewish mediaeval thinkers. *See* also *n.* 30, *above.*

42. So Dunlop, whereas Asin translates السياسة المدنية by 'political government ! *siyasa* is usually the designation for Plato's *Republic* and Ibn Bajja refers to it so on p. 49 (*see n.* 13 *above*). Galen's summary bears this title and Alfarabi refers to it as the book *fi-l-siyasati* in his *De Platonis Philosophia* (*loc. cit.*, p. 20 of text, line 14). Ibn Sina likewise in his *Aqsamu-l-'ulum.*

43. *tadbir*, 5.18-6.2.

Alfarabi summarises the contents of the *Republic* in his *Book of Agreement*, *etc.* (*Philos. Abhdlg. loc. cit.*, 5) thus : فان افلاطون هو الذى دون السياسات وهذبها وبين السير العادلة والعشرة الأنسية المدنية وابان عن فضائلها واظهر الفساد العارض لافعال من هجر العشرة المدنية وترك التعاون فيها

We would underline that corruption and decay are the result of man abandoning political society and note the contrast with Ibn Bajja. *Cp.* also § 25 on the *Republic*, p. 19f. of text in *De Platonis Philosophia*, *loc. cit.*

The household, in Plato's view, is a part of the State and peculiar to man.[44] Since it is a part of the state its *tadbir* was not discussed in the political art. *For, he* (Plato) *explained there what a household is and how it exists. Its best existence is that it should be a common possession.*"[45] Further, since the household is a part of the state, it follows that its character depends upon that of the state. It is perfect only in the Ideal State, not in the four imperfect states.[46] The perfection of the household is therefore not intended for its own sake *but in order to make the state perfect and for man's natural goal.*[47] Ibn Bajja denies economics the character of an independent science for this reason and says that its discussion is a part of man's government of himself or of politics. It is therefore bound up with particular circumstances prevailing at certain periods as can be learnt from the many books on the subject, *e.g.*, *Kalila wa Dimna*. This view runs counter to that held by Ghazzali and Ibn Sina who both adopted the threefold division of the practical sciences into Economics, Ethics and Politics which, as is well known, goes back to Aristotle.[48] The *Ideal*

---

44. Alfarabi who is strongly dependent on Plato's *Republic* deals in his *k. al-siyasat*, 39 with the units of association of which the household is the smallest as part of the street which in turn is part of the village which is part of the city. The city-association, *al-madina* is the first perfect unit. For its sake the smaller units in themselves defective exist.

45. *tadbir* : 6.2 ff.

Dunlop changes the first *sina'a* to *siyasa* and translates *Republic*. He notes that this 'correction seems necessary, but the passage remains obscure.' He translates the second *al-sina'a al-madaniyya* by *Politics*. In his note he refers to " Aristotle's *Politics* (i, 3 seq.), here apparently ascribed to Plato. There seems to have been no Arabic version of the *Politics*, however. The last part is correct and Ibn Rushd's statement that he commented upon Plato's *Republic* because he had not yet seen Aristotle's *Politics* holds good for the Falasifa to date. (*See SAIPT*, 7). It may be noted in this connection that Asin whenever *al-'ilm al-madani* or *al-sina'a al-madaniya* which are used by Ibn Bajja synonymously, occur makes a reference to Aristotle's *Politics*. This is very misleading and we have failed to locate even one of the numerous references so given, also in other places.

There is, moreover, no need to go outside Plato quite apart from the difficulty to ignore the text which clearly means Plato whether we adopt Dunlop's correction or not. It would be easiest to make the change since Plato nowhere in the *Republic* explicitly deals with economics. But *oikos*, household, and 'economics' are, though briefly, dealt with both in the *Politikos* and the *Nomoi*. It is here that we have to look for the source of Ibn Bajja's statement. Both treatises were known to the Falasifa, at least in Summaries (*see* Alfarabi *De Platonis Philosophia*, *loc. cit.* §§18 and 27) Alfarabi's Summary of the *Laws* will soon be published. We know from Hunain b. Ishaq that Galen wrote a Summary of the *Politikos*. The source for Ibn Bajja's statement may therefore be sought in *Politikos* 258E-259D, esp. 259B and such passages in the *Laws* as *Book* III, 680B-E, *Book* V, 729, 737, 739, 740 and 742. It is by no means impossible that even *Republic* 369f. on the beginnings of social and political organisation can be claimed, esp. 369D.

Political art or science comprises all these Platonic writings and more as is so evident from Alfarabi's *De Platonis Philosophia*. One may even think of Alfarabi's treatises and certainly the *Nicomachia* is included.

46. The basis for the four imperfect states is naturally Plato's *Republic*, 445DE and 544C. There are four states mentioned in the *mad. fad.* of Alfarabi, 61, apart from the Ideal or perfect state. We cannot agree with Asin who in his *n.* 6 on p. 36 of his translation refers to the *k. al-siyasat*, 57. There are, however only three mentioned in addition to the Ideal State and we are not justified to see in the *nawabit* of this passage (*see* later) " perfect individuals who live isolated in the imperfect states," for there they are compared to " darnel in the wheat."

Whenever Ibn Bajja mentions four other states he means the four mentioned in the *mad. fad.*. *See n.* 51, *below* for a full treatment.

47. *tadbir* (Asin, 7.8 f. What follows in our treatment is a summary of this page 7.

48. This view is confirmed by another passage in the *tadbir* (p. 57 beg).. where Ibn Bajja enumerates economics among such '*crafts and faculties*' as rhetoric, strategy, medicine, etc.

Barker (*loc. cit.* 273) sees in the passage in the *Politikos* 259B " there is one science of all of them : and this science may be called royal or political or economical " the starting point of Aristotle's *Politics* which

State is characterized by the absence of physicians and judges because its citizens are united in love and never quarrel among themselves. All its actions are just, its citizens live on a sensible diet excluding illness. By contrast, the four simple states have need of both, physicians and judges. The further removed these states are from the Ideal State the greater is their need for these two ' classes ' and the more respected the ever-growing number of physicians and judges will be.[49] It is to be noted that Ibn Bajja follows Plato in this respect without the transmission through Alfarabi. Ibn Rushd repeats these statements in his *Paraphrase* on the *Republic*.[50] It must further be pointed out that though Ibn Bajja is not interested in the actual government of the state—as has been stated repeatedly—he does see the close connection between the character of the state and that of its individual citizens. Thus, the art of medicine and the administration of Law have great political importance. They stand for imperfection with Ibn Bajja, their need is due to the absence of love and social peace resulting in unjust actions and false opinions. He contents himself, however, with a description of the Ideal State in which—to repeat—the philosopher can reach ultimate happiness in the contemplation of the *Intelligibilia*, leading him to the union with the (Active) Intellect. It is for this reason that the discussion of the Spiritual Forms in their grades is bound up with the character of the states and their ways of life. Only if we view the state under the aspect of individual perfection and blessedness can we understand why Ibn Bajja contents himself with simply contrasting the Ideal state which he briefly characterizes, with the four imperfect states. Their different character, their transition from one to the other as Plato describes it in

---

emphasises' the distinction between the State and the household and therefore between political and economic science.'

Ibn Sina in his *Aqsam al-'ulum* distinguishes three practical sciences : Ethics taught by Aristotle's *Nicomachia* comes first, next economics as set out in *Bryson* dealing with the regimen for the household which man shares with his wife, children and servants, and last Politics which is taught by Plato and Aristotle. (*See* Ibn Sina, *Tis' rasa'il*, Istanbul 1298 p. 73f. or p. 140b in the Latin version contained in Alpagus : *Avicennae Compendium de Anima*, etc. Venice 1546.) The whole passage is most interesting and important (*see* L. Strauss : *Eine vermisste Schrift Alfarabis* in : *MGWJ*, 1936 where he traced that part of Falqera's *Reshit hokmah* which is not to be found in Alfarabi's *k. tahsil* to Ibn Sina's *Aqsam*).

For Bryson consult M. Plessner, *Der Oikonomikos des Neupythagoraers ' Bryson ' u. s. Einfluss a. d. islamische Wissenschaft*, Heidelberg, 1928. Alpagus has ' liberberus ' which is *k. birus*, *birus* being one of the forms in which Bryson occurs in Arabic (according to Plessner p. 8 and *n.* 10). Falqera (*ed.* David, Berlin 1902) p. 58 for *wehaq-qosim* read *wehaq-qibusim*=*ijtima'at*.

It seems that Ibn Bajja did not know Ibn Sina's writings. But he knew Ghazzali's as his frequent polemical references show. Yet, either he did not know Ghazzali's threefold division into Politics, Economics and Ethics in that order or he deliberately ignored it and, perhaps in opposition to it, denied economics the rank of an independent science.

(*See* Ghazzali, *maqasid al-falasifa*, Introduction to Part II, Metaphysics, *fi taqsim al-'ulum*, 3f.) In Yehudah Hal-lewi's *Al-Khazari*, *ed.* Hirschfeld § 35 we find the same order as in Ibn Sina. Finally, it is to be noted that Ibn Sina's summary of Politics betrays his interest in all aspects of the *Republic*, *e.g.*, constitutional changes as we find it in Ibn Rushd's *Paraphrase*. We were unable to obtain a copy of Ibn Sina's *k. al-siyasa*, *ed.* Cheikho in *Al-Mashriq*, 1906.

49. *tadbir* (Asin), 9 : Ibn Bajja mentions four simple (*al-basita*) states. This must be in contradistinction from the mixed states, *i.e.* composed of elements of two or more of the imperfect states. *Cp. Republic*, III, 404-409.

50. *See* PG, 163 with *ns*.

his *Republic* appear to him irrelevant. He only once distinguishes them by names such as Plato or Alfarabi give them. The usual distinction he draws is between simple and composite imperfect states, no doubt an echo from Plato's *Statesman* and *Laws*. The latter especially contains a description of the normal constitution as a mixture of monarchy and democracy. Guided by his own attempt at Syracuse to influence as a philosopher-statesman the course of political life, Plato advocated in the *Laws* the co-operation between a tyrant and a young philosopher. We see in the *Laws* the source for Ibn Bajja's composite states. When he speaks now of three, now of four or even of five states he thinks of Plato no less—where four and five are concerned—than of Alfarabi who mentions five in his *k. fi ara'i ahli-l-madinati-l-fadilati*,—Plato's Ideal and four imperfect states, as well as seven which may be traced to Plato's *Statesman* where two classifications are given, first five and then seven different constitutions ; and four in his *k. al-siyasatu-l-madaniya*—the Ideal and three imperfect states. Alfarabi uses a mixed terminology, partly a literal translation of Plato's constitutional terms, partly coining possibly his own terms, modelled upon the meaning of Plato's different constitutions, as he understood them, and adapted to Islamic conceptions and conditions prevailing in his own time.[51]

After this digression, we resume the analysis of Ibn Bajja's discussion which we follow in order to make clear—as far as we can understand this difficult text—his own train of thought. For, it seems to us that we are not justified to take political statements out of their context since, as we stated earlier on, they are used as illustrations and analogies in the first place. General observations no less than references to actual

51. Plato regards in the *Rebublic*. *Book* IV, 445D, monarchy and aristocracy as a single form and four vicious forms in addition: timocracy, oligarchy, democracy and tyranny (VIII, 544 C.). In the *Politikos* 302C-303 A Plato sub-divides the constitutions thus : the Ideal perfect State of the *Republic* is set apart, then come three Law States : monarchy, aristocracy, democracy and then three Arbitrary States : tyranny, oligarchy, extreme democracy (*see* Barker, *loc. cit.*., 289f).

These re-appear in the *mad. fad.* of Alfarabi, p. 62, some with names reminiscent of Plato's designations in the *Republic*, 544C : *al-jama'a*, *al-taghallub*, *al-karama*, *i.e.* democracy, tyranny and timocracy. Of the others *al-jahiliyya* is applied to the state in which ignorance as opposed to knowledge in the sense Plato uses these terms in the *Republic* is the characteristic of its inhabitants (*see Republic*, V. 476-478). It is used in the *mad. fad.* and in the *k. al-siyasat* (57 a.o.) and may well have the specific Islamic meaning of the term in adaptation of the Platonic sense. *Al-fasiqa* the wicked state is characterized by knowledge of God and the good, but its actions are those of the ignorant state and for that reason it is wicked or vicious. (*mad. fad.*, 62). It occurs also in the *k. al-siyasat*. Next we meet with *al-dalla* (in *mad. fad.* 61 and 63 and *k. al-siyasat*, 57.12), the state in error. This error consists in holding false opinions on God, the Active Intellect etc. Just like Plato, Alfarabi sub-divided the ignorant states in both books (*see mad. fad.* 62 and 80, *k. al-siyasat*, 58 ff.) Since Ibn Bajja nowhere goes beyond four we cannot enumerate them all the more so since *al-jahiliyya* is employed as a collective term including timocracy, democracy and tyranny. The fourth, oligarchy, must be meant by *al-baddala* because it is transformed from *timocracy* (*Republic*, 550) and, in fact, it is defined by Alfarabi (*mad. fad.* 62) as that in which the citizens help each other to acquire wealth etc. On p. 63 the term is applied to opinions and actions which have changed from those of the ideal State to others, false ones. (The term used here and p. 80 is *mubaddala*, on p. 61 *mutabaddala*). Is it possible that *al-nadhala* of *k. al-siyasat* is corrupted from *baddala*? The Hebrew version (*sepher hahathhalot*, *ed* Filipowski, p. 47) has *hahamuda* which though usually meaning carnal desire occurs once in the form *himud* together with *mamon*, desire for money. It is neither the equivalent of *nadhala*, vile, nor of *baddala*, but as 'desire' could perhaps be interpreted to mean plutocracy ?

Narboni (*ed.* Herzog, p. 8) does not translate *al-basita* but gives instead these four terms : *kohanit*, *mamonit*, *qahalit* and *nissuhit*. We shall come back to these terms in *n.* 72, *below*.

political events and situations serve as justification, we are inclined to think, for the *mutawahhid*, the philosopher, the *homo sapiens* who isolates himself from uncongenial society organized in an imperfect state in order the better to overcome the animal part of his nature as an important step towards reaching his truly human goal : to know himself by knowledge of the *Intelligibilia* with the help of the most excellent of the three grades of *Spiritual Forms* in preparation of the union with the Intellect which draws him as near to God the Creator as is in man's nature.[52]

A basis for this anti-political and anti-social view may be found in Plato's *Republic*, Book VI. But whereas in the *Republic* it is assumed that the philosopher ought to be the ruler yet he cannot benefit the state by his philosophic rule because the people reject him as useless and consequently deny him honour and esteem which are due to a true ruler. Ibn Bajja's *mutawahhid* neither considers it his duty to benefit the community of citizens nor has he any other intention than ruling himself by withdrawing from Society. Besides, we find in Ibn Bajja's treatise nothing of the grave dangers Plato finds inherent in the very virtues of the philosopher against which he must guard lest the virtues turn into defects and vices.[53]

VI

In addition to just actions which, as has been noted, is characteristic of the Ideal State, it possesses also *only true opinions*. It is due to both that *to every citizen in it is given the best his natural disposition warrants. There is no false opinion in it, its actions are exclusively excellent in the absolute meaning* (of the term). *Yet, every action outside even if good is so in relation to an existing corruption.*[54] Consequently, if opinions should arise in the Ideal State different from those of its citizens, they must be false, just as actions not in keeping with its proper actions are wrong. There is, thus, no room in the Ideal State for discourses putting forward views and deeds in opposition to those appropriate to it. " *This is possible in the four states.*" But just as false opinions may arise there and men may be led by their nature or taught by others to actions, so, right opinions and

52. *See* the passages from the *risala* quoted in *ns.* 30 and 31 and those from Alfarabi there and in *ns.* 35 and 36, *above.*

53. *Republic*, VI, 487B to 497A, esp. 489ABE and 491AB.

It cannot be overemphasized that Alfarabi and Ibn Rushd do not allow the philosopher to withdraw from even the imperfect society. Though Ibn Bajja is aware that highest perfection and blessedness is not within reach for his *mutawahhid* he insists on his withdrawal to reach as high a degree of both as is possible through *tadbir*, self-government. Alfarabi and Ibn Rushd follow herein Plato who states in the *Republic* VII, 519 and 540 that the philosophers are only allowed to retire to the *Islands of the Blest* after they have done their duty by the state, *i.e.*, *ruling for the public good. See* concluding paragraph of this article.

54. *tadbir* (Asin) 9.6 ff.

Dunlop (p. 66) reads و این الرأی کاذب فیها and وجوده with this translation : " How could a view in it be false ?" and " the corruption of its existence " for our " an existing corruption." *al-fadila* we rendered "excellent", in connection with *madina* always "ideal" in the sense of perfect contrast to the four non- or imperfect states. *See* also *tadbir*, 9.12-14,

good conduct are possible in an otherwise imperfect state. This axiom leads Ibn Bajja to justify the existence—in these four states—of beings different from the general run of that society. " *Those who fasten on a true opinion which did not exist in that state or there exists the opposite of what they believe, are called al-nawabit. Whenever their beliefs occur very often and prominently this term is applied to them; in a specific sense. In a general sense it is used for those whose opinions differ from those of the citizens of the state be they true or false. This term is transferred to them from the plants growing spontaneously among a cultivated field. Now, we would attribute this term exclusively to those who hold true opinions. It is evident that it is of the essence of the Ideal State that there are no ' nawabit ' in it if this term is used in its specific sense because there are no false opinions represented therein; nor in a general sense, for when does it become diseased, its affairs corrupted and itself imperfect ? But in the four (imperfect) ways of life the ' nawabit' are to be found and their existence is even the reason for the coming into being of the perfect state.*"[55]

Ibn Bajja then states that all ways of life existing in his as well as in former times are composed of the five ways, most of them of the four (imperfect) ways of life. He leaves the explanation to those who examine the ways of life in his own time. " *But the three classes which either exist or can exist are the nawabit, the judges and the doctors. The blessed ones, in so far as they can at all exist in these states, enjoy an isolated blessedness. For the just government is only the government of the isolated, be he one or be they more than one, whilst neither nation nor city-state are in agreement with their opinion. The Sufis allude to them by their term ' the strangers '! For, though they live in their own countries and among their friends and neighbours—they are strangers in their opinions, they travel in their thoughts to other planes which are for them like homelands...*"[56] Already Munk noticed that this characterisation of the ' strangers ' is in part borrowed from Alfarabi. Steinschneider following up Munk's remark, quoted the Hebrew translation of Alfarabi's *k. al-siyasat.*[57] On the basis of the incomplete text of the *tadbir* in the form of Narboni's *Commentary* we were at that time not able to gauge

55. *tadbir* (Asin), 10. 7-11.2

Ibn Bajja uses mostly the term كاملة for the perfect ideal state in his *k. tadbir* for the more usual فاضلة.

56. *tadbir* (Asin) : 11: 3-14.

Cp. Plato, *Republic*, IX, 580B : monarchy, timocracy, democracy, tyranny. Like Alfarabi Ibn Bajja is fond of using the combination امة او مدنية here and often. The use of سيرة, سير reflects Plato's emphasis on *bios*, ' way of life ' in the various states. This is also a trait borrowed from Alfarabi, possibly. Note the *isolated* blessedness *if* it is possible.

Cp. also *PG*, 165.

57. *PG*, 165, *n.* 34. As stated there we had only the German translation at our disposal. Now, as the result of a study of the relevant passage in the *k. al-siyasat*, 50.7 ff. it is clear that only men living under the rule (*ri'asa*) of the *ra'is* who has received the gift of prophecy by the emanation of the Active Intellect on to his passive by the mediation of the acquired intellect, are capable of reaching *sa'ada* (which we translate by ' blessedness ' or the usual ' happiness ') and become, in Alfarabi's phrase الناس الفاضلون والاخيار والسعداء ' If they form a nation (*umma*) this nation is *fadila*, do they unite in one domicile under such a prophet-philosopher-king (for this is the meaning of this *ra'is*) there comes into being the *madina fadila*. Yet, if they are dispersed over a number of domiciles the inhabitants of which are ruled by a different kind of *ri'asa* then they are *only* excellent (*not su'ada* !) and are *strangers* in those places. *See* also *n.* 63, below.

the significance of that dependence on Alfarabi nor could we realize the full importance of Ibn Bajja's deliberate deviation though we 'conjectured that Ibn Bajja, taking up a side-line of Alfarabi's consciously turned to an individualistic-mystical concept and thus paved the way for Ibn Tufail.' That guess is now fully confirmed as the following analysis will show.

Alfarabi mentions the *nawabit* once in connexion with the states in contrast to the Ideal State : the ignorant, vicious, and erring states. "*Then the nawabit in the Ideal State. The nawabit in the states are in the position of the darnel among the wheat or the thorns that sprout among a cultivated field or the other herbs which are useless or damaging to crops and plants.*"[58]

Whereas here the *nawabit* are purely negative, a danger to the Ideal State within which they grow,[59] as well as in the other states, Alfarabi paints a rather complex picture of "*the nawabit in the excellent states*" towards the end of his treatise. He distinguishes six main classes of varying degrees of error and imperfection making them heretics in the worst case (*al-mariqa*). Yet—and this is decisive for Ibn Bajja's entirely positive evaluation of the *nawabit*—there are others who "*isolate themselves in it and distort* (?) *it with themselves and with others in speech but in doing so they are not opposed to the Ideal State but follow the right road and seek after truth....*"[60] This kind of *nawabit*, guided by the imaginative faculty can ultimately reach true understanding. But be it noted that Alfarabi says nothing about reaching his goal : ultimate happiness or blessedness. This, as has been stated before, is possible only for the citizen in the full meaning of the term and is therefore impossible for him who isolates himself.

It will be clear from these statements that Ibn Bajja though dependent upon Alfarabi in his explanation of the term *nawabit* not only turns its meaning into the direct opposite by restricting it to those who hold right views, but excludes them from the Ideal State altogether. Since they arise spontaneously in the imperfect states they must needs live in isolation from an otherwise corrupt society. By adhering to a discipline (*tadbir*) befitting a philosopher they are capable of reaching their goal and even, presumably if they become numerous enough, can be the means for an Ideal State coming into being. The contrast to the view held by the majority of the Falasifa, notably by Alfarabi and Ibn

---

58. Alfarabi, *k. al-siyasat*, 57.11 ff.

Dieterici-Bronnle translate : "the officials in the vicious state" for : ثم النوابت فى المدينة الفاضلة فان النوابت فى المدن Perhaps they read الفاسقة for الفاضلة

59. In the *mad. fad.*, 61, 18 نوائب of Dieterici's text must be corrected to نوابت in the light of the passage in *k. al-siyasat* referred to in the previous *n*. The translation assumes *nawa'ib* as correct: "Also individuals are often in opposition to it (the Ideal State) as *representatives* (or: deputies) of these" (other states). The same translation is used in the *k. alsiyasat*, 74.8 where Dieterici must have read again *nawa'ib*. Our text correctly reads *nawabit*.

60. Alfarabi,*k. al-siyasat*, 74.20 : 75.2 :

Dieterici-Bronnle and the Hebrew translator must have read تخيلون for يختلون of the Hyderabad edition.

Rushd could not be more pronounced. The perfect, ideal state is possible in their view only on the basis of the perfect, divinely revealed Law, a view which Plato came to adopt more and more in his advancing years.[61] As a rule, they follow Plato in assuming a downward trend of change from one state to another. Without the philosopher who is at the same time lawgiver and prophet[62] no ideal state can come into being and exist. For Ibn Bajja, on the other hand, human beings like the *nawabit* who are *the strangers* and whom he evidently equates in his mind with the *mutawahhid*, can help in the birth of the perfect out of the imperfect states.[63]

---

61. *Cp.* E. Barker, *loc. cit.*, 304 ff.;on the connection between law and religion esp. 351 ff. *See* also *SAIPT*, 9 f. on the interaction of Politics and Law. *Cp.* also Ibn Bajja's dictum (*tadbir*,12) : والحكومة طب المعاشرات *Hukuma*, not *shari'a!*

62. Ibn Rushd leaves this an open question. *See Maimonides, etc.*, 198, *n.* 2.

63. Alfarabi certainly did not identify the *nawabit* with the *strangers* as Ibn Bajja does. The latter's explanation of the term and his explicit statement that it is used by the Sufis raises the point where the term *nawabit*, spontaneous growth, originated. We do not know Sufi literature well enough to be able even to suggest that in its metaphorical sense, applied to the political sphere, it stems from those who coined the term *ghuraba'*. Moreover, the juxtaposition of *nawabit* and *ghuraba'* appears to have originated in Ibn Bajja. Its etymology points to *nabata*, grow, as is clear from Alfarabi's definition which Ibn Bajja took over in substance. We are indebted to Prof. Arberry for references to Jahiz where the term is used as name of a sect. M. Horten in his *Speculative und Positive Theologie d. Islam*, Leipzig 1912) mentions *nawabit* in his Glossary as a " sect who were at the same time adherents of Muawia and Ali." This designation of sect tallies with one of Alfarabi's groups mentioned above.†

In the *Sepher hag-gedarim* of Menahem b. Abraham Bonafos (late XIVth or early XVth century) we find a lengthy entry under the heading *someah ham-medina* which contains what we find in Alfarabi and Ibn Bajja together with some additions. It contains the greater part of the Arabic, more than Narboni brings—who naturally must have made his Paraphrase from a complete text. On the other hand, Narboni's account contains additional matter (Herzog, 8 f.) which is a comment of his own. This is sandwiched between *Tadbir* (Asin) p. 11, end of line 2 and the middle of line 7 thus : ". . . . *he explained that it was his intention in this treatise to present the ' rule ' of these ' plants ' and that their self-government was in accordance with that of the perfect State so that they would have no need of the three kinds of medicine for the Lord was their physician. Further, the happiness of these ' plants ' would be that of the isolated one and their ' government ' would be the government of the isolated one. . . .*

Note that from " Further " Narboni translates almost literally—though narrowing the application down to the *nawabit* only— from *tadbir*, 11.9 : فانما يكون لهم سعادة المفرد His ' three kinds of medicine ' take the place of line 8 *bal* to 1.9 *fa'innama.* Lines 3-7 are missing. The ' three kinds of medicine ' stand, of course, for the three classes. Narboni supplies the motif for their absence : God.

Munk, *Mélanges*, 390, *n.* 1 gives this explanation: "*C'est à dire, de la médecine des corps, de la médecine morale et de la justice* '—which throws an interesting light on the concept of the *nawabit. Cp. tadbir*, 12.8 f. : " *medicine of the souls, of the bodies, of the societies.*" *See* also *n.* 56, *above.*

It is difficult to find the origin for the *nawabit* as used by Alfarabi and Ibn Bajja in the Greek *phuton.* Jahiz, as just mentioned, uses the term without giving a derivation, for a sect on which he wrote a little treatise (*fi-l-nabita*) where once the plural *nawabit* occurs. G. van Vloten edited this treatise under the title of a paper he read to a Congress of Orientalists in 1897 : *Les Hachwia et nabita*, published in : *Actes du XIe. Congres International des Orientalistes*, Paris 1897. It is likely that Alfarabi knew this treatise and that his use of *nawabit* to designate heretics was influenced by Jahiz.

One might think of passages in the *Republic* of Plato such as IX, 591, esp. DE and 592A, or, VI, 491A. But most probable of all is a passage in VII, 520 B3-5 which is quoted in the concluding paragraph of this article. The spontaneous, untended growth in uncongenial soil and the consequent aloofness from society is strongly reminiscent of Alfarabi's definition, quoted in this article, but even more of Ibn Bajja's meaning and use of the term. The French translation by Leon Robin (p. 1109) runs: "*car c'est spontanément qu'ils y ont poussé. . . .*" *See n.* 81, *below.*

But there is no certainty. Unfortunately, one has so far not discovered the full text of Galen's Summary of the *Republic* and it is therefore impossible to know whether Ibn Bajja had this or the other likely passages before him. A passage in the *Timaios* (90 A) :" . . . .*like a plant whose roots are not in earth, but in the heavens. . . .*" which has some bearing on our problem is not contained in Galen's Summary which is shortly to be published under the title *Galeni Compendium Timaei Platonis* as Vol. 1 of *Plato Arabus*. We are indebted to the Editor, Dr. R. Walzer, for having kindly lent us the final proofs of this book.

See also Asin's *n.* 14 (on p. 41 of his translation).

He is conscious that something extraneous to nature affects the *mutawahhid* wherefore his regimen has to be studied and worked out by analogy with the physician and the regimen he prescribes for the patient. This applies likewise to the isolated *nabit* (*al-nabit al-mufarrad*), "*how he can reach blessedness if it does not exist or how he can remove from himself the accidents that hinder him from* (*reaching*) *happiness or what is possible of it.... but it is not possible in the three ways of life or a mixture of them.*"[64]

VII

Next, we meet with the familiar statement that man has certain features in common with the inanimate and the animal, which Ibn Bajja discusses on the basis of the three-fold division of the soul into a nutritive, generative and augmentative part. The faculties of sense, imagination and memory are therefore animal faculties whereas the cogitative faculty is exclusive to man. Following Aristotle in his *Nicomachian Ethics* Ibn Bajja finally states that the human actions properly so called stem from his free will (*ikhtiyar*), by which he understands "*the will which arises out of reflexion.*" Discussing the nature of human actions he says that "*the majority of human actions in the four ways of life or what is mixed together of them consist of animal and human elements. It is rare to find the animal element isolated from the human element for man in his natural state.... cannot but think how to act....But the man who acts* (*solely*) *because of the* (*right*) *opinion and judgment without any regard for his animal soul or what takes place in it, is more worthy that his action be* (*considered*) *divine than human. Therefore, such a man is necessarily excellently endowed with the ethical virtues.*[65]

This is, as it were, the prelude to the ensuing rather lengthy discussion of the *Spiritual Forms*, another expression for the *Intelligibilia*. In order to preserve their superiority and pure spirituality Ibn Bajja terms them *Universal Spiritual Forms* in contradistinction to the inferior *Individual Spiritual Forms* which are bound up with *Matter*. These two groups are the second and third, with a first consisting of the *Forms* of the Celestial Bodies or Spheres, and a fourth represented by the Ideas which exist in the faculties of the soul, imagination and memory. The *Universal Intelligibilia* are the *Active* and the *Acquired Intellect*.[66]

---

64. *tadbir* (Asin), 12.2-9.

Dunlop thinks (p. 78, *n.* 1) that 'three' is probably a slip for 'four'. But no change is necessary in view of Alfarabi's *k. al-siyasat*, 57.11 where three states are opposed to the Ideal State. The whole passage is interesting for Ibn Bajja's contention that medicine and judicature are no sciences since they do not exist in the Ideal State, and for his attack on Galen.

65. *tadbir* (Asin) : 15.14-16.2 and 16.5-12. *See* also p. 14.

Note again the four ways of life or what consists of a mixture of them. He obviously thinks of the many shades of mixed social and political organisations which fall under the *jahiliyya* or under the *jama' a*, as described by Alfarabi in his *k. al-siyasat*, 58 and 70.

al-fada' ilu-l-shakliyya must, in the context, mean *ethical virtues*. The Hebrew version has *ma'alot hat-tekhuniyot* (Herzog, 10) and in the *risala* (37 = MS. 93a. 18) : *ham-middot*. *Cp.* Aristotle's *Nicom. Ethics* Book VI, ch. ii. 2-5 and also Book III, ch. ii. 1-5.

66. See *tadbir* 19.

His dependence upon Alfarabi is obvious. How far he was directly influenced by Alexander of Aphrodisias's treatise *On the Spiritual Forms* which he mentions in his *k. ittisal* or by Alfarabi's Commentary on Alexander we are not competent to judge. We confine ourselves therefore to those passages within his discussion which have a direct bearing on *Politics* in general and on the *mutawahhid* in particular.

In his discussion of the errors to which man is subject in his perception and the resultant false spiritual forms, Ibn Bajja emphasizes that it is not his intention to enumerate the classes of government but only "*the true government because it is the most excellent 'tadbir' and because it is just possible that through it the mutawahhid may attain essential blessedness. As for the employment of a lie it enters only to promote the attainment of blessedness of the inhabitants of (the imperfect) states ; yet not through a pure lie, rather through ambiguous lies. All this is exhaustively dealt with in the Political Science.*"[67] He himself is only concerned about the *tadbiru-l-mutawahhid* (self-government of the unitary, the man who segregates himself from society). The false spiritual forms are found in the existing ways of life, *e.g.*, hypocrisy and ruse. The use of sophistry misleads—fine psychological insight is thus shown by Ibn Bajja—not only the *vulgus* but even the principal citizens of these states into imagining this to be prudence (*hikma*), the very prudence which Aristotle mentions '*in the sixth*' (Book of the *Nicomachia*).[68]

Claiming that man loves the spiritual forms by nature he maintains that "*The end of all human actions—provided man is a part of the state—is the state. But this is the case in the Ideal State alone.*" Yet, in the other four imperfect states, the simple or mixed, the people consider all these forms from the point of view of pleasure they derive from them as an end in themselves. Therefore, what are in the Ideal State introductions are ends in the others.[69] We are inclined to interpret this statement in the sense that only in the perfect or ideal state is man part of the state, *i.e*, a citizen.

In his analysis of the various classes of human actions, Ibn Bajja remarks that what is considered noble by some ways of life is considered ignoble by others. Thus, such actions bring down dynasties without affecting personal nobility, however. As an example he cites the conduct at the time of the *muluk al-tawa'if* more even than what happens at the time of his writing this treatise.[70]

---

67. *tadbir*, 29.6-15.

On *al-'ilmu-l-madani see n.* 45, *above.* Asin refers again to Aristole's *Politics without* reason. Rather might one look to the *Republic* as the likely source, *e.g.*, Book II, 381 to end, Book III. There are very few references in Ibn Bajja's writings to Education. Ibn Rushd commented fully in his *Paraphrase* on this kind of education through stories and fables. We hope to deal with this matter in the edition of the *Paraphrase*.†

68. *See n.* 41, *above. Cp. Nic. Eth., Book* VI. chs. v. 1-2 ; viii. 2, 4 ; xii. 6, 9, 10.

69. *tadbir*, 37.9-15.

A very concise description of the difference between the true citizen of the perfect state and the selfish in the other states.

70. *tadbir* ; 39.11-16 and 40.3-9.

A remarkable comment on an actual political situation not long closed.

In connection with the spiritual forms in children and by analogy or contrast in animals—based upon Aristotle's *History of Animals* and *On Animals* which he commented upon in a separate treatise—, he stresses that filial affection varies with the various ways of life since this quality derives as much from instinct as from convention. It is greater in democracies than in other ways of life for mutual help, as can be seen among the Arabs and Berbers.[71]

Another reference to contemporary history is made when the qualities of old age, above all wisdom, are discussed. Prudence and counsel are naturally not to be expected in childern. Yet, the children of the refined and noble families in his time were wrongly credited with them and accepted as rulers. "*This is the gravest and most powerful reason for corruption in it, whichever of the four states it is. Is it that of the Imam* (?) *then this is in no way possible. Mostly it happens in the timocracy* (?), *then in the democracy, then in the tyranny.*"[72]

If our conjecture is plausible the text becomes reasonably clear. The State presided over by the *Imam* would then represent the Islamic equivalent to Plato's aristocracy—[73] at least in theory, though reality

71. *tadbir* : 51.5-52.2.

Asin, p. 87 of his translation, refers in *n.* 105 to Alfarabi's *k. al-siyasat*, 69 for an identical definition

72. *tadbir* : 54.3-7.

Asin in his *n.* 112, p. 91 justifies his translation for *al-iqamiyya* on etymological grounds as 'stable' but says that he does not know its technical sense because neither the context nor Alfarabi offer any help. Indeed, this term does not—to our knowledge—occur in any of Alfarabi's three treatises likely to contain It. We are led to our emendation through Alfarabi's *Imam* in his *k. tahsilu-l-sa'ada* (Hyderabad 1345), p. 43 where the *Imam* is equated with the philosopher, lawgiver and king (*See SAIPT*, 8 with *ns.*) Besides, Ibn Rushd—following Alfarabi—uses the same terms. The Hebrew translator renders *imam* by *kohen, priest,* (*See* our *Maimonides* ' etc., 198) whilst we are not aware of the term *imamiyya* occurring in any treatise on *Politics* we have seen, it is in itself a legitimate formation. What confirms us strongly in our conjecture is, however, the fact, noted in *n.* 51, *above*, that Narboni uses the term *kohanit* (which Steinschneider in his *Alfarabi*, p. 66, noticed and rendered by 'priestly') in the first passage where the four imperfect states are mentioned. Unfortunately, our present passage does not occur in Narboni's *Commentary*. But the term *Kohanit* is a literal translation of *imamiyya* on the basis of "*imam equals kohen.*" Now, we find in Ibn Rushd's *Paraphrase on Plato's Politeia* towards the end of the second *Book* this passage : "*States that are excellent in actions alone are priestly and it has already been told that such a priestly state existed under the ancient Persians.*" (MS. Munich f. 30a). There are further references to priestly states and priestly parts of states in the beginning of the third *Book* of this *Paraphrase* which will be dealt with in their context at a later date. These passages are found in the Latin version of Jacob Mantinus in : *Aristotelis Opera Omnia*, vol. II, Venice, 1550, on pp. 186b. *v.*, 20 *sqq.*; 187 a, *v.*, 69/*r.*, 1*sq* and 27; 187b, *v.*, 19 *sqq.* This reference to the Persians must come from Ibn Bajja (*tadbir*, 11.4 f.) who mentions five states "*apart from what Abu Nasr tells of the way of life of the ancient Persians.*" Asin cannot trace this in Alfarabi. Unfortunately Ibn Bajja does not name the *sira*. In Messer Leon's *Rhetoric* (*nofet suphim*)—quoted in J. Klatzkin's *Thesaurus Philosophicus*, etc., *s. v. kohanit* (II, p. 67)—there occurs a passage definitely linking the priestly state with Aristocracy : "*the rule of the best—its actions and opinions are exclusively excellent—is called priestly and it is said that it existed among the ancient Persians.*" Perhaps Alfarabi repeated what he read in a Greek or Hellenistic source ? Yet, he may have culled his knowledge from Arab geographers or historians which must be verified.

(Ibn Rushd does not mention Alfarabi in the passage quoted earlier on in this note). *See* on this question the account by Prof. A. Christensen in his *L'Iran sous les Sassanides*, 2nd. ed. Copenhagen 1944, pp. 97 ff., with references to Tabari on pp. 107 ff. We hope to deal with this question later on. It appears that the office of *wazir* goes back to Sassanian influence. At the time of the Arab conquest of Persia one of these priests governed Persia (*see* Christensen, *op. cit.*, 119).

Ibn Rushd's *Paraphrase* contains considerable material borrowed from Alfarabi and also some from Ibn Bajja. We hope to deal with this in a separate article. Ibn Rushd treats fully of timocracy and oligarchy much in the same way as Alfarabi. In view of Narboni's term *mamonit* Asin may be right in suspecting oligarchy in the missing term.†

73. Ibn Rushd enumerates in his *Paraphrase* five constitutions (in the beginning of his third *Book* (MS. Munich f. 30b) and says if the first excellent constitution is divided into the rule of the king and the rule of the best (*aristoi*) there are six. In this he follows closely Plato. Further subdivision brings the number to eight.

might look somewhat different. Only in this context is the sequel intelligible: that corruption is out of the question. Where we read 'timocracy' Asin would read 'oligarchy.' It is difficult to decide either way. If Alfarabi can be taken as the source for Ibn Bajja's terms both constitutions are possible. At any rate, democracy and tyranny seem well established through our text and they make it probable if not certain that the two other terms are also borrowed from Plato's four constitutions in the *Republic*. Herein lies the interest of our passage that, apart from the conjectural first term, all are going back to a Greek source and conception which is highly characteristic for Ibn Bajja. For, in all other places where four or three imperfect states are mentioned there is never, as stated above, a name given to them.

Ibn Bajja turns next to a consideration of the ends in respect of the *mutawahhid* : corporeal, individual and universal spiritual forms. "*If he is a part of the Imam-state*[74] *his ends have already been discussed in the Political Science.*" It depends on the nature of one of the imperfect states of which he is a part and on his actions in conformity with his being a *mutawahhid* which of the ends it will be. The case of the Ideal State has likewise been expounded in *Political Science*. Naturally in it he will exercise his powers of investigation, judgment, reasoning and reflection in his endeavour to attain all his ends. Yet, if his rational faculty is not functioning his is an animal action without any connection with the human element. Because of his animal actions he cannot become a part of the state and must needs live in isolation.[75]

The philosopher is the virtuous divine man. By comprehending the simple substantial intelligences he becomes himself one of these intelligences and thus reaches his ultimate end. These intelligences are described in Aristotle's *Metaphysics*, *De Anima* and *De Sensu et Sensibili*.

Finally, "*it is clear that the mutawahhid* (who is not a part of the Ideal perfect State), *ought not to associate with merely corporeal beings nor with any whose end is a spirituality mixed with corporeality. Rather should he seek the company of the adepts in the sciences. These men are now more numerous, now less and even non-existent in some ways of life wherefore the mutawahhid is obliged in some ways of life to retire altogether from the society of men as much as this is possible for him. He should not mix with them except in necessary matters and in necessary measure. Or, he should emigrate to ways of life in which the sciences are* (practised)—*if such do exist*—. *This is not in opposition to what is said in Political Science nor to what is made clear in Physics. For it is made clear there that man is a citizen by nature and in Political Science that retreat is*

74. We read again *imamiyya* and *huwa* for *hiya*. The passage is *tadbir* : 54, new chapter (1)—55.1.

75. Asin (*n.* 117, p. 92 f.) quotes a long passage from Alfarabi's *k. al-siyasat*, p. 57 about men who are like domestic animals or wild beasts—this passage follows the one on the *nawabit*. They are, if 'domesticated,' just good enough to be servants but not citizens. No doubt, Ibn Bajja has this passage in mind. This is clear from his closely resembling treatment on p. 55 of his *tadbir*.

wholly bad. But this is only so in essence, it is good by accident."[76]

In other words, since we are dealing not with the Ideal State of the *Republic* with its '*pattern set up in the heavens*', but rather with imperfect states on earth in our own time a realistic reading of the situation forces us to discard—in practice—the ideal standard in order to save the divine soul of striving man. This can be done only by avoiding contamination with the impurity and evil of imperfect human society through retreat. A life in retreat is incompatible with the assertion of man being a *zoon politikon* who shares fully in the social life of the State. But, postulates Ibn Bajja, circumstances force the *mutawahhid* to set himself apart and, if necessary, cut himself off entirely from social life.

In conclusion we would point out once more the striking feature of Ibn Bajja's departure from Alfarabi before and from Ibn Rushd after him. Both adhered closely to the Platonic idea of the civic obligation of the philosopher. When Ibn Bajja states in his *k. ittisal*[77] that Plato describes the state of the blessed metaphorically as that of one who gazes into the sun he understands this to mean that man perceives the *Existing Things* as they really are. This, for him, is the highest grade of ascent to the Union[78] and assures Blessedness. He thus deliberately ignores Plato's explicit insistence on service to the community. This, Plato expresses in Book VII of the *Republic*—still within the metaphor of the Cave—thus : "*Then when they are fifty, those who have come safely through and proved the best at all points in action and in study must be brought at last to the goal. They must lift up the eye of the soul to gaze on that which sheds light on all things, and when they have seen the Good itself, take it as a pattern for the right ordering of the State and of the individual, themselves included. For the rest of their lives, most of their time will be spent in study ; but they will all take their turn at the troublesome duties of public life and act as rulers for their country's sake, not regarding it as a distinction, but as an unavoidable task. And so, when each generation has educated others like themselves to take their place as Guardians of the commonwealth, they will depart to dwell in the Islands of the Blest.*"[79]

It is this insistence on (the best) *rule of the commonwealth* in contrast to the *self-rule of the philosopher in isolation from the community*, which Plato illustrates in the same Book VII : "*It is for us, then, as founders of a commonwealth to bring compulsion to bear on the noblest natures. They must be made to climb the ascent to the vision of Goodness, which we called the highest object of knowledge, and, when they have looked upon it long enough, they must not be allowed, as they now are, to remain on the heights, refusing to come down again to the prisoners or to take any part in their labours and rewards, however much or little these may be worth. . . . . The law is not concerned to make any*

76. *tadbir* : 78.6-16.
Here the term *al-'ilmu-l-madani* may well refer to Alfarabi's *k. tahsil*, p. 14, quoted in *n.* 36, *above*.

77. p. 20.3 f.

78. *See n.* 37, *above*.

79. 540A–C2.

one class specially happy, but to ensure the welfare of the commonwealth as a whole. By persuasion or constraint it will unite the citizens in harmony, making them share whatever benefits each class can contribute to the common good ; and its purpose in forming men of that spirit was not that each should be left to go his own way, but that they should be instrumental in binding the community into one.'"[80]

Ibn Bajja would keep his philosopher on the summit of his beatific vision, he would not bring him down into the cave of social obligation, of civic duty. For him, there is no law that holds sway over all citizens alike. He seems to hold with the philosophers ' " *compeers in other states* " who " *may quite reasonably* refuse to collaborate : *there they have sprung up, like a self-sown plant, in spite of their country's institutions* ; *no one has fostered that growth, and they cannot be expected to show gratitude for a care they have never received.*"[81]

Ibn Bajja freed himself from the beautiful vision of the *Ideal State*, and, pondered, instead, over the possibility how to attain blessedness; or at least partial blessedness and perfection in the existing—far from ideal—states. The result of his reflection is the *tadbiru-l-mutawahhid*; the self-government of the speculative philosopher who retreats into his own self and strives for perfection by withdrawing from society.[82]

---

80. 519D-520A 4.

81. 520B-5. The passages quoted are taken from the English translation by Cornford. (*The Republic of Plato*, Oxford, 1941).

82. Finally, a word about certain discrepances between the Arabic original and the extracts from it contained in Narboni's *Commentary*.

Asin noticed some additions in Munk's French version in his *Mélanges* based upon Narboni. They are of the kind we have given an example in *n.* 63, *above*. We must not forget that we do not deal with a translation but with a Summary made by a man whose claim to be a philosopher in his own right is a strong one. Asin did not notice our example nor a few similar ones.

But in a contribution to *Al Andalus* VII, 1942, fas. 2 : *Un texto de al-Farabi atribuido a Avempace por Moises de Narbona* he charges Narboni with adding a whole long passage from Alfarabi to his Summary as an epilogue of Ibn Bajja's and states that Munk did not suspect such plagiarism.

There is no doubt that the passages in Munk set against extracts from Álfarabi's *maqala fi ma'ani al-aql* are identical. We compared the passages cited by Asin with the Hebrew text edited by Herzog (p. 20 f.) And yet, we are not prepared to agree without reservation to Asin's charge. Immediately after the first passage Alfarabi is actually mentioned and no new subject is introduced. The quotations fit into the context quite naturally. They could therefore belong to Ibn Bajja just as much as to his Commentator. Verbal agreement between Alfarabi and Ibn Bajja is not infrequent in the three treatises we considered for this article.

Another factor, though not by itself valid, is a marginal note found in a MS. Herzog used for the constitution of his text, and quoted by him as *n.* 9, on p. 20. It refers to the beginning of the first passage discussed by Asin. It states that Ibn Rushd apparently referred to this profound passage in his *On the possibility of union* as one in which nobody else preceded Ibn Bajja. The writer of the gloss is of opinion that this passage is the source for Ibn Rushd's boast in his Long Commentary on *De Anima*, where he enlarged upon this statement here, that he alone solved the problem of *union*. Be that as it may, there are other reasons which make us hesitate. The Hebrew text contains the end of the text edited by Asin in a literal translation on the last line of p. 19. The first suspect passage begins on the last line of p. 20. Asin's text ends abruptly and has this note obviously from the hand of the copyist : *Completed is what was found of this treatise*. Is it not possible that Narboni had a more complete copy of the *tadbir*? Or, alternatively, Narboni, the Commentator, summed up the realisation of the aim of the *mutawahhid* : that he becomes completely free from matter and by drawing near to the Acquired Intellect as much as possible, gains the possibility of union with the Active Intellect, in the manner of Alfarabi and Ibn Bajja in the *risala* and the *ittisal*.

4

THE PLACE OF POLITICS IN THE PHILOSOPHY OF IBN RUSHD[1]

THE significance of Political Philosophy for the philosophy of Islam and Judaism in the Middle Ages has been recognized in recent years, and the importance of Plato's *Republic* and *Laws* together with Aristotle's *Nicomachean Ethics* for the *falāsifa* is becoming increasingly evident. Attention has been drawn to Alfārābī's political treatises, to Ibn Bājja, to Averroes' Commentaries on Plato's *Republic* and on Aristotle's *Nicomachean Ethics*, to Ibn al-Ṭiqṭaqa and to Ibn Khaldun. The reception of Platonic and Aristotelian political ideas conditions—in varying degrees—the attitude of the *falāsifa* to the State as such, to the Muslim State in particular, and therefore to the *Sharīʿa* of Islam and to Greek philosophy, both practical and theoretical. This is already clear from the writings of Alfārābī, but in his attempt at blending and harmonizing Greek-Hellenistic and Islamic conceptions no Alfarabian philosophy proper with distinct features of a definitive, authoritatively formulated synthesis emerges. It was left to Averroes—to use the name by which Ibn Rushd was generally known to the West—to work out a peculiarly Islamic religious philosophy. He establishes in unequivocal terms the supreme authority of the *Sharīʿa* and its identity of purpose with *falsafa*, *religious* philosophy in the *Faṣl al-maqāl*, the *Manāhij*, the *Tahāfut al-tahāfut* and his Commentary on Plato's *Republic*. The last named forms the main subject of the present article. In an earlier study it was considered in connexion with his Commentary on Aristotle's *Nicomachean Ethics* already, but not with his other treatises just mentioned. This is, however, necessary in order to gain a correct, balanced view of his philosophy, and especially of his political thought. It is equally important to see his political Commentaries against the background of his active life as *qāḍī* and of contemporary Muslim history in the Maghreb.

The views here offered are the result of a study of the Commentary on the *Republic* in this setting. At this juncture they are still provisional. Some aspects require further study, others will remain hypothetical as long as we have to rely on the Hebrew version of the lost Arabic original of this as well as of his Commentary on the *Nicomachean Ethics*, and as long as Ibn Rushd's theological and legal treatises are not found. But it is hoped that my views will

[1] This article offers an interpretation of Ibn Rushd's Commentary on Plato's *Republic* in the context of his other writings. It is the result of work on the edition of the Hebrew version of the Arabic original which is presumed lost. Text, English translation, and explanatory notes now await publication in the *Plato Arabus* of the *Corpus Platonicum Medii Aevi* of the Warburg Institute.† Though reference to this forthcoming publication is made constantly the present article forms the general conclusions drawn from it and warrants separate publication, the more so since it contains matter not connected with the edition of a text. It should be read in conjunction with my article published in *Islamic Culture*, xxii, No. 1, of January, 1948, under the title: 'Some Aspects of Islamic Political Thought', especially pp. 9 ff., with my 'Avicenna's Influence on Jewish Thought', in *Avicenna: Scientist and Philosopher. A Millenary Symposium*, edited by G. M. Wickens, London, 1952, pp. 66 ff., and also with my 'The Place of Politics in the Philosophy of Ibn Bājja', in *Islamic Culture*, xxv, part i (Jan., Apr., Jul., Oct., 1951), 1952.†

help in a much needed, extensive study of all extant works of Ibn Rushd and of the historical and literary sources of 11th- and 12th-century Maghreb.

I. Critique of the Muslim State of his Time

1. The nature of the Commentary on the *Republic* is clear proof that it is more than a substitute for the *Politics* of Aristotle—though it is this too, as Averroes himself tells us; for it differs fundamentally from his other Commentaries. In the first place it contains a comparatively large number of references to the political history of the Maghreb in the 11th and 12th centuries which—as is stressed in the notes on these passages in my edition—are far more than illustrations: they represent a critique of a Muslim philosopher who is a disciple of Plato and Aristotle, whose political philosophy he takes very seriously and applies to his own civilization and its State and Society, past and present.

Then we meet with strong criticism of certain persons and classes of contemporary society, like the *mutakallimūn*, on the lines of his criticism and strictures in his religious-philosophical, polemical treatises (*Faṣl, Manāhij, Tahāfut al-tahāfut*). This criticism is an important aspect of his opposition to dialectical as against demonstrative arguments and of his claim that the speculative philosopher is alone qualified and entitled to search for and explain the inner meaning of those passages in *Qur'ān*, *Ḥadīth*, and *Shar'* which require expert interpretation by and for the adept of philosophical sciences. In other words, the correct interpretation of religious beliefs and convictions is the business of the *failasūf*, the religious philosopher. It is for this reason that Averroes stresses his exclusive concern for the theoretical statements contained in the *Republic* and insists on the employment of demonstrative proof.

Finally, seen in the context of his philosophy as a whole, Averroes' references to the *Sharī'a* of Islam—often in contrast to Plato's νόμος and its use in Aristotle—constitute perhaps the most important of the distinguishing features of this Commentary. For the *Sharī'a* is not merely adduced as an illustration of Plato's argument, as a clever stratagem to secure a superficial adaptation to Islamic concepts and conditions for the benefit of Muslim readers and for his own safety. Nay, it serves to explain the religious law of Islam in terms of the Ideal Constitution on the basis and with the help of Plato's discussion of the Ideal State and its deviations.

Just as Plato measures the character of State and individual by the standards of the Justice that inspires the law of the Ideal State, so does Ibn Rushd contrast the contemporary Muslim scene with the rule of the *Sharī'a* in the time of the four *khulafā rāshidūn*.

2. Averroes stresses the obligation of the speculative philosopher to remain in the state and fulfil his duties of citizenship. If he were to isolate himself—as Ibn Bājja advocates in his *Tadbīr al-mutawaḥḥid*—he would forfeit highest perfection and ultimate happiness. Averroes is thus a true disciple of his masters in Political Science, Plato and Aristotle, as I have stated elsewhere. Since

the philosopher cannot rule except in the Ideal State, he must serve the community in another capacity. In his Commentary on *De Partibus Animalium* (Venice edition, f. 103b) Averroes tells us that the performance of his public duties occupied much of his time : ' Nobis tamen non est concessa huiusmodi facultas hac nostra tempestate, neque in hac provincia nostra, immo si aliquid incidentur scivimus de his rebus, est quid minimum. Cuius rei veritatem cognoscet qui nostram hanc tempestatem viderit, vel hanc provinciam nostram, scil. Andalugiae : et quot damna passi sumus nos, et alij homines sunt passi multos labores ad necessarias res adipiscendas, quibus conservatur sanitas corporea . . .' Similar passages in the Commentary, e.g. his comment on *Republic* 567 about the people of Cordova under Ibn Ghāniya, or about himself at the end of this and in others of his Commentaries reflect his preoccupation as *qāḍī* and as personal physician to the Almohad *amīr al-mu'minīn* Abū Ya'qūb Yūsuf—in succession to Ibn Ṭufail. Remembering what Plato said about judges and physicians and particularly Aristotle's definition in the *Nicomachean Ethics* (x, 9, 1180b) of jurisprudence as a branch of political science, we realize how well qualified Averroes was to observe the political scene and to pronounce upon it.

If the office of *qāḍī* under the Almohads corresponded to what it was under the Almoravids who preceded them, it meant for its holder much more than applying *fiqh* in the law courts. It constituted the highest civil authority as we know from Ibn Rushd's grandfather Abū Walīd, Grand Qāḍī of Cordova, who crossed over to North Africa in 1126 to secure the active help of the Almoravid *amīr al-muslimīn*, 'Alī b. Yūsuf b. Tāshfīn, against the Christian threat to Cordova. (It is not without irony to find the grandson criticizing the very man whom the Almoravid ruler appointed governor of Eastern Spain—with residence in Cordova—Yaḥya b. 'Alī b. Ghāniya as a result of the grandfather's mission, if my identification of him with the Ibn Ghāniya of our Commentary is correct.)

His office enabled Averroes to gain insight into the administration of the Almohad State and thus offered ample opportunity to test Plato's theories in practical politics. Yet this would not account sufficiently for the telling criticism of contemporary events and persons. It cannot be ruled out entirely that the unfavourable judgment on the Almoravids was proffered at least partly for personal motives in order to cover up his family's connexion with these enemies of the now ruling dynasty. This applies in particular to the criticism levelled against a member of the Banū Ghāniya, symbol and rallying point of Almoravid opposition. In his comment on Plato's discussion of the transformation of the timocratic into the plutocratic man and their corresponding states Averroes says : ' In general, the transformation of the timocratic into the hedonistic man is obvious, be it that he takes delight in money or in the other remaining pleasures. The same seems to apply to the timocratic and the hedonistic state. For the plutocratic and the hedonistic state belong to the same category. We often see kings becoming corrupted into such like men. Similarly there is in our time the kingdom of the men known as Almoravids. At first they were imitating the constitution based on the Law—this under the first of them [Yūsuf b. Tāshfīn]—then they changed [it] under his son ['Alī b. Yūsuf b. Tāshfīn] into the timocratic [constitution] together with an admixture in him of the love of money as well. Further, it changed under his grandson into the hedonistic [constitution] . . . and perished in his time. The reason was that the constitution which was opposed to it at that time resembled the constitution based on the Law.' (III. xi, 4–5.) A similar comment is offered with regard to the transformation of the Ideal State—' the government of the Arabs in the earliest period '—into the timocratic one. ' For they used to imitate the ideal constitution and then were transformed in the days of Mu'āwiya into timocratic men ; and so it seems to be the case with the constitution that exists now in these islands.' (III. ix, 13.) The end of III. xi, 5, and ix, 13, seem to refer to the Almohads, in the first passage to Ibn Tūmart and 'Abd al-Mu'min, in the second to Averroes' two masters, Abū Ya'qūb Yūsuf and Abū Yūsuf Ya'qūb al-Manṣūr. A similar comment is again offered in connexion with the transition of democracy into tyranny and the corresponding rulers : ' You can discern this from the democratic rule that exists in our time, for it frequently changes into tyranny. Take for example the rule existing in our own country, i.e. Cordova, after 500 [A.H.]. For it was almost completely democratic, [but] then after 540 [A.H.] it turned into tyranny.' (xv, 13.) If we compare this comment with that in xi, 5, quoted above, we notice that what is called timocracy there is called democracy here. The contradiction can perhaps be resolved by assuming that ' democratic ' refers to the Council of the Almoravids as representing the *jamā'a* of Almoravid Islam in the Maghreb ? Further, when discussing tyranny and its effect on the citizens smarting under it, Averroes says : ' All these acts of tyrants are, indeed, evident to the men of our own time, not through a dissertation alone, but also through their sense-perception and evidence.' (III. xvi, 7.) It is difficult not to refer this courageous utterance to Averroes' own experience and it may be explained as referring to the administration rather than to the Almohad caliph himself. It may, however, apply to the *mulūk al-ṭawā'if* and the Almoravids, especially Ibn Ghāniya. There is support for this interpretation in Averroes' comment on the change human dispositions undergo in the wake of a change in the laws governing State and Society : ' You can discern this in the qualities and morals that have sprung up among us after the year 40 [540 A.H.] among the rulers and dignitaries. For because the timocratic constitution in which they had grown up was weakened, they came by these vile character traits which they now [exhibit]. Of them he only perseveres in the excellent virtues who is excellent in accordance with the religious laws, and this is rare among them.' (III. xix, 5.) This outspoken criticism of Almoravid rule is significant, together with ix, 13 and xi, 5, in that it shows two important trends in Averroes' political thought. In the first place Averroes is quite in keeping with the orthodox interpretation of the Ideal Muslim Polity under the four *khulafā rāshidūn* which was perverted by the *mulk* of Mu'āwiya, for which Averroes uses the Platonic term ' timocracy '. He is clearly in earnest when he applies Platonic observations and thought-categories to Islamic civilization, and thus considers Platonic notions—conditioned by Greek concepts and institutions—as fully valid general principles, applicable to Muslim concepts and institutions. The analogy is not simply an illustration but the outcome of the recognition of Greek political thinking as relevant to Islamic thought and practice. Yet, Averroes made one very important modification and this is the second trend in his political thought : he saw Greek thought with the eyes of an orthodox Muslim who acknowledges the absolute authority of the *Sharīʿa*. In this sense, his assertion about the religious laws, just quoted, clearly implies two related concepts : the identification of the Ideal State with the Islamic, i.e. *Sharīʿa*, State, and the conviction of the superiority of the excellent religious law. But he is realist enough to add that its observance is rare. We also note that in his critique of contemporary Muslim history in the Maghreb he attaches great importance to the year 540 A.H. as a turning point in the Platonic sense.

Since these quotations are at least in part clearly directed against Almohad administration an ulterior motive, assumed as not entirely unthinkable, is not very likely in the man who wrote the *Faṣl* and the *Manāhij*. Nor is it very plausible that he attacked the Almoravids in order to distract attention from his criticism of the existing Almohad State. It seems more reasonable to see in these criticisms, together with his references to family-associations centred in a household and his identification of ' *imām*-states ' or ' *imām*-parts ' within existing states—which will occupy us presently—a concerted effort on the part of an exponent of practical philosophy in the meaning Aristotle gave to this term, to influence the course of history by subjecting contemporary politics to a sustained critique. This critique takes the *Sharīʿa* as its norm and is waged with the weapons which Plato's and Aristotle's political philosophy furnish. There is, therefore, meaning and significance in the parallels drawn as a matter of course between the vices, defects, faults, and errors which Plato adduces as evidence for the uselessness of philosophers in his day, for the necessary transformation of the various constitutions from one to another as the result of the bad character of the rulers on the one hand, and recent and contemporary Muslim history in Spain on the other. These parallels are intended as object lessons for his countrymen. The judge-physician turned political critic as the disciple of Plato and Aristotle. However, an element of uncertainty remains since we cannot be sure—in the absence of the Arabic original—whether the Hebrew translator renders accurately Ibn Rushd's thought.

3. There remains one further group of references to contemporary states : the *imām*-state, *madīna imāmīya* in Ibn Bājja. Averroes clearly distinguishes between two kinds of ' priestly ' states, as we have to translate literally the Hebrew equivalent. The one known as having existed among the ancient Persians is quoted by Ibn Bājja on the authority of Alfārābī. It is possible that such a reference was contained in Alfārābī's lost Commentary on the

Nicomachean Ethics where Aristotle, however, refers to Persian rule as tyrannical, as Plato does in his *Laws*. Averroes says in II. xvii, 5 : ' States that are excellent in deeds alone are called " priestly " ' [i.e. they are *imām*-states], with reference to the ancient Persians. (We shall come back to this definition presently.) The other *imām*-state is linked with tyranny by Averroes and connected with contemporary Muslim states. In III. iv, 11, he speaks of the democratic state as in utmost opposition to the tyrannical one. Economic power is in the hands of the ruling family ; *bayt* has here the meaning of *dawla*.

Averroes goes on : ' For this reason the " priestly " part in them is to-day completely tyrannical.' In III. v, 6, he points again to ' the similarity that exists between the *imām*- and tyrannical states in that the " priestly " parts . . . are transformed into the tyrannical ones and disparage him whose aim in respect of them is " priestly ", as is the case . . . in the states to be found in our time '.

What connects the two kinds of *imām*-state is naturally the word *imām*, defined by Averroes in II. i, 6, as the one ' whom one follows [as chief] in his actions '. This definition, together with the equation of philosopher with *imām* is borrowed literally from Alfārābī. If we are justified in treating the adduced passages as a whole for the purpose of their application to Averroes' own State it appears that a dynasty is meant which is inspired by the *Sharī'a* and whose head looks upon himself as *imām* in the sense this word has in orthodox Sunnite Islam. III. v, 6, may then be interpreted as an attempt to exculpate the caliph Abū Ya'qūb Yūsuf, his patron, from complicity with his ministers responsible for the administration of the Almohad State. For Ibn Rushd emphasizes the caliph's intention to be the *imām*, as represented by his father 'Abd al-Mu'min, the founder of the dynasty. In that sense Leo Africanus speaks in his *Descriptio Africae* of the Almohads as *pontifices*. (But his statements must be treated with reserve.) There is a possibility that these passages refer to the Almoravids. Yet this seems unlikely since Averroes criticizes and condemns them elsewhere in his Commentary—with the exception of their founder—and the phrase ' in this our time ' rather points to the Almohads. I can only say with Averroes : ' this is a matter for [further] consideration '.

4. *The Position of Women*.—Ibn Rushd's critical attitude to State and Society of his time is also shown in his outspoken pronouncement on women and their status in contemporary Islam. It is also an interesting application of Plato's ideas about the equality of women as far as civic duties are concerned. The relevant passages are found in the first treatise of the Commentary (xxv, 6–10). It is for our purpose sufficient to quote paragraphs 9 and 10—Averroes' application to his own time and place : ' Yet, in these states the ability of women is not known, only because they are being taken for procreation alone therein. They are therefore placed at the service of their husbands and [relegated] to the position of procreation, for rearing and [breast] feeding. But this undoes their [other] activities. Because women in these states are not being fitted for any of the human virtues it often happens that they resemble plants. That they are a burden upon the men in these states is one of the reasons for the poverty of

these states. For, they are found in them in twice the number of men while at the same time they do not support any (or: carry on most) of the necessary [essential] activities, except for a few, which they undertake mostly at a time when they are obliged to make up their want of funds, like spinning and weaving. All this is self-evident.'

This pronouncement runs counter to Islamic teaching and practice and is the more remarkable since it is made by an orthodox member of the Muslim community which was ruled by the *amīr al-mu'minīn*, and moreover by a practising lawyer steeped in *fiqh*. He openly attacks their way of life as the result of the official attitude. It is clear that Plato's ideas must have drawn Averroes' attention to the wastage of human labour so detrimental to the State, and led him to advocate a reversal of orthodox Muslim policy. It is the more surprising that this realistic criticism of the position of women in Islam and its bad effect on the economic health of the nation should have gone unnoticed, together with his repeated critical remarks about the contemporary Muslim state as a whole and some of its prominent classes. For as far as I am aware no trace can be found in the sources that his enemies and opponents used them against him. Yet it may well be that they meant this criticism when they allegedly cast doubt upon his orthodoxy, though the sources give different, conflicting reasons for his temporary disgrace.

5. '*Philosophers*' *and Dialectic Theologians*.—Ibn Rushd's criticism so far discussed has been rather guarded with the exception of the last example. But his defence of *ḥikma* (or *falsafa*) and the *falāsifa* is bold and explicit as is his criticism of the 'false' philosophers, the 'sophists' of his own day, and his attack upon the theologians, especially the *mutakallimūn* among them. Since he identifies himself with Plato's strictures on the 'sophists' in the latter's time no quotation of the relevant passages is required. Averroes' own contribution is simply a reference to so-called philosophers in his own time and the extension of the term 'sophist' to the *mutakallimūn*. Berber fanaticism created an atmosphere singularly uncongenial to the unhampered development of a speculative philosophy which was conscious—in the vein of Plato and Aristotle—of its political obligation to the community. The true philosophers were, no doubt, few and could pursue their search for truth only under the protection of the Muslim rulers. Our sources tell us that the two masters of Averroes were highly educated men with a strong bent for philosophy, as the life and work of Ibn Ṭufail and Averroes clearly show. But the rulers had to reckon with the opposition of the *'ulamā* and *fuqahā*, who wielded absolute authority over the masses. Especially the *mutakallimūn* viewed *falsafa* and the *falāsifa* with hostile suspicion. (It is possible that Averroes' temporary disgrace in 1195 on the eve of the caliph's departure for a *jihād* against the Christians was an expedient to appease these groups and the masses under their influence.) In such an atmosphere philosophy could not flourish except for a few elect, fearless personalities. It is mainly for this reason that Averroes stands out as the last thinker of note in the Muslim West, with whose passing religious philosophy

declined. Another contributory reason was naturally the Christian advance leading in the end to the reconquest of the whole of Spain.

In order to understand Averroes' opposition to *kalām* and its adherents, the *mutakallimūn*, one must recognize that both *falāsifa* and *mutakallimūn* claimed the right and the duty of rational explanation of the beliefs and convictions of the Muslim *jamā'a* which lived under the absolute authority of the religious law—the *Sharī'a*. It was Averroes' aim—once he had convinced himself of the inadequacy of *kalām* authoritatively to interpret the religious beliefs and convictions of Islam, and of the danger to what he understood to be their purity, for the maintenance of orthodoxy and a united *jamā'a*—to establish the superiority of *falsafa* as the exclusive custodian of the *Sharī'a* and its sole legitimate and authoritative interpreter. He achieved this by applying the Aristotelian distinction between dialectical and demonstrative arguments to Islam. It is for this reason that he wrote his three complementary treatises, *Faṣl* with *Ḍamīma* and *Manāhij*, in defence of the superiority of the *Sharī'a*; and he deduced from the identity of aim between *Sharī'a* and *falsafa* the warrant of the latter for the interpretation of the former with the help of demonstration. It is precisely in this context that we must understand his insistence, in his Commentary on the *Republic*, on demonstrative arguments and his attack upon the *mutakallimūn* when he stresses—as Alfārābī did before him in his *K. taḥṣīl al-sa'āda* (ed. Hyderabad, 45, 5 ff. and, before, already 43, 18 ff.)—that the philosopher must have the right religious beliefs and convictions. The Platonic demand that right beliefs and convictions are absolutely essential in the philosopher-statesman is simply brought into line with the overruling authority of the divinely revealed prophetic law, the *Sharī'a*.

It is, therefore, necessary to deal with Averroes' insistence on *demonstrative argument* in the wider context of the relation between *Sharī'a* and *falsafa*.

II. Religious Law and Religious Philosophy

1. In discussing the various ideas about the Highest Good Averroes states (II. vi, 4): 'But as for that which the religious laws in our own time think of this matter it is what God wills. But the only way to know what this matter is that God wills . . . is [through] prophecy. This knowledge is, if you investigate the laws, divided into abstract knowledge alone—such as our religious law commands regarding the perception of God—and into practice—such as the ethical virtues it enjoins. Its intention with this purpose is in essence the intention of philosophy . . .' He expresses the same idea in the *Faṣl* thus *al-ḥikma hiya ṣāḥibat al-sharī'ati wa-l-ukht al-raḍī'a* (ed. Gauthier, 32) and in another passage he uses almost identical terms: (22) *maqṣūd al-shar' innamā huwa ta'līm al-'ilmi-l-ḥaqqi wa-l-'amal al-ḥaqq wa-l-'ilm al-ḥaqq huwa ma'rifat-Allah ta'āla wasā'iri-l-maujūdāt 'alā mā hiya 'alayhi* . . . It is the merit of the distinguished interpreter of Muslim philosophy, Léon Gauthier, to have recognized and convincingly demonstrated the signal importance of the *Faṣl*

al-maqāl as the decisive treatise of Averroes' philosophy, and I am in substantial agreement with his analysis. Yet I am, to my regret, unable to agree with a number of his conclusions, and a few observations are necessary here. The title of Gauthier's profound and important book: *La théorie d'Ibn Rochd sur les rapports de la religion et de la philosophie* already indicates a misunderstanding of the fundamental character of the correlation between *Sharī'a* and *falsafa*, *religious* law and *religious* philosophy. This has arisen from the translation 'religion' for *shar'* or *sharī'a* instead of 'la loi religieuse'. Averroes is very concise and careful in his terminology and uses *dīn* or *milla* if he wants to express *religion* meaning *faith*. We shall never understand Islam, Judaism, and their religious philosophers unless we recognize that an all-embracing, comprehensive, perfect 'law' is the core and pivot of both religious ways of life, binding upon elect and masses alike, in its preceptive parts of moral and ceremonial laws no less than in its theoretical part: its teaching about God, the Universe, man's place in it and his relation to God, in other words right beliefs and convictions. But there is this important difference between the elect philosophers and the masses of varying degrees of intellectual receptiveness—a distinction made by all *falāsifa* and their Jewish followers: the philosophers *must* attempt a rational interpretation of these beliefs and convictions—apart from those inaccessible to human reason—and their results will of necessity agree with the findings of pure reason. The masses, on the other hand, must *accept* these beliefs and convictions in their external sense. There can thus be no question of Faith *versus* Reason, but it is rather a contrast between intelligent and naïve, unquestioning faith. Gauthier's distinction between religion—which is 'd'ordre pragmatique'—and philosophy—which is 'de l'ordre de la vérité pure' misses this vital point. In fact, he himself raises objections to his formulation that 'la doctrine philosophique qui s'en [in the *Faṣl*] dégage est un rationalisme sans réserve' and admits that—according to the *Faṣl*—there are texts in the religious law of Islam which nobody has a right to interpret—their external sense must be accepted by *all* men (109)—or that philosophical interpretation must not go so far as to deny what is stated in the text of the Qur'ān or *Ḥadīth*. His answers that the understanding of those texts is accessible to all three kinds of arguments (persuasive, dialectical, and demonstrative), and that revelation cannot teach anything which reason cannot apprehend do in no way, to my mind, invalidate his objections. Like several other scholars, he attributes to Averroes a rationalism quite alien to the Middle Ages and akin to the rationalism of 18th-century *Aufklaerung*. This is clear from his statement (108): 'Peut-être vaudrait-il mieux dire que le symbole révélé, la religion indispensable à la masse, est utile, mais que la philosophie seule est pleinement vraie.' Or (120): 'L'enseignement dogmatique donné par les religions n'a point pour fin, comme celui de la philosophie, la vérité spéculative, mais seulement l'utilité morale de tous pour la vie future.' It is well to remember that the medieval philosopher is a unitary personality and not split into traditionalist in so-called religion and sovereign intellect in philosophy; the more so since in the Middle Ages there did not exist a speculative philosophy in abstract purity and sovereign independence, but only a religious philosophy which was conditioned by a revealed law that taught truth to perfection ; and, we may add, there was only one truth which both ' religion ' and philosophy sought after, albeit by a different method. The real problem is how to harmonize the findings of human reason with the help of the demonstrative arguments of the speculative philosopher, with the teachings of a law divinely revealed through prophecy and embodied in the *Sharī'a*. To this problem Muslims and Jews devoted their minds trained in the traditional science of *fiqh* (*halakhah* among the Jews). They fully and unreservedly acknowledged the authority of their prophetic law. Consequently they met the challenge of Greek and Hellenistic philosophy as religious minds. This challenge was in the name of sovereign human reason. The answer Muslim and Jewish medieval religious philosophy gave represents its signal, original contribution to the culture of the West. Gauthier has shown convincingly that the charge of irreligion levelled against Ibn Rushd is completely unfounded and utterly false. It is the more surprising that he should have come to such a conclusion (41) : ' pour les philosophes, rationalisme ésotérique, absolu, pour le vulgaire, fidéisme exotérique absolu : pour les théologiens qui forment une classe hybride, semi-rationalisme et semi-fidéisme, c'est-à-dire license de s'adonner entre eux au petit jeu des interprétations dialectiques, inconsistantes et variées, mais à la condition expresse de ne s'y livrer qu'en secret, avec défense d'en rien communiquer au vulgaire, sous peine des plus sévères châtiments.' Nor is his categorical assertion, I regret to say, tenable (111) : ' En résumé, le Façl el maqâl d'Ibn Rochd est le plus profond commentaire qu'on ait jamais donné de cette formule célèbre : Il faut une religion pour le peuple . . . Loin de subordonner en quoi que ce soit la philosophie à la religion, ce traité, en somme, subordonne catégoriquement la religion à la philosophie.' But he is right in stressing the essential unity of the ' dogmatic ' treatises (*Faṣl* and *Manāhij*) and the *Tahāfut al-tahāfut*. He sees the key to this unity in ' la théorie philosophique commune à tous les falâcifa, de l'intuition mystique dont l'inspiration prophétique n'est qu'un cas particulier '. I think we can agree with this if we substitute *intuitive reason* in the Aristotelean meaning of the term for Gauthier's *intuition mystique* which may be correct for Ibn Bājja and Ibn Ṭufail, but certainly not for Averroes.

The writings of Alfārābī and Avicenna and particularly Averroes' Commentaries on Plato's *Republic* and on Aristotle's *Nicomachean Ethics* show, indeed, the connexion between *Sharī'a* and *falsafa*, but also equally clearly the vital link of both with Politics, which Gauthier does not seem to have noticed, but L. Strauss has. This will be elaborated later on, in connexion with Averroes' spirited defence of the *Sharī'a*. For the moment the place Averroes assigns to demonstrative argument in philosophy and theology must be more fully illustrated.

2. *Demonstrative Arguments*.—In the Commentary on the *Republic* Ibn Rushd distinguishes two main groups of arguments—borrowed from Aristotle—and

assigns their use to two corresponding groups of men : demonstrative arguments are used by and for the elect few—the metaphysicists—and dialectical, rhetorical, and poetical arguments are used in teaching the masses. The second group includes the *mutakallimūn*, who use *jadal*, dialectical argument, and are unable to rise to *burhān*, demonstrative proof. It is characteristic for Averroes the religious philosopher to attack the dialectic theologians. The reason is that *falsafa* and *Sharīʿa* both teach true knowledge, that is knowledge of God and Existing Things. It can be gained only by means of *aqāwīl burhānīya*, demonstrative arguments. Averroes aims to establish—in the *Faṣl*—a claim for the *falāsifa* alone to possess a legitimate title to the interpretation of the parts of the *Sharīʿa* which require interpretation by means of *burhān*. The masses must be satisfied with the plain, external meaning, and the philosophers must not divulge the results of their rational inquiry to them since it would lead to confusion and error, even schism. For the masses are incapable by natural disposition of rising to an understanding of the hidden, inner meaning of revealed truth. But the philosopher must bring about unity between the infallible truth of the *Sharīʿa* and the truth of the philosopher arrived at by demonstrative argument.

From the point of view of the *Sharīʿa* a third group had to be included by dividing the second group of arguments into dialectical on the one hand, and rhetorical and poetical on the other. Averroes is not opposed to the interpreters of tradition as long as they restrict themselves to *fiqh* and its interpretation. But he resents their intrusion into the realm of doctrine. For dialectical arguments are insufficient for the rational interpretation of beliefs and convictions. This is, in his opinion, the preserve of the philosophers. But as a devout Muslim he is not only conscious of the intellectual inferiority of the *mutakallimūn*, but apprehensive lest heresy and schism be the result of the divisions in their interpretation which they divulge to the masses. This criticism is directed in the first place against the Ashʿarites. The *Sharīʿa* contains all three classes of arguments and thus appeals to all three classes of Muslims. Consequently, it teaches each class in a manner appropriate to it, truth which cannot contradict that arrived at by demonstration (*Faṣl*, 7).

Gauthier makes out a good case for the *Faṣl* agreeing with Almohad doctrine as modified by the successors of the Mahdi Ibn Tūmart. That Averroes was in full agreement with the religious policy of the two caliphs whom he served, is evident from the concluding sentences of the *Faṣl* and does not contradict his criticism of the political and economic organization of their State with which I have dealt before. He has learnt from Plato as well as from Muslim history to distinguish between the ideal *Republic* and the imperfect States which represent its perversion. The object of the Almohad revolt was to replace Almoravid misrule by pure orthodoxy and to reform Muslim Spain. He says (*Faṣl* 33) : ' Allah has removed many of these evils [hatred and enmity through sects, e.g.], follies and erroneous ways through this ruling power and has made a path for many good things, and in particular for those who follow the way of speculation and are eager for a knowledge of the truth . . . He has called the masses—in respect of the knowledge of God—to a middle way which is far above the low level of the *muqallidūn* [who relied in their interpretation of *fiqh* on the authority of an independent interpreter, *mujtahid*] but below the disputatiousness of the *mutakallimūn*. He has awakened the elect to the need for complete theoretical inquiry into the root-principle of the *Sharī'a*.' This may mean that the Almohads have caused the masses of the people—kept ignorant under the Almoravids—to be instructed in the plain, external meaning of the *Sharī'a* and have encouraged the *falāsifa* to apply demonstrative arguments to the interpretation of the inner meaning of it. A brief description of their religious policy is therefore necessary, in accordance with I. Goldziher's authoritative exposition.

The most important feature of Ibn Tūmart's revolutionary doctrine seems to me to be his insistence on knowledge of the *Sharī'a* in addition to the observance of its regulations. Faith must be supplemented by knowledge of God. It does seem to me that Averroes takes his cue from here for his justification from Scripture of rational endeavour to acquire a knowledge of God as revealed in the *Sharī'a*—which is based on Qur'ān, *Sunna*, *Ḥadīth*, and *ijmā'*. Averroes must also be in agreement with Ibn Tūmart in his exclusion of *ẓann* and *ra'y* from interpretation as subjective. But he would presumably not agree to the exclusion of *qiyās 'aqlī* from the *uṣūl al-fiqh*. (Ibn Tūmart allowed only the use of *qiyās shar'ī* in legal deduction.) Nor would he follow Ibn Tūmart in matters of theology, bearing in mind his opposition to Ash'arism. We know that he wrote a large commentary (*sharḥ*) on Ibn Tūmart's *'aqīda*, which is unfortunately lost. The gradual estrangement of the second and especially the third Almohad caliphs from Ibn Tūmart's theology, combined with their almost exclusive concern with *fiqh* helped Ibn Rushd to persist in his anti-Ash'arism without incurring the disfavour of his masters. This applies in particular to his strong opposition to the use of *ta'wīl*, allegorical interpretation, of which Ibn Tūmart had approved. Abū Yūsuf Ya'qūb declared himself against *taqlīd* and *furū'* and, according to al-Marrākushī (134) ordered the burning of Malikite *fiqh* books. On the other hand, Ibn Tūmart's branding of the Almoravid adherence to *tajsīm*, anthropomorphism, as *kufr*—thus raising his opposition to a religious revolution and his war against them to a *jihād*—was upheld. Though the matter requires further careful study it seems to me at the moment that Averroes tended more to the views of Ibn Ḥazm, especially where he differed from Ibn Tūmart. Points of contact between Averroes and Ibn Ḥazm—following Goldziher's monograph *Die Zahiriten*—are briefly these, which are of immediate relevance to my interpretation of Averroes' thought. Ibn Ḥazm seems to go further than Ibn Tūmart would, in allowing a departure from *ẓāhir*, clear, external meaning, when sense-perception and experience necessitate a different interpretation. Averroes also adopted Ibn Ḥazm's stand on the interpretation of words in legal texts in accordance with their grammatical meaning (*Faṣl*, 9), but he does not admit of Ibn Ḥazm's distinction *ḥaml al-lafẓa 'alā-l-ḥaqīqat al-shar'īya muqaddam 'alā ḥamlihi 'alā-l-ḥaqīqat al-luġawīya*. But this is of lesser import than the conclusion Averroes draws from the *'arabīya*: if this is the practice of the *faqīh* how much more is the *failasūf*, who possesses knowledge by proof, entitled to interpret in conformity with Arabic usage. For the *faqīh* works only with *qiyās ẓannī*, whereas the *'ārif* works with *qiyās yaqīnī* (*Faṣl*, 9, 5–7). This juxtaposition of syllogism based on (subjective) opinion, and syllogism of certainty, i.e. demonstrative proof, sums up tersely the difference between the *failasūf*, who as *'ārif* has certain knowledge, and the *mutakallim*, who lacks certainty.

Averroes has support for his unconditional rejection of *ta'wīl* and of dogmatic speculation as practised by the Ash'arites in Ibn Ḥazm who likewise only recognized *fiqh* and rejected *kalām*. Averroes, as we know from lists of his works, participated actively in *'ilm al-fiqh*. As a philosopher, following in the tradition of Plato and Aristotle, he attached great importance to jurisprudence whilst criticizing its practitioners for their worldly interests (*Faṣl*, 7, 10 ff.). His principal opposition is, however, directed against the dialectic theologians, and this for two main reasons, as stated before: the inadequacy of their method and the consequent absence of certainty and unanimity as well as their divulging of false notions to the masses ignorant of the proper method of study and therefore without discernment. Both combined result—to repeat—in confusion, heresy, and schism. In this sense he identifies them with the Sophists (*Manāhij*, 76). He does not hesitate to appeal to the *imām*, the Almohad caliph, to suppress this grave danger to the purity of Islam and the security of the State. For notwithstanding his deep interest in philosophical speculation—of which more will be said when his attitude to Plato and Aristotle is being examined—he was principally concerned with the inner meaning of the *Sharī'a*, in particular its teaching of God and Existing Things. This will be clear from our next point.

3. *The Supremacy of the Sharī'a and the Place of Prophecy in the Philosophy of Averroes.*—The identity of purpose between philosophy and *Sharī'a* has already been discussed. The superiority of the latter over even the general law without which no nation can live or formulate particular laws suited to its society, consists in that it is the expression of the will of God. It is for this reason that the Highest Good of man, his end as a rational being, is therein contained. It is superior to what man can devise. The philosopher aims at knowledge identical with that which God demands in the *Sharī'a*. To know God's will is possible only through prophecy, as we learnt earlier on from Averroes' own words. Prophecy is the source of the *Sharī'a*; it consists—to anticipate a fuller examination presently—of the revelation which legitimizes the prophet: the Qur'ān. If we want to understand Averroes' view that it is only possible for the religious philosopher to gain that knowledge we must remember that for him as an orthodox Muslim Muḥammad was the seal of the prophets. Therefore prophecy is extinct and—with striking similarity to the Jewish idea that the wise, i.e. wise in the Torah, are the heirs and successors of the prophets—the philosopher in Islam is heir to the prophet in knowledge of God. It is significant that Averroes stresses this point at great length in the *Faṣl*, expounding the nature of the three classes of men corresponding to the

three kinds of arguments, and polemizing against the *mutakallimūn* and in particular against al-Ghazāli. He even invokes the highest Muslim authority, the *imām*, to guard and protect the *falāsifa* and their writings—in which they interpret with their superior method of demonstration what requires interpretation in the *Sharī'a*, namely, abstract knowledge—and, moreover, to see that these writings do not fall into the hands of the two other classes.

If we are justified in reading this statement in conjunction with Averroes' characterization of the founders of the Almoravid and Almohad dynasties, particularly the latter, who were animated by the desire to restore the rule of the *Sharī'a*, it follows that the Ideal State is that built upon the *Sharī'a* and the Ideal Ruler is the *imām* who, as *amīr al-mu'minīn*, is charged with implementing the *Sharī'a* and guaranteeing its strict observance by the ideal society, the Muslim *jamā'a*. That this concept was not confined to the realm of the ideal is evident from two facts reported in our sources of this period. Ibn Tūmart wrote a treatise on the Imamate—*fī imāma*—which Averroes may have known, and Abu Ya'qūb Yūsuf ordered his *'ulamā* to collect all traditions concerning *jihād* and combined them into a *K. al-jihād* for practical guidance in his wars against the Christians and the Almoravid resisters.

The *Sharī'a* as divine law has much in common with the general law which is man-made. This will engage our attention in the final section. The ' political ' character of law needs no stressing. The *Sharī'a* is the law of the Muslim State and aims at the happiness of all its citizens, the elect philosophers as well as the masses. Its perfection and superiority over man-made laws consist in its divine character. Divine means revealed by Allah through Muḥammad, his messenger. This is unequivocally Averroes' view notwithstanding his doubt whether the Ideal Ruler—who combines in his person the qualities and functions of philosopher-king-lawgiver and *imām* in one—should also be a prophet. In this doubt he may have been influenced by the laws of the *Sharī'a* about the *khilāfa*, and he may have left the question an open one for the reason that prophecy was certainly not one of the requirements in the *khalīfa*, the vice-gerent of the prophet Muḥammad. On the other hand, the *falāsifa* had no difficulty in harmonizing accomplishment in the theoretical sciences, demanded of the philosopher-king, with the *'ilm* required of the caliph. This *'ilm* meant ability to make independent decisions (of *fiqh*) and pass judgments on points of law (*ijtihād*). For the *Sharī'a* teaches true beliefs and convictions and—as we have seen from Averroes' claim for the philosopher to be the only qualified and authorized interpreter of the *Sharī'a*—*'ilm* certainly covers knowledge of God, the angels and all Existing Things. In other words it is identical with the knowledge that the metaphysicist strives to attain.

The Ideal Muslim State is founded on the *Sharī'a*, i.e. prophetically revealed law. It is of crucial importance to realize that Averroes is interested in prophecy exclusively under the aspect of the *Sharī'a* and, consequently, offers an explanation of prophecy which hardly, if at all, differs from the traditional orthodox definition. For him, the prophet is the Lawgiver, sent by Allah. He is at pains in his *Manāhij* to show that the working of miracles is no proof of prophetic status by itself, but only an additional and—for him—unimportant confirmation. He says that miracles cannot be proved *bi-l-shar'*, through the religious law, nor *bi-l-'aql*, by reason (93, in Mueller's edition). This view is directed against the *mutakallimūn* who maintain that a prophet can be recognized by the miracles he performs. Averroes' intention is to free prophecy from miracles. But, he says, one must believe that he who performs them is virtuous and does not lie—as Plato's philosopher-rulers do! As a Muslim Averroes cannot deny that Muḥammad performed miracles, and it is for this reason that he admits them as a secondary confirmation of prophecy, valid only in conjunction with and in addition to the sole relevant criterion: the Qur'ān, *al-kitāb al-'azīz*, by which Muḥammad called upon the people to obey the will of Allah. This alone is the true legitimation of prophecy.

The Qur'ān is the miracle that confirms the *nubuwwa*, the prophetic character, of Muḥammad. It is through the Qur'an that we know prophets exist.

These prophets lay down laws (*sharā'i'*)—not *nawāmīs* like Plato's *νομοθέτης*—by dint of a revelation (*waḥy*) from God for man to whom they announce knowledge (*'ilm*) and good actions (*al-af'āl al-jāmila*). These laws enable man to reach perfect happiness and forbid him vicious religious convictions (*i'tiqādāt fāsida*) and bad actions. This is the act of prophets (*Manāhij*, 98).

Averroes is most insistent on the legislative function of the prophet by means of divine revelation. Not the dividing of the sea during the Exodus from Egypt but the giving of the Law from Sinai made Moses a prophet (99). The political character of prophecy is inherent in Islam, but brought into relief through the Greek concept of *νόμος*.

Apart from the Qur'ān in the case of Muḥammad and the Torah in that of Moses it is the authentic witness of successive, uninterrupted tradition (*naql tawātur*) which proves the existence of prophets; just as *naql* attests to the existence of philosophy and the philosophers (100). (We note that in the latter case it is *naql* without *tawātur* which seems to be reserved for Islam.)

Averroes further insists that the *Sharī'a* contains both theoretical and practical laws—as has been stated before. Only he has the necessary knowledge to lay down these laws to whom was vouchsafed through revelation knowledge of God, happiness, and the good deeds that lead to it. He alone knows the obstacles that prevent man from attaining happiness. Averroes, the disciple of Plato and Aristotle, knows that many things contained in the *Sharī'a* are also to be found in human laws. But, he avers (101), it is revelation which enables us to understand them, or at least most of them. Yet, there seems to be a certain weakening of his rigidly orthodox position expressed in his qualifying statement that their understanding is *best* obtained through revelation.

One might be of the opinion that in dealing with Islamic doctrine Averroes could not very well be anything but traditional. The more significant is therefore the fact that Averroes should give the same definition of prophecy and prophets and make the same assertion about the *Sharī'a* in an admittedly philosophical treatise, written in defence of the *falāsifa* against al-Ghazāli's attack upon them. For we find in the *Tahāfut al-tahāfut* that the prophet lays down 'religious laws which conform to the truth and impart a knowledge of those actions by which the happiness of the whole of creation is guaranteed' (ed. Bouyges, p. 516). The *Sharī'a*, he says towards the end of this treatise, leads to the happiness appropriate to each individual. It is necessary for the ethical virtues, the speculative virtues, and the practical arts. For without the last-named man cannot live in this world, nor can he live in this world and the world-to-come without the speculative virtues. But it is the ethical virtues without which he cannot attain the two others to perfection.

It is relevant to interpose here that the aim of the *Sharī'a* is identical with that of Political Science as defined by Aristotle in the *Nicomachean Ethics* and repeated by Alfārābī in his *K. taḥṣīl al-sa'āda* and by Averroes in his Commentary on Plato's *Republic*.

Exactly as in the *Manāhij* Averroes makes the ethical virtues in man dependent on previous knowledge of God and how to honour Him—which only the *Sharī'a* teaches. Averroes asks there the question how the prophetic lawgiver can know to what extent the individual is capable of reaching happiness and by which method he procures it. In his answer he makes an important distinction—which is fundamental for his outlook as a religious philosopher—between the knowledge of the prophetic lawgiver and that of the speculative philosopher. The former possesses knowledge which is absolutely certain through devotion to the theoretical sciences, i.e. *yaqīn* as the result of demonstrative proof and in particular, through laying down religious laws and establishing regulations and making pronouncements about the circumstances of the Hereafter (*Manāhij*, 101). The latter has only the knowledge he gained from a study of the speculative sciences to guide him and consequently lacks the knowledge of *waḍ' al-sharā'i'* on the basis of the Qur'ān and, through that, the means to make the masses happy. In other words, the prophetic lawgiver must be a philosopher. Yet he not only states in the *Tahāfut al-tahāfut* that whilst the prophet is also a philosopher not every philosopher is a prophet—a stock-in-trade of the *falāsifa* and their opponents—but proceeds to clarify the difference between philosophy and *Sharī'a*—notwithstanding the identity of their aim—thus: philosophy explains the happiness of some (elect) intellects and the study of philosophy marks man out as a human being. The religious laws, however, aim at instructing the masses (*al-jumhūr 'āmmatan*) and leading them to happiness (582). A little later on he exhorts the philosophers to choose the best religion, which is naturally Islam, just as in his view it was Judaism in the time of Israel, and Christianity in the time of Rome. For him it is Muḥammad who, with the Qur'ān, has brought the final revelation to mankind. That Averroes should have defined prophecy and proclaimed the superiority of the *Sharī'a* in the *Faṣl al-maqāl* and the *Manāhij* in the same way as in the *Tahāfut al-tahāfut* and—at least as far as the *Sharī'a* is concerned—in the Commentary on the *Republic* proves beyond doubt, to my mind, that he was a sincere, orthodox Muslim. In any case, it is very strange that—as far as I am aware—Averroes nowhere expounds the theory of prophecy current among the *falāsifa*. Al-Ghazāli attacks this theory in his *Tahāfut al-falāsifa*, but Averroes counters the charge merely by stating the orthodox Muslim conception, buttressed by arguments taken from political philosophy. His brilliant vindication of the *Sharī'a* puts him in a class apart among the *falāsifa*. It is true that they have all recognized its excellence and paid tribute to its divine character. Averroes alone among them has endeavoured not only to defend it and establish its authority unchallenged and unchallengeable, but also to stress its political necessity as the only Law guaranteeing the happiness of *all* who acknowledge its authority and live by its regulations.

In this he resembles Maimonides among the Jews. Both have the same attitude to the prophetic law. But Maimonides is a strong exponent of the psychological explanation of prophecy as first expounded by Alfārābī. This theory is, as is well known, inextricably bound up with the neo-platonic theory of emanation. It is interesting to observe that Gauthier bases his exemplary analysis of this psychological theory of prophecy on Maimonides' account in his *Guide to the Perplexed*. That Averroes should not even mention it is strange and I know of no other explanation than that he rejected it in favour of the orthodox one which he so forcefully expounded. This matter requires investigation. Gauthier is convinced that Averroes shared the view of the *falāsifa*, especially in the formulation of Avicenna, by implication (130 ff., 138, and especially 143 ff.). He adduces Averroes' treatment of the prophetic intellect in the *Tahāfut al-tahāfut* (532 ff.) as evidence for his view. But I cannot find any reference to the emanation of the Active Intellect in the way propounded by Alfārābī and after him by Avicenna and Maimonides; and I am convinced that Averroes rejected it. He did so not only because for him revelation (*waḥy*) took the form of the *kitāb al-'azīz* and was supplemented by *certain knowledge* as a result of it, but perhaps also because of his deeper and purer understanding of Aristotle's Theory of Knowledge. For I am not aware of a treatment of the intellect other than that in his Commentaries on *De Anima* and *Metaphysica*. This exposition is, if I am right, entirely free from collusion with the Theory of Emanation. Moreover, in the passage of the *Tahāfut al-tahāfut* Averroes refutes a charge brought by al-Ghazāli against the *falāsifa*, with Avicenna's argument, since it was Avicenna in the first place who was attacked. That does not necessarily mean that Averroes made Avicenna's view his own. His further statement (516) that the Active Intellect of the *falāsifa* is identical with the *malak* (Angel) of the *Sharī'a* has, to my mind, no connexion with the Theory of Emanation. But I repeat: this problem needs further serious consideration. If it is as I believe it to be we would have in Averroes' rejection of the Theory of Emanation by ignoring it the clearest indication of the orthodoxy of his position in respect of Prophecy and its most important result: the *Sharī'a* as the Ideal Constitution of the Ideal State. But the problem is as complex as the human mind itself. Revelation occupies the first and dominant place. Yet this does not mean that Averroes assigns to the intellect an inferior position. For he demands of the prophetic lawgiver knowledge of all Existing Things, without which perfect knowledge of God is not possible. If there is here a contradiction it is—at least for Averroes—more apparent than real. For him the Qur'ān, that miracle of Revelation, does not only prove the *nubuwwa* of the lawgiver, it also demands speculation about God, the angels and all Existing Things by means of demonstrative proof.

Whilst Averroes—to my mind—differs from Alfārābī and Avicenna in his concept of prophecy, he shares Avicenna's view that prophecy and *Sharī'a* are necessary for the survival of mankind. But how can we explain Averroes' doubt as to whether the philosopher-king-lawgiver-*imām* should also be a prophet ? ' As for the stipulation that he be a prophet there is room for thorough investigation. We will inquire into it in the first part of this science, *in sha'a-llah*. But perhaps if this were so it would be [stipulated] on grounds of perfection [or : of the highest good] and not out of necessity.' (II. i, 7.) One possible explanation might be that he envisaged a secular State, i.e. a State based on a law which was not the result of prophetic revelation. But why then should he insist on the qualification of *imām* ? Therefore, it seems to me more likely to look for the reason for his hesitancy in Averroes' orthodoxy. The *Sharī'a*, the direct result of Muḥammad's prophetic mission, was already in existence. Therefore no new prophet was possible nor necessary. But, we notice at once, no new lawgiver would be required either. If he simply followed Alfārābī in this whole chapter why did he take exception to the prophetic qualification only ? Was it because he did not agree with the current theory of prophecy ? Or had he simply not yet come to a definite conclusion at the time of the composition of the Commentary ? This would perhaps also explain why Averroes did not redeem his promise in his Commentary on the *Nicomachean Ethics*, if we are justified in placing its date very near that of the Commentary on the *Republic*. May not the answer be found in the two treatises in which the *Sharī'a* as the prophetic law is so vigorously championed, in the *Faṣl* and the *Manāhij* ? It could possibly be assumed that the *Faṣl al-maqāl* and the *Manāhij* are of the realm of ' Political Science, Part I : Theory ', since they are concerned with the *Sharī'a* and its object of leading man to perfect happiness. Now this is exactly the objective of Plato's Royal Art, Aristotle's Master Art, the science of Politics which is concerned with the Highest Good and to it the *Nicomachean Ethics* is devoted on which Averroes wrote a Commentary as well, referred to frequently in the Commentary on the *Republic*. Just as this Commentary is Averroes' own contribution to ' Political Science, Part II : Practice ', so is his treatment of the prophetic lawgiver and the *Sharī'a*—in addition to the justification of *falsafa* by this *Sharī'a*—the Islamic counterpart to his Commentary on the *Nicomachean Ethics*. This is only a suggestion and further research is necessary, hampered unfortunately by the absence of the Arabic originals of both his

Commentaries on the *Republic* and on the *Nicomachean Ethics*, of some of his religious-philosophical treatises, and of his legal writings in particular if we bear in mind that Jurisprudence is part of Political Science.

III. Political Realism

Although Averroes considered the Islamic State based on the *Sharī'a* the most excellent State imaginable he was equally emphatic that of the States not based on revealed prophetic law Plato's Ideal Republic was the best and its coming into being as Plato described it. This is clear from his own words: 'It is right that you should know that the manner which Plato described is the best of its coming into being. But it is also possible for it to come into being in a different manner, yet after a long time. This is when there will over a long time be a succession of excellent kings over these states and they will not cease to influence these states gradually until in the end of time matters will come to the best government. Their influence will work in two ways at once, i.e. by their activities and works and by their convictions. This will be easy or not easy according to the laws in existence at a given time, and to their being near to this state or far [from it]. In general, their influence towards excellent deeds is more likely than towards good convictions in this time.' (II. xvii, 3.) This is obviously the description of a secular State and may perhaps be connected with the hesitancy about the prophetic qualification, notwithstanding the possible objections I have raised myself earlier on. Prophecy in a secular State is not necessary, but would make for perfection. If Averroes posed this question merely as a Muslim, he could certainly not admit that prophets would appear after Muḥammad had been the last and most perfect of all prophets. But as a realist investigating the question of the origin and nature of the State, he recognized the existence of the secular State. The study of Plato's *Republic* and no less of contemporary States though theoretically under the *Sharī'a*, taught him this. As a Muslim, and no less as a disciple of Plato, he insisted on a State-law which, however, varies with the kings who rule the State. To recognize the mutual influence between rulers and laws is in itself a sign of political realism. It has already been remarked that he also recognized the close affinity between the divinely revealed law of Islam and the general law promulgated by the lawgiver of the secular State. All stages from complete identity to contrast are noted in various passages of the Commentary; e.g. when speaking of corrective punishment in the Ideal as well as the imperfect States he says: 'The same is the case with laws which follow [the pattern of] the human laws in this our divine law, for the ways which lead in it to God are two: the one of them by persuasion and the other by war.' (I. vii, 11.) Or when dealing with the objection that the coming into being of the Platonic State was impossible because nobody would be in possession of all the qualities required of the ruler he says: 'The answer is that it is possible for men to grow up with these natural qualities . . . and to develop together with this by choosing the general law, the adoption of which none of the nations can escape. In addition, their own particular (religious) law should not be far from the human laws. Philosophy should already be perfected in their time. This is like the situation that prevails in this our time and in our religious law. If it so happens that such like men are rulers . . . then it is possible that this state exists.' (II. iii, 1–2.) Without the Arabic original it is impossible to ascertain the exact meaning of the terms *nīmūs* and *tōrāh* here. Normally *nīmūs* renders *nāmūs* and *tōrāh* renders *shar'* or *sharī'a*. But it is strange to find the combination *tōrōṯ anūshiyōṯ*, unless 'human' here means truly human because divinely revealed. The distinction between general and particular laws is derived from Aristotle, who in his discussion of Justice distinguishes between natural, legal and conventional law (*Nic. E.* V, 7, 1134b). Finally, in I. xxix, 3, Averroes discusses the rules of war and says: 'But what Plato thinks is at variance with what many lawgivers think.' He uses the term *tōrōṯ*, religious laws, which corresponds to *sharā'i'*. In all such passages a definitive interpretation is very difficult owing to the uncertainty of Averroes' terminology. But two observations are beyond doubt. In the first place, we note the close connexion between *Sharī'a* and *νόμος*—their precise relationship will be the subject of the final section—and philosophy and secondly, the resulting connexion between law and politics, as understood by Plato and Aristotle.

Averroes' political awareness and realistic approach have already been noticed in previous sections and it remains now to assess their significance in the context of Political Thought in Islam in general. There can be no doubt that his study of Plato's *Republic* and of Aristotle's *Nicomachean Ethics* has sharpened his own political sense, trained through experience as judge and citizen. To hold office was, moreover, a family tradition with the Banū Rushd.

If we are justified in seeing in the passage about the origin of the State a recognition of the secular State in conjunction with his positive attitude to Plato's Ideal State and its deviations, which he took so seriously that he applied their characteristics to the contemporary scene, we will have to look upon Averroes as a forerunner of Ibn Khaldun. His attitude to law, just touched upon, is another pointer in this direction. And yet, he has not advanced on the road to the Power-State, described with so much insight by Ibn Khaldun, as far as Ibn al-Ṭiqṭaqa. His preoccupation with law and justice—without overlooking the speculative element of intellectual perfection—goes hand in hand with a strong historical-political sense. This is brought into play in his defence of Plato against Galen's strictures, when Averroes draws a line between the city-state of Plato and the *οἰκουμένη* of Galen; or when he recognizes the laws regulating prayer and sacrifices and enjoining humility as integral parts of the general law of the State, though they vary with every nation, religion, time, and place, just as other laws and injunctions vary. But before all his statement—in connexion with regulations governing prayer and other religious observances and, in particular, the teaching about God, the angels, and the prophets—that '*al-sharā'i' hīya al-ṣanā'i' al-ḍarūrīya al-madanīya*' (*Tahāfut al-tahāfut*, 581) shows great political insight and reminds one forcibly of Ibn Khaldun's attitude to religion, as I have shown elsewhere. To refer to religious laws as 'necessary political institutions' is of course quite compatible with the Muslim position and the all-embracing character of the *Sharī'a*, but it seems to me that the use of the term *madanīya* points to the recognition of the political sphere as on a par with other spheres of the life of the State which are all held together by the *Sharī'a*, but have a significance of their own. His views on the place of women in the State—discussed before—fall in this category, and his resulting awareness of the political importance of Economics have their origin in the *Republic*, it is true. But by applying them to his own environment and by enlarging on them Averroes has developed them further and clearly foreshadows Ibn Khaldun. His keen interest in education and his realization of its political importance are further proof of this realism. His condemnation of Arab poetry springs as much from his recognition of its political harmfulness as from his orthodoxy. His insistence on the philosopher's fulfilment of the civic duties is another case in point.

Tentatively I would add a further indication of a significant development of a Platonic idea in the direction of Ibn Khaldun's concept of the *'aṣabīya*. Averroes uses the term, rendered into Hebrew by *qibbūṣ* (association, community) often in the meaning of Plato's σύνταξυς (τοῦ ἄρχοντος). In these passages (e.g. I. xxvii, 2 ; III. iv, 7, etc.) it seems to emphasize the corporate life of the State, almost a social-political force : the group ; especially when it is used in union with *shittūf*, Plato's κοινωνία, a community organized on the principle of fellowship. *If* this interpretation is correct, we have in this term—specific to Averroes—a clear indication of his political interest and of his advance towards Ibn Khaldun with his concept of the State as an independent entity with laws and tendencies of its own, and of the group as a political factor. Whether Ibn Khaldun was influenced by Averroes is a matter for investigation. He certainly polemizes against the political views of the *falāsifa*. But this is not the place for such an inquiry and I must reserve it for another occasion. At any rate, Averroes started from Plato (*Rep.* 462*d*), and we now examine in summary fashion his attitude to his source and to Aristotle.

IV. Averroes, Plato, and Aristotle

Far from looking upon Plato's *Republic* merely as a substitute for Aristotle's *Politics*, which was inaccessible to him, Averroes used the *Republic* as a guide to the understanding of the State as such and, in particular, of contemporary Muslim States. To comment on it—as I tried to show in the first section of this article—was a necessary, self-imposed task of the philosopher who could not live in the Ideal State, but had at least to offer a considered judgment on his own State. By so doing he may have hoped to influence affairs by contrasting the existing, imperfect, with the Ideal State. His method of commenting upon what was most likely Galen's Summary of the *Republic* in Ḥunain b. Isḥāq's translation is dealt with in the Introduction to the edition and translation of the Hebrew version. Suffice it to stress that Averroes comments only on Plato's theoretical statements. This follows from his insistence on the use of demonstrative arguments only in philosophy. He therefore leaves out of account Books I and X, notably the myth of Er, but offers a very substantial commentary on Books II–IX, often preceded by or interspersed with theoretical digressions. Throughout his Commentary he illustrates the Muslim's genius for absorbing, adapting, and entirely transforming ideas and institutions from another culture or civilization.

Although Averroes was the Commentator *par excellence* and felt inclined to assume the role of political critic, there must be a deeper, more compelling reason still for the way in which he commented on the *Republic* which differs so greatly from some of his other Commentaries and shows—in parts—such striking resemblance to his ' dogmatic ' polemical writings. This reason is to be found in what I have called elsewhere the ' common ground ' between Plato and Aristotle on the one hand and the *falāsifa*, especially Alfārābī, Avicenna, and Averroes, on the other. It is the dual aspect of the central problem of Islamic philosophy: the political character of prophecy and the affinity between *Sharī'a* and νόμος which manifests itself in the concept of the prophetic lawgiver. This affinity will be discussed in the final summing up, but it is to be borne in mind in the present context and in the next section—Averroes' relationship to Alfārābī.

Averroes treated the *Republic* very seriously and attached great importance to its leading ideas no less than to Plato's practical advice in matters of the education of philosophers and guardians, of the participation of women on an equal basis in all offices of state and civic duties generally, and of the principle of one occupation for one person. He entirely agrees with Plato's definition of the four cardinal virtues—supplemented by Aristotle's discussion in the *Nicomachean Ethics*—and the method of developing and perfecting them. In all this he shows a keen analytical mind by testing Plato's ideas on the political reality, not to speak of his conscious application to his own times, as we have seen before.

But he applies another test as well, namely the opinion of Aristotle to which he accords greater authority if Aristotle differs from Plato. Yet he sides with Plato against Galen, an example of which has been given before. This submission of Plato's thought to the judgment of Aristotle finds its explanation, in the first place, in Averroes' own systematic mind, trained in the method of Aristotle's logical writings and attaching—as repeatedly mentioned—the greatest importance to theoretical statements. It must be emphasized, however, that substantial agreement exists between Aristotle and Plato on moral and political questions. Aristotle is adduced as corroborating evidence as a rule, very rarely as overriding authority, and couched in such phraseology as: ' If this is not the opinion of Plato, it is, however, the opinion of Aristotle, and is undoubtedly the truth '. (I. xxii, 3 end.) Another instance is his criticism of Plato's opinion of the order of transformation of States from one to another in his comment on *Nic. E.* VIII, 10, 1160b, which—it is interesting to note—is not made in the

Commentary on the *Republic*, and I quote it in the Latin translation : ' Et istud est, quod narravit Arist. et est diversum viae vel semitae Platonis, qui videt quod principatus regni primo permutatur ad principatum honoris, et principatus honoris ad principatum divitiarum et principatus divitiarum ad principatum congregationum et principatus congregationis ad principatum tyrannidis. Et verisimile est quoniam quando perscrutatio exquaesita fit de hoc, patet quod res est, quae currit cursu naturae in compermutatione istorum principatuum est, ut dixit Arist. non ut dicit Plato.' (Ed. Venice, 1550, *f.* 59b. *r.*) Aristotle holds that monarchy is perverted to tyranny and timocracy to democracy. Aristotle's systematic treatment of the theoretical sciences, together with his logical categories, lifted many a Platonic argument out of the realm of persuasion or dialectic on to the plane of demonstrative proof. The *Analytica Posteriora* and *Physica* are largely responsible for that. As a result, Averroes often presents Plato's ideas in the modification Aristotle gave them. This has naturally an important bearing on the correct understanding of Averroes' text. Ibn Rushd is fully aware of the limitations which the mental climate of his time imposed on Plato, as can be seen from his recognition that the education of the philosophers could not have begun with logic in Plato's time (since it only became a philosophical discipline with Aristotle's *ὄργᾶνον*).

Similarly, Plato's cosmology and psychology are understood by Averroes in the systematic modification of the *Physica* and the *De Anima*, just as Plato's *Ideas* are understood in the modified form of Aristotle's treatment in his *Metaphysica*.

In this context Ibn Bājja has served as an important link, for he treated of Spiritual Forms at great length—thanks to his study and understanding of Aristotle, which has greatly influenced Averroes.

It would fall outside my province to examine whether or not Averroes' reference to Plato's view on *Universalia* and *Intelligibilia* represents Plato's original idea or rather Aristotle's modification of it.

What strikes the reader of this Commentary is the effortless, natural combination of Aristotle's theoretical philosophy with Plato's political thought and ideal. But though Averroes be prepared to bow to Aristotle's superior judgment, he does so critically, as he says in the *Faṣl* that it is our duty to examine carefully what our predecessors have written on a subject of theoretical philosophy, according to the requirements of demonstration and then concludes : *famā kāna minhā muwāfiqan lilḥaqq qabalnāhu minhum wasararnā bihi washakarnāhum ʿalayhi wamā kāna minhā ghayr muwāfiqin lilḥaqq nabahnā ʿalayhi waḥaḏirnā minhu waʿaḏarnāhum.* (6.)

Since the *Nicomachean Ethics* is for Averroes the theoretical basis for Plato's practical treatise it is not surprising to find Aristotle's fuller and more explicit distinction between leading and subordinate arts, though this distinction is already made by Plato, just as is the definition of Politics. That he adduces the *Nicomachean Ethics* in explanation of Plato's statements is a matter of course. It is particularly noticeable in economic affairs and in the realm of Law and

Justice, though Averroes has also drawn on the *Laws*. Thus, Averroes adopts Aristotle's differentiation of Justice and Equity and the identity between political and legal equity, the distinction between natural and human law and also—as already mentioned—between a general, universal law and particular laws, suited to specific nations and varying with time and place.

This blending of Platonic and Aristotelian thought and argument is a characteristic feature of the Commentary and thus of Averroes' political philosophy. It is no less interesting than his adaptation of typically Greek concepts to Islam and Muslim notions. It can be expected that much of this adaptation goes back to Averroes' Arabic source, though exactly how much cannot be ascertained since Ḥunain's translation of Galen's *Summary* must be presumed lost. Thus, Ḥunain may have changed Plato's 'gods' into 'angels' or 'demons' and made 'houses of prayer' out of 'temples'. But it is doubtful who replaced the Delphian Apollo by 'what the Most High commanded through prophecy', Ḥunain, or perhaps rather Ibn Rushd. The latter is probably responsible for substituting Arab for Greek poetry, and Plato's 'lands' are certainly replaced by 'trees' (I. xxix) with reference to *jihād* by Averroes himself. But these and many more similar instances throughout the Commentary are of minor importance than 'the weightier matters of the Law'.

It does not matter so greatly whether a Platonic idea was accepted in its Platonic form and connotation or in its Aristotelian modification and development, except under the strictly historical aspect. But it is important to state once more that Averroes' exposition of the *Republic* cannot be appreciated in many passages without our realizing that he studied and often understood Plato in the light of Aristotle's systematic philosophy. This is apparent in his comments on the *Republic* and, particularly, in his summaries of Plato's argument in the form of introductions of varying length. It is in these introductions as well as in the digressions of a theoretical nature—notably the long excursus II. vii–xiii, intended as a theoretical basis for the discussion of the education of philosophers—that Averroes' skilful blending of the *Republic* with the *Nicomachean Ethics* with the help of *De Anima*, *Physica* and *Metaphysica* as well as of the *Analytica Posteriora*, brings out the essential unity of the two parts of Political Science. It is on that unity that Averroes' own political thought is based. A striking example is the beginning of the Commentary, especially from I. ii, 2 to the end of viii. Averroes summarizes here the detailed comment of Books II, 376–IV (end) in the form of an extended paraphrase of Platonic passages, which are explained with the help of Aristotle's definitions—e.g. Courage—and blended with Alfārābī. The latter is, however, not quoted but simply incorporated without acknowledgment, the usual procedure. Averroes adds his own observations and welds the various strands into a concise, clear, coherent whole.

Almost without exception he follows Plato where practical politics is concerned. This can best be seen in his unreserved acceptance of the idea of law as the basis of the State. He did so as a traditionalist, Almohad Muslim, who saw in the *Sharīʿa* the equivalent of Plato's Constitution of his Ideal Republic. The community of the faithful with the *amīr al-mu'minīn* at the head *is* the Ideal Polity. But it is the study of Plato which has heightened the understanding of the *falāsifa*, chief among them Averroes, for the political significance of the divinely revealed, prophetic law.

That Averroes, echoing Aristotle, criticized the *Republic* as incomplete—in the Epilogue of his Commentary on the *Nicomachean Ethics*—because Plato had dealt with two only of the three classes of the State, the guardians and the philosophers, does not, to my mind, invalidate the assertion that in his interpretation of the *Sharīʿa* of Islam he was a disciple of Plato, whose philosopher-king was the ideal *imām* of the Muslim State. This *imām* was the *khalīfa* of the prophet-lawgiver. Hence the equation—since Alfārābī—of philosopher-king with *imām* and lawgiver-prophet, though, as we have seen, Averroes thought that the prophetic qualification was perhaps not necessary.

V. Averroes and Alfārābī

It is in his capacity as *qāḍī* and *faqīh* no less than as philosopher that Averroes studied and commented upon the *Republic*. Parallels adduced from the *Laws* make it almost certain that he knew this treatise as well. One passage in particular about first, second, and third laws (III. iv, 4) suggests autopsy, though it is naturally possible that he owed his knowledge of the *Laws* to Alfārābī's Summary (which I have so far been unable to consult in F. Gabrieli's edition as *Plato Arabus* III). He refers in our Commentary (I. i, 1) to other political writings of Plato. Again from parallels it appears that this included a knowledge of the *Politikos*. How much of these other treatises he knew direct or through Alfārābī must still be investigated. We know from Ḥunain b. Isḥāq that Galen's Summaries of Plato's treatises included the *Politikos* (Bergstraesser, 50) and Ibn Abī ʿUṣaibiʿa mentions it twice, first under *Aflāṭūn* and then under *Ḥunain*. Alfārābī gives a short description of the *Politikos*, without mentioning the title in his *De Platonis Philosophia* (ed. R. Walzer/Fr. Rosenthal as *Plato Arabus* II) V, 13. I am almost certain that Averroes used the Summaries of the *Laws* and *Politikos* that existed in Arabic. But I am not sure about the *Philebos*, though a number of passages in the Commentary would suggest that he knew it, or at least of it. It may, however, be due to his source of the *Republic*.

The fact is that Alfārābī's writings exerted considerable influence upon Averroes, in ideas no less than in literary dependence. The explanatory notes on the text provide clear evidence of it in abundance, and I must content myself here with some general remarks, illustrated by a few examples. But an important reservation must be made first. With the possible exception of Al-Kindi, Abū Naṣr Alfārābī seems to be the first Muslim philosopher to have introduced and adapted the philosophy of Plato and Aristotle. Most of the political part of his independent treatises is taken from Plato, chiefly from the *Republic* and the *Laws* and the *Timaios*. Many an idea and many a formulation to be met with in these treatises—*Al-madīna al-fāḍila*, *K. al-siyāsāt al-madanīya* and *K. taḥṣīl al-sa'āda*, to name only the three more important ones which are accessible, though not in satisfactory critical editions—is derived from Aristotle. We will do well, therefore, to pause before we credit Alfārābī with the transmission of what Averroes might very well have taken over direct. Yet there is unmistakable literary borrowing on a large scale, as I hope to have established in my notes. Besides, there can be no doubt that Alfārābī determined the thought of all subsequent *falāsifa*—and their Jewish followers—by his decisive combination of the neo-platonic theory of emanation with the phenomenon of prophecy in the Islamic sense—though not in the case of Averroes, as I have tried to show—and, as a result thereof—by his equation of prophet and philosopher, of philosopher and lawgiver and of lawgiver and *imām*. Plato's *Laws* and Aristotle's *Nicomachean Ethics*—both of which he commented on—with their stress on law led him to a consideration of the *Sharī'a* in relation to the νόμος and to a recognition of the essential similarity of outlook between the two. The superiority of revealed prophetic law was clear to him just as much as to his successors. But in contrast to Averroes, e.g. he concentrated on the qualifications necessary in the prophet-philosopher-lawgiver-king-*imām*, his intellectual perfection and happiness and on the theoretical part of Political Science. The practical implications for the State, its government, and the ordinary citizen which arise from the correspondence between *Sharī'a* and νόμος hardly interested him. He was a metaphysicist in matters political and not a statesman. Whereas Averroes often follows Alfārābī word for word his interest is at least equally divided between the individual perfection and happiness of the rulers and the citizens, especially the former, and the actual political reality. The result is that he incorporates Alfārābī's treatment of the speculative sciences, of the arts, even of the various constitutions of Plato's *Republic*, in his own Commentary. His systematic mind and great practical experience combined made him summarize and compress a lengthy, often vague statement of Alfārābī's whose terminology he uses at the same time. (I am naturally not referring to Platonic terms which, in both authors, go back to the Arabic Summary of the *Republic*.) But he differentiates more and consequently his vocabulary is not only more concise, but also more varied and richer.

In metaphysical and political questions—though not in matters logical—he has accepted much without criticism, giving it simply in his own name. Apart from a significant and unusually worded reference to Alfārābī's *K. al-siyāsāt*—' . . . and it will be transferred here from there ' (I. x, 6)—and another reference, presumably to Alfārābī's Commentary on the *Nicomachean Ethics*, Averroes never quotes his great precursor. In an earlier study I have already stressed the great dependence of Averroes on Alfārābī. The same applies to Ibn Bājja and to Avicenna in respect of Alfārābī. Needless to add that Averroes was far from being a mere copyist. In using earlier *falāsifa* he transformed his source-material, imprinting upon it the clarity of his own mind and the conciseness of his diction. Moreover, his superior knowledge and understanding of Aristotle and his Commentators served as a check and made him use his predecessor's writings critically and judiciously. All the same, the eminence of Alfārābī stands out clearly and Averroes' own exposition constitutes a skilful and impressive blend of his Platonic original with Alfārābī's digest and Aristotle's modification of it, seen against the dominating position of the *Sharī'a*. To this he added his own observations and comments based upon theoretical knowledge and practical political experience.

In two respects Averroes differs from Alfārābī and both are typical of the man and of the commentator of a work forming part of Practical Philosophy. The one feature has been fully discussed earlier on: the application of Plato's analysis to the contemporary scene which is entirely absent from Alfārābī's treatises. It is this which lends Averroes' treatise colour and distinction. The man of affairs was able to infuse a topical interest into an otherwise purely academic discourse with the result that the Commentary—though deprived of the personal element of the Platonic Dialogue—is much more realistic. The performance of his public duties enabled him—to repeat—to gain valuable insight into the workings of government, administration and, not least, into the minds of those engaged in these duties. The philosopher's world is one of speculation and of action combined: Averroes practised this pronouncement of Aristotle's all his life, except for the short spell of enforced exile.

The second element is no less interesting: it concerns Averroes' political terminology. There can be no doubt that the *falāsifa* as a group adapted Greek ideas—or what they understood to be such—to Islamic concepts and conditions. In this, Alfārābī led the way and coined the terms, except those which go back to the translators from the Greek either direct or through the medium of Syriac. If I am right in my interpretation, Alfārābī uses two sets of political terms. The one set is Platonic and presumably goes back to Ḥunain's text. The other is Islamic, in fact Quranic. (This is fully discussed in my notes to II. xvii, 6; III. iii, 1; x, 2, and particularly xviii, 8, and cannot be reproduced here.) On the whole Averroes keeps to the Platonic terms since he comments on Plato's text, except in the case of *madīna jāhilīya* and *madīna imāmīya*. The latter term is borrowed from Ibn Bājja, as I have shown elsewhere. The ' State of error ', *madīna ḍālla*, is in a category apart, since the word stands in Plato not as a technical term for a constitution, but rather as a characterization of the four other—imperfect—States. Thus it is used by Averroes. Yet, in Alfārābī it has the theological connotation it has in the Qur'ān. Another term used by Averroes in connexion with Plato's four or five imperfect States is *basīṭa*, ' simple ', which is used by Ibn Bājja from whom Averroes, no doubt, borrowed it. It is another instance of the importance of Ibn Bājja for Averroes' political thought as a link between him and Alfārābī.

In spite of his considerable literary dependence upon Alfārābī Averroes stands out clearly by contrast. For if we compare the two outstanding intellects we find that Averroes is preoccupied with the *Sharī'a* in its theoretical and practical parts ; for it teaches—as he says—abstract knowledge and moral actions alike. This—in any case in this form—is wholly absent from Alfārābī. The explanation may be found in what I called before the exclusively theoretical interest of the philosopher Alfārābī as against the eminently practical concern of the philosopher-judge-political scientist-critic Averroes.† It is, however, possible that we have to modify our view on Alfārābī once we know his Summary of the *Laws*. Nor do we know how he commented on the *Nicomachean Ethics*. The place where we would expect to find a clear reference to the *Sharī'a* is where Alfārābī contrasts the true philosopher with the masses, and where he speaks of their knowledge and education (in the *K. taḥṣīl al-sa'āda*). He does so in a way clearly foreshadowing Averroes, as I state in my notes to the text. But it is curious that he should not mention the *Sharī'a* in connexion with the Lawgiver—who is not called *wāḍi'u-l-sharā'i'* as always in Averroes' *Faṣl* and *Manāhij*, but *wāḍi'u-l-nawāmīs*, corresponding to Plato's philosopher-lawgiver, *νομοθέτης*. This is the more striking since the equation of the philosopher-lawgiver with the king (or first ruler) and *imām*, as well as that of philosopher and prophet, is Alfārābī's combination of neo-platonic and Islamic concepts. No doubt the problem of *Sharī'a* versus *falsafa* was not as acute in Alfārābī's day as in Averroes' Spain or even in Avicenna's East, which might have something to do with this strange omission.

VI. Sharī'a and *Νόμος*

This completes our survey of the various elements which together make up Averroes' political thought. His work constitutes the consummation of Muslim philosophy. It contains elements of Alfārābī, Avicenna, and Ibn Bājja, but is much more than a restatement of their ideas, with corrections as the result of a deeper understanding of Aristotle. Lucidity, penetrating analysis, concise diction characterize the Commentator with a master's grasp of the essentials of any problem in any branch of philosophy dominated by Aristotle. The analysis of his political thought has shown that Averroes was possessed of qualities which distinguish him from his predecessors in this branch of philosophy as well. He surpasses Alfārābī, to whom he owes more than to any other of the *falāsifa*. He was anticipated by Ibn Bājja in introducing references to contemporary history in his *tadbīr al-mutawaḥḥid* (40, 3 ff., 'this time', 'this land', 'in the way of life of the *mulūk al-ṭawā'if*'), but only as illustrations. His critique is to be understood as an original contribution to Political Science and foreshadows the independent attitude of an Ibn Khaldun. He goes far beyond the other *falāsifa* in his awareness of the political character of the *Sharī'a*, especially in seeing ordinances regulating religious observances as political institutions. But though he has considerably widened the realm of politics in agreement with his Greek models, it is still encompassed by the all-embracing religious law and not yet an independent realm subject to a law of its own as we find it with Ibn Khaldun. The beginnings are there, and they are important, as we have seen in the matter of the origin of the State not bound by an overriding religious law. On balance, it seems that the Law of God and not the ' Reason of State ' is the guiding principle of his political philosophy.

Since it is this which singles him out among the *falāsifa* whose work he has not only epitomized but also completed and perfected, it is necessary to state once more in what the principal contribution consists which Muslim (and Jewish) philosophy has made to medieval thought and left as its permanent legacy to the West. Islam met Christianity in the Maghreb, whence its influence spread over the Mediterranean lands and its adjacent territories. This contribution consists, according to Gauthier, of ' the agreement between philosophy and religion ', as evolved in Averroes' *Faṣl al-maqāl.* If we—in the light of my remarks earlier on—substitute for Gauthier's wording Averroes' own statement on the identity of aim and purpose between *Sharīʿa* and *falsafa,* we are in a position to understand Muslim philosophy correctly and at the same time to comprehend that it was from the beginning, and remained throughout its development from Al-Kindi to Averroes, *religious* philosophy. We can also understand why and how a philosopher who applies the canons of Aristotelian logic and adheres to Aristotle's metaphysics can at the same time be—and actually is—an ' orthodox ' Muslim.

For Muslim philosophy did not become what it is through the sudden onrush of alien ideas which were embedded in Greek and Hellenistic philosophy, once this had found a refuge in the East and was made available to Muslim theologians in Arabic translations. We usually think only of the challenge this philosophy threw out to established orthodoxy. In reality heterodox and heretical minds fastened on philosophical concepts to use them in their attack on orthodoxy (and, no doubt, discredited philosophy in that process).

This challenge could have been met by refutation and need not have led to a basically Muslim type of ' philosophy '. That *ḥikma,* in the sense of *falsafa,* could arise and fully develop, producing a succession of *falāsifa* is, to my mind, due to the ' common ground ' supplied by the central position of Law in both Islam and Plato-Aristotle. Law in Islam means divinely revealed, prophetic law. Though Law is for Plato not divine in this sense, it has also a connexion with the god from whom it ultimately originates, though not by means of a direct revelation. It aims at educating the citizens towards highest perfection—a following of the god. Since the ruler must obey and implement this law which the philosophers have established, his office is likened by Plato to a ministry of the gods. There is thus a definite religious element in Plato's concept of the Law. But the difference in religious thought between a Muslim and a Greek is the difference between Revelation and Myth. We should therefore not over-rate the influence which this religious element may have had on the *falāsifa,* for they were fully aware of the difference between *nawāmīs*—man-made laws—and *sharʿ* or *sharīʿa*—prophetic, divinely revealed law. Even if Averroes is doubtful whether the philosopher-king-lawgiver-*imām* must also be a prophet, he is emphatic that the Ideal Law of the Ideal State can be no other than the *Sharīʿa* of Allah through his prophet Muḥammad.

But where Muslim and Greek political thinkers agree is in this: there can be no State or responsible rule without Law. Law, in the view of Plato and Aristotle, is not only necessary to guarantee the necessities of life—and, indeed, life itself; its real—higher—purpose is to bind ruler and ruled alike, to enable man to reach his destiny as a rational human being.

Towards the end of his Commentary (III. xxi, 4) Averroes once more remarks adversely on Plato's tales and makes the significant comment that many men who are guided by their religious laws attain the virtues demanded of man without these tales. If we recall his discussion of the *Sharī'a* in the *Faṣl*, we are at once reminded of his statement that there are texts which must be accepted in their external meaning by all three classes of men. One of these classes is constituted by the masses (*jumhūr* or *'awāmm*), who are only capable of understanding persuasive (i.e. rhetorical and poetical) arguments. We must therefore ask what difference there is between Plato's persuasive arguments used for teaching the masses and Averroes' corresponding arguments. The answer is instructive in that it reveals the fundamental difference between *Sharī'a* and νόμος. In the first place, only the truth of revealed law is accessible to all three classes equally. Therefore these statements—about the existence of God, of the angels, about happiness in this world and the next, about reward and punishment in the next world, etc.—are not only true but also clear in themselves. In other words, they require no interpretation and they lead all believers to happiness and perfection.

The masses of Plato's Ideal State, which is guided by philosophers who obey the law which they themselves have first to lay down—even be it with the help of God—cannot see the truth with the naked eye, as the Allegory of the Cave tells us. Divine revelation is replaced by a tale or fable. Fiction approximating to truth occupies in the νόμος the place which the reality of *waḥy*, revelation in the shape of the *kitāb al-'azīz*, occupies in the *Sharī'a*.

Plato allows his rulers to use lies, ruse, and subterfuge—a fact which cannot be explained away by the expedient that it is for the good of the masses and of the State. No such provision is made in the *Sharī'a* since it would be incompatible with its ethics, quite apart from the fact that it would be unworthy and unthinkable of Allah. We have seen Averroes' aversion against miracles as proof for prophecy which, significantly, stems from his apprehension that what is unprovable may be untrue.

The analogy between the elect few and the masses in the *Sharī'a* and in Plato's *Republic* is no mere accident. In both education plays a vital part. In Islam it serves the purpose of maintaining the *Sharī'a* and guaranteeing its observance, thus leading the Muslim to Allah. In the *Republic* education is necessary to create and maintain the Ideal State in justice and to guarantee that philosophers and guardians will be born and properly brought up.

In both States a departure from the Law leads to deviation. Under the *Sharī'a* deviation leads to error, heresy, and schism. Under the νόμος deviation leads to a transformation of the Ideal Republic of philosopher-kings, through a process of progressive deterioration, until right beliefs and convictions have been perverted into their direct opposite.

Both agree that right beliefs and convictions alone promote justice and happiness, for the sake of which the State exists. If we allow for different, even opposite, views about what constitutes right beliefs and convictions—as different as prophetic revelation is from myth on the one hand and from sovereign human reason on the other—there still remains an essential similarity in conception and aim between the two. This, I submit, is the reason why the *falāsifa*, chief among them Averroes—exactly like Maimonides among the Jews—were attracted to Plato's (and Aristotle's) ideas about law and justice. Yet they were fully conscious of the fact which only Averroes has so clearly formulated—that the *Sharī'a* alone guarantees the whole of mankind happiness—provided they are all Muslims—whereas the νόμος of the philosopher makes provision for happiness based upon theoretical knowledge for the elect few only. The *Sharī'a* is all-comprehensive in another way as well. It draws what we call 'Politics' into its orbit and treats political rights and duties, especially the latter, as religious duties, like prayer, fasting, and charity. For it does not recognize that there is a sphere divorced from religion, a secular realm from which God and His perfect Law are excluded. This political nature of Islam facilitated the reception of Platonic notions. In principle, Plato makes the same comprehensive claim for his law devised by philosophers. Yet striking as the similarities are, they must not blind us to the contrast between *Sharī'a* and νόμος.

For the *Sharī'a* as the declared will of God is not only starting point and centre for the *falāsifa*; it postulates certain beliefs and convictions which determine their speculation, circumscribe it, and exclude from rational interpretation some of its fundamental pronouncements. It provides—and this is important—in these doctrines a bond that unites the elect few and the masses as *muslimūn*, as believers in Allah, to Whose Will—announced through Muḥammad—they willingly submit.

On the other hand, we have the νόμος, the imposing creation of the sovereign reason of free but fallible men, whose errors are excused by Averroes because they are striving to know the truth. The νόμος recognizes the gulf that separates the elect from the masses as final: it can offer neither Faith nor Hope nor Charity to bridge it.

SELECT BIBLIOGRAPHY

A. Sources

Ḥunain b. Isḥāq: *Ueber die syrischen u. arabischen Galen-Uebersetzungen*, by G. Bergstraesser, Leipzig, 1925.

Alfārābī, Abū Naṣr: *Risāla fī arā'i ahl al-madīna al-fāḍila*, ed. Dieterici (Alfarabi's Abhandlung Der Musterstaat), Leyden, 1895.

K. taḥṣīl al-sa'āda, Hyderabad, 1345.

K. al-siyāsāt al-madanīya, Hyderabad, 1346.

De Platonis Philosophia, ed. Fr. Rosenthal and R. Walzer, as *Plato Arabus II*, London, 1943.

Ibn Al-Athīr : *Kāmil*, x–xii, ed. Tornberg, Leyden, 1864, 1851, 1853.

Ibn Abī 'Uṣaibi'a : *'Uyūn al-anbā'*.

Ibn Bājja, Abū Bakr b. al-Ṣā'igh : *K. tadbīr al-mutawaḥḥid*, ed. Asín Palacios, Madrid-Granada (*El Régimen del Solitario*), 1946.

Ibn Ḥazm, Abū Muḥammad 'Alī *K. al-fiṣal wa-l-nihal*, see also M. Asin Palacios, *Abenházam de Cordova*, Madrid, 1927–1931.

Ibn Khaldun : *K. al-'ibar*, ed. De Slane (part dealing with the Berbers, translated as *Histoire des Berbères*).

Ibn Rushd (Averroes) : *Faṣl al-maqāl*, ed. L. Gauthier, Alger, 1948.

Manāhij, ed. Mueller.

In : *Aristotelis Opera Omnia*, Venice, 1550.

Commentary on Plato's 'Republic', ed. Erwin I. J. Rosenthal, Cambridge, 1956, 1966, 1969.

Commentary on Aristotle's Nicomachean Ethics, MS. Heb. Add. 496 of Cambridge University Library (in Hebrew).

Tahāfut al-tahāfut, ed. Bouyges, Beyrouth.

Ibn Tūmart : *K. muḥammad b. tūmart mahdī al-muwaḥḥidīn* (*Le livre de Mohammed Ibn Toumert*, Alger, 1903), ed. Luciani.

Al-Marrākushī, 'Abd al-Wāḥid : *History of the Almohads*, ed. R. Dozy, Leyden, 1847, and the French translation : *Histoire des Almohades*, par E. Fagnan, Alger, 1893.

Al-Maqqarī : *The History of the Mohammedan Dynasties in Spain*, ed. and trsl. Gayangos, London, 1843.

Renan, E. : Appendices III, IV, and V in his *Averroès et l'Averroïsme*[2].

B. Descriptive Literature

Bel, A. : *Les Benou Ghânya*, Paris, 1903.

Dozy, R. : *Recherches sur l'histoire et littérature de l'Espagne pendant le Moyen Age*[2], Leyden, 1860.

Dozy, R., and E. Lévi-Provençal : *Histoire des Mussulmans d'Espagne*, III, iv, Leyden, 1932.

Gauthier, L. : *Ibn Thofail : sa vie, ses œuvres*, Paris, 1909.

La théorie d-Ibn Rochd sur les rapports de la religion et de la philosophie, Paris, 1909.

Ibn Rochd (Averroès), Paris, 1948.

Goldziher, I. : 'Materialien zur Kenntnis der Almohadenbewegung,' in *Z.D.M.G.*, xli, 1887.

Die Zahiriten, Leipzig, 1884.

'Mohammed Ibn Toumert et la Théologie de l'Islam dans le Nord de l'Afrique au xie. Siècle,' Alger, 1903 (introduction to *Le livre de Mohammed Ibn Toumert*).

Munk, S. : *Mélanges de philosophie juive et arabe*, Paris, 1859.

Renan, E. : *Averroès et l'Averroïsme*[2], Paris, 1861.

Rosenthal, Erwin I. J. : 'Averroes' Paraphrase on Plato's "Politeia"', in *Journal of the Royal Asiatic Society*, October, 1934.

'Maimonides' Conception of State and Society', in *Moses Maimonides*, ed. I. Epstein, London, 1935.

'Politische Gedanken bei Ibn Bāǧǧa', in *M.G.W.J.*, 1937, 3. Heft.

'Some Aspects of Islamic Political Thought', in *Islamic Culture*, xxii, January, 1948.

'The Place of Politics in the Philosophy of Ibn Bājja', ibid., xxv, part 1, 1952.

'Avicenna's Influence on Jewish Thought', in *Avicenna : Philosopher and Scientist*, ed. G. M. Wickens, London, 1952.

'Mediaeval Judaism and the Law', in *Law and Religion* (vol. 3 of *Judaism and Christianity*), ed. E. I. J. R., London, 1938 ; sections on 'The Philosophers and Divine Revelation' and 'Divine and Human "Law"'.

Rosenthal, Erwin I. J. *Ibn Khalduns Gedanken über den Staat* (Beiheft 25, *Historische Zeitschrift*, München und Berlin, 1932).

Ibn Khaldun, 'A North African Muslim Thinker of the Fourteenth Century', in *Bulletin of the John Rylands Library*, xxiv, 2, 1940.

Steinschneider, M.: *Alfarabi*, St. Petersburg, 1869.

Strauss, L.: *Philosophie und Gesetz* Berlin, 1935.

Postscript

After the MS. had been accepted for publication in this *Bulletin*, Gabrieli's edition of Alfārābī's *Compendium Legum Platonis*, referred to above, p. 270, was published. I have since compared this text with the passages in Averroes' Commentary which, to my mind, betray an acquaintance with Plato's *Laws*. Although Averroes may have known Alfārābī's Paraphrase the absence from it of 697, on which I assume Averroes' threefold division of the laws in III. iv, 4 is based, and of 903*c* and, in particular of 961*e*, 962*a*, makes it practically a certainty that he knew the *Laws* in a much fuller version. Moreover, Alfārābī stops in Book IX. As I have shown in an Addendum to the introduction to my edition of Averroes' Commentary on Plato's *Republic*, there are other passages—apart from those just mentioned—which may have served as background to Averroes' comment, but are not contained in Alfārābī's Summary. On the other hand, passages which are found in Alfārābī as well—though only in part—may suggest a link with Plato. Yet, it is much more likely that both authors knew and used Galen's Summary of the *Laws*, each for his particular purpose. For Alfārābī see Gabrieli's *Praefatio*, Xf. and especially XIV with n. 19. Averroes' purpose has been stated in this article, and may be summed up as a critical interpretation of Plato whose views he applied to his own times and circumstances as a representative of practical philosophy. How much of this different attitude, approach, and purpose is due to Averroes' fuller understanding of Aristotle and his commentators can as yet not be determined. A first examination of Alfārābī's Summary has so far not led to any modification of my views such as I envisaged on p. 273 above.

5

THE PLACE OF POLITICS IN THE PHILOSOPHY OF AL-FARABI

IN recent years students of Islamic philosophy have paid more and more attention to Al-Farabi, 'the Second Teacher,' and his dominating position has been generally recognized.[1] But a critical appraisal of his philosophy as such and in relation to his sources as well as to his successors among the *Falasifa* has barely been attempted. The reasons are not far to seek. Although hitherto unknown or unpublished texts, like *On Plato's Philosophy*[2] and Tal*kh*is *nawamis Aflatun*,[3] have added to our knowledge of his literary output,

1. See, e.g., Ibrahim Madkour: *La Place d'al-Farabi dans l'école philosophique musulmane*, Paris 1935 ; L. Strauss: *Philosophie und Gesetz*, Berlin 1935 ; Erwin I. J. Rosenthal: *Maimonides' Conception of State and Society* -(*M*) in *Moses Maimonides*, ed. I. Epstein, London 1935 ; H. K. Sherwani: *al-Farabi's Political Theories* in *Islamic Culture*, July 1938, pp. 288-305. In view of the similar title of this interesting estimate of Al-Farabi's originality as a political thinker, it may be said that my present study treats the problem from a different angle altogether. So, to avoid repetition, the reader is referred to my earlier articles published in *Islamic Culture* : *Some aspects of Islamic Political Thought (SAIPT)* (XXII, i, 1940) and *The Place of Politics in the Philosophy of Ibn Bajja* (XXV, Part I, 1951 *(PIB)*; *The Place of Politics in the Philosophy of Ibn Rushd* (*PIR)* in *BSOAS* XV, 2, 1953. *Cp.* also R. Walzer : *Islamic Philosophy* in : *The History of Philosophy Eastern and Western*, London 1953. Further literature is quoted in my articles just mentioned. M. Steinschneider, *al-Farabi*, St. Petersburg 1869, a pioneer work of great learning, is still invaluable.
2. *De Platonis Philosophia* ed. Fr. Rosenthal and R. Walzer, vol. II of *Plato Arabus*, London, 1943.
3. *Alfarabius Compendium Legum Platonis* ed. F. Gabrieli, vol. III of *Plato Arabus*, London, 1952.

   Until D. M. Dunlop's edition of the hitherto unpublished text of the *Fusul al-madani* from a complete MS. is available, the reader is referred to the same author's English translation of the Bodleian Fragment under the title: *Al-Farabi's Aphorisms of the Statesman* in: *IRAQ*, XIV, 2, 1952 pp. 93-117. This translation is quoted in the last section of this article. It is difficult to judge the work by the English translation of a fragment ; but it is apparent that it adds to our knowledge of Al-Farabi's treatment of Political Philosophy in some important details. A proper evaluation must, however, wait for the publication of the complete text.†

no adequate critical editions of his major works extant are available, so that the textual basis for such a critical assessment of his contribution is still lacking. A far more serious handicap is the nature of his work, since much of his writing is diffuse, repetitive and lacking in clarity and precision. Besides, the absence of important texts which would provide the missing link between the last representatives of Hellenism and the first Arab philosopher, al-Kindi, greatly impedes the task of establishing the origin and development of ideas embodied in the writings of Al-Farabi. His theory of prophecy is a case in point. To point to Plotinus, Proclus and Porphyry helps us only a little more than thinking of Hermetic and Iranian influences. Yet, this theory is of great importance for the subject-matter of the present study which would have been written earlier if my search for Al-Farabi's possible sources had been successful. For the time being I must abandon hope of tracing the theory. Until experts in Greek and Hellenistic philosophy and its Oriental Gnostic and Hermetic offshoots will provide a solution we must, I think, assume that, apart from the so-called Theology of Aristotle which has provided him with the concept of emanation, Al-Farabi himself has originated the psychological explanation of prophecy.† I shall deal with it in its proper place later.

It is clear from the foregoing remarks that the following treatment of Al-Farabi's political thought can only be tentative. A further reservation is necessary: in isolating Al-Farabi's political thought we must bear in mind that it is only a part of a whole philosophy derived from Plato and Aristotle and evolved by a Muslim. The result is a blend of Greek-Hellenistic thought with Islamic tenets in an attempt to accommodate one with the other. How closely politics is linked with philosophy as a whole, in particular with metaphysics, ethics and psychology, is clear from the structure of the three more important of Al-Farabi's political treatises upon which this study is based: *al-Madina al-Fadila, al-Siyasa al-Madaniya* and *Tahsilul-Sa'ada.*[1] The title of the first of these treatises is indicative of this dependence of politics on philosophy as a whole; it is in full: *risala fi Ara'i ahli-l-Madinati-l-Fadilati,* and it begins with a lengthy disquisition on the One, God, includes a cosmology and covers the whole range of the theoretical, philosophical disciplines. Of its 34 chapters only the last 9 are political in subject-matter. The first half of the *siyasa* contains Al-Farabi's theory of the soul and the intellect, and of the heavenly substances, while the second half deals with man and his perfection in the State. Both treatises are based on Plato's *Republic* and

1. The following editions were used: *Madina Fadila* ed. F. Dieterici, Leiden 1895; *Philosophische Abhandlungen* ed. F. Dieterici, Leiden 1890; *K. al-Siyasa, al-Madaniya*, ed. Hyderabad, 1346 *H.*; *K. Tahsil al-Sa'ada*, Hyderabad, 1345 H. The *K. al-Tanbih 'ala sabili l-sa'ada* is of no importance for our problem; I am, moreover, doubtful whether it is rightly attributed to Al-Farabi. Neither its rather elementary nature nor its style and diction can approach his other works. But this is a matter for detailed investigation.†

Timaios and on Aristotle's *Nicomachean Ethics* ; the structure and sequence of their political parts take Plato's discussion of the ideal and of the imperfect States as a pattern. The *Tahsil* is the most important, independent and mature of the three, and deserves the designation 'political' in the theoretical sense more so than the other two. It begins with a statement on the twofold happiness of man in this and in the other world, which can only be attained if man lives in political organisation in a nation or city-state. It describes the way of life of man seeking perfection, and defines happiness as the highest good sought after for its own sake,[1] and Political Science as concerned with the means by which men, living in political association in States, attain their happiness according to their natural disposition.[2] Both definitions and their underlying philosophy are taken over from Aristotle.[3] This is why Al-Farabi is so much concerned with the nature and destiny of man in relation to God and the universe, and the large space he assigns to psychology and epistemology in his political treatises. So we understand why he examines in the *Tahsil* certain knowledge (*haqq yaqini*) as opposed to opinion (*zann*) and persuasion (*iqna'*), emphasizes instruction (*ta'lim*) and education (*ta'dib*), and concentrates rather on epistemology than on psychology in describing human existence and the end of man. This end is happiness. Happiness is highest perfection, that is, intellectual perfection on the foundation of moral perfection. His dependence on Plato[4] and Aristotle[5] in the realm of political philosophy is, indeed, very strong, but it is by no means confined to it, as his treatise *The Book of Agreement between the ideas of the two philosophers, the divine Plato and Aristotle* clearly shows. For it is not only an attempt to establish harmony between their views but also between philosophy and revelation. The aim of the study of philosophy is the perception of the Creator, and the philosopher must strive to imitate (or, to resemble) God.[6] This is ultimate happiness, and Al-Farabi's principal concern in his political philosophy is based upon Plato in the first place.

We must, therefore, not expect to find a theory of government as such, a concern with power and its end. If Al-Farabi describes the various constitutions of the perfect and imperfect States he does so in relation to man's ultimate perfection and happiness, and because he

---

1. *Mad. Fad.* 46.14. Happiness is defined *ibid.* 46.7 ff.
2. *Tahsil* 16.4 ff. See also *PIB* 197 with n. 35.†
3. *N (icomachean) E (thics)* I. ii, 1094 ab.
4. See *PIB* 189 with n. 10.
5. Plato and Aristotle have shown Muslims "a way by which the matter of these statements of the *Shari'a* (that is, of the Creation out of nothing, the dominion of God (*rububiya*), etc. becomes clear and it (the *Shari'a*) is utterly correct and true." See *Abhandlungen*, 25.
6. *Ibid.* 53 and *PIB* 197 with n. 37, where the source for Al-Farabi's *al-tashabbuhu bi-l-khaliq* was traced to Plato's *Theaetetus*, but it may equally or even more likely be Plotinus (*Enneads* I, 2).

found them discussed in Plato's *Republic* and Aristotle's *Nicomachean Ethics*. But as a Muslim he believes in Reward and Punishment and in a Hereafter, and knows that Happiness is twofold, in this and in the next life. *This* happiness is guaranteed by the *shari'a* alone. Some of its assertions, like the Creation out of nothing, Divine Providence extending to the particulars, the Creator's dominion over the whole world, would have caused confusion among men but for the philosophy of Plato and Aristotle which brought certain proofs for the truth and correctness of the divine laws. These two philosophers have shown the way to faith. Starting from physics we proceed to demonstrative, political and religio-legal questions. Men of insight and intelligence deal with demonstrative questions, men of judgment with political, and men of spiritual inspirations (*ilhamat ruhaniya*) with the religious.[1] Al-Farabi states clearly the difference in method between the philosopher who uses demonstrative arguments and the religious teacher who relies on revelation and inspiration. This distinction has been employed by all subsequent *Falasifa*.

This brief account of Al-Farabi's general attitude as a Muslim disciple of Plato and Aristotle may serve as background for a more detailed description of his political thought, in so far as it can be extracted from the three treatises in question.

Al-Farabi starts from the necessity of political association. Man cannot provide himself with the necessities of life or with everything needed for the attainment of his perfection, without the help of many others of his kind who singly supply every one of his many needs. Therefore man's perfection can only be realized in association with others in communities, which are either perfect or imperfect. The former are three, of large, medium and small size. The large association comprises *ma'mura*, the whole inhabited earth; the middle-sized one nation in a part of the civilized world, and the small the people of a city in a part of the territory of a nation. Any community smaller than a city is not a perfect State. It is to be noted that the need for political association—described in similar terms in both the *Madina Fadila* and the *siyasa*[2] —is stated more concisely in the *Tahsil*. Here Al-Farabi simply states that it is man's natural disposition to be in need of others, and that he must join with others in political association because in isolation he cannot reach his share of perfection. Therefore he is called *hayawan insi* or *hayawan madani*, Aristotle's *zoon politikon*,—and the science by which man inquires into the actions and habits necessary to attain perfection is, thus, *the human or political science*.[3]

This is derived from Plato and Aristotle, of course. Plato's view that

1. *Abhdlg*. 25 ff.
2. *Mad. Fad.* 53.7 ff.: *siyasa* 39.10 ff.
3. *Tahsil* 14.9 ff.

one person should have no more than one occupation is echoed in Al-Farabi's emphasis on the need of many persons who must co-operate mutually to satisfy their many requirements. Further, Al-Farabi's division of perfect States according to size is also influenced by Greek political thought. *Madina* (city) as the smallest political unit in which man can reach perfection is Plato's *polis*. The large association comprising the whole civilized world may well be due to Al-Farabi's Islamic background[1] and is undoubtedly in agreement with the universalism of Islam as a way of life and with the claim of the Islamic empire. But I am inclined to attribute it rather to a blend of this Islamic concept with that of the *Oikoumene* of Hellenism. 'Perfect' on account of size must not be confused with 'perfect' on account of quality. This is clear from Al-Farabi's definition of the Ideal State as one whose citizens help each other to obtain those things by which true happiness is reached.[2] Al-Farabi conceives of true happiness as a state of the soul in which it exists free from matter and tends towards pure substances free from corporeality.[3] Political Science shows man the way in a gradual ascent from a perception of the physical world and its Intelligibles to that of the spiritual world with the help of metaphysics in search of the principles of Existing Things, that is of Reality. It teaches man to distinguish what is good for the purpose of his end, from what is evil, to seek Good and to shun Evil. Ethical virtues must be joined by intellectual virtues and practical arts in order to prepare man for the acquisition of speculative virtues through the speculative sciences, which alone enable him to perceive Reality, and thus to reach highest perfection and ultimate happiness.[4] Man lives in the State in which alone he can reach happiness; therefore these virtues and arts are political or civic. What applies to man also applies to 'cities' and nations. Virtues and arts can be acquired in two ways: by teaching and education. The former is carried out by words alone and leads to speculative virtues, while in the latter are used words and deeds and ethical virtues and practical arts are produced.[5] Aristotle distinguishes between rulers and ruled, or masters and servants, and between master arts (like Political Science which had already been termed a "royal art" by Plato[6]) and subordinate arts. Al-Farabi adopts this same distinction and illustrates it by an analogy between the State and the human body. There is a hierarchy in the body from the head,

1. So Madkour, *op. cit.*, 183, quoted from Carra de Vaux's *Avicenne*, 104. See also *PIR*, 265, where I discuss this question of *oikoumene* in connection with Averroes and Galen.
2. *Mad. Fad.* 54.5 ff.
3. *Mad. Fad.* 46.7 ff.
4. *Tahsil* 2.
5. *Tahsil* 29. The whole section, from p. 22 on, contains a detailed description of the virtues and arts, and has served as a basis for Ibn Bajja and Averroes in relation to Politics.
6. *NE* I. ii, 1094 b; *Politikos* 304.

that is, the heart, down to the lowest and smallest of the members whose degree is determined by their nearness or remoteness from the heart. Those members nearest to the heart rule and are ruled, those furthest removed from the head only serve, but all alike are united in serving the purpose of the heart. It is the same with the State, and when all parts of the State serve the purpose and end of the 'head' or ruler we have the *Madina Fadila*, the Ideal State. But while the members of the body are naturally disposed to their functions, men in the State are guided by will and choice. Leadership or rule is possible on two conditions only: fitness by natural disposition, and volitional quality and habit. As for the arts, some are both ruling and serving, others only subordinate, but the highest art is solely ruling. It is the art of government, exercised by the ruler exclusively, whom nobody must dominate.[1]

This ruler is called by Al-Farabi in the *Madina Fadila* and in the *Siyasa al-ra'is al-awwal*, the first ruler, who is, in the *Tahsil*, identified with philosopher, king, lawgiver and *Imam*. In the two first-named treatises the first ruler is by nature disposed to receive a revelation. This is described more briefly in the *Siyasa* as contact of the soul with the Active Intellect by mediation of two intermediaries, the passive and the acquired intellects, Al-Farabi explicitly refers to the *Kitab al-nafs*, presumably in the form Alexander of Aphrodisias commented on and transformed Aristotle's *De Anima*. He says that this man is understood as 'an angel (*malak*) in reality' by the ancient philosophers.[2] The emanation is in form of a revelation enabling its recipient to define things and direct actions towards happiness.[3] The political significance is more evident still in the *Madina Fadila* where Al-Farabi differentiates between the first ruler's imagination and intellect. God mediates to his theoretical and practical reason a revelation which makes him a philosopher, and then to his imaginative faculty, making him a prophet, a warner, capable of directing men to their happiness. This man has reached the most perfect stage of humanity and the highest degree of happiness: 'He is the *Imam*, the first ruler over the Ideal City-State, the ruler over the Ideal Nation and over the whole inhabited earth.'[4] Those ruled by him are "the excellent, best and happy citizens."[5]

Before we discuss the qualifications required of the first ruler as set out in the *Madina Fadila* immediately after the above passage,

1. This passage briefly sums up the relevant matter in *Mad. Fad.* 54-57.
2. *Siyasa* 49. 14f. This is rather surprising in view of Al-Farabi's statement (*ibid.* 3.19) that the Active Intellect is called *al-ruh al-amin waruh al-quds*, usually identified with the angel Gabriel who mediated God's revelation to Muhammad, as we know, *e. g.* from Averroes's *Tahafut al-Tahafut*, ed. Bouyges, 516.10. However Al-Farabi goes on to say that this is only the case if there is no intermediary between such an (angel) man and the Active Intellect.
3. *Siyasa* 49.4-50.2.
4. This is a summary of *Mad. Fad.* 57.17-59.13.
5. *Siyasa* 50.7 f. *al-nasu-l-fadilun wa-l-akhyar wa-l-su'ada.*

we must turn to the *Tahsil* for a fuller definition of the ruler and his functions in connection with the fourfold perfection necessary for the attainment of happiness.

Imam and king must study the speculative sciences.[1] The king is compared to the master of a household and to a leader of young people who are taught and educated either willingly or unwillingly. Education is indispensible, without it nobody in cities or nations can reach perfection and happiness. Education in speculative virtues is by means of certain proofs, in the other virtues and arts by means of a persusion. Persuasion and imagination, both of which the king must possess in perfection, are appropriate means of teaching the masses who serve the State only by their arts and crafts. Political leadership belongs to the elect alone. This is quite in keeping with Plato's views on education and on the three classes in the *Republic*. In fact, Al-Farabi refers in his *Tahsil* to Plato in developing his own ideas on education for citizenship and thereby to happiness. In his introduction to his *Talkhis* on Plato's *Laws*[2] he states approvingly that Plato had refrained from disclosing and explaining the sciences to the people in general, but had followed the path of allegory and enigma so that knowledge might be withheld from the uninitiated. 'The first ruler is the most elect of the elect......who aims at the complete fulfilment of his aim and purpose. He possesses knowledge of the Intelligibles by means of certain proofs and perceives Reality thereby. This is the foremost and most perfect science with regard to rule, and the other master-sciences are under the rule of this science.... the aim of it is the utmost happiness and ultimate perfection which man can reach.'

This science is called Wisdom or Philosophy; it originated with the Chaldaeans, that is Iraq, migrated from there to Egypt, then to the

1. What follows is based upon *Tahsil* 29-38; in particular 29.18 ff., 31.8 ff. and 36.8-38.9.
2. *Op. cit.*, 4. *Cp.* for the discussion of the distinction between the few elect intellects and the masses also M. Asin Palacios: *La Tesis de la Necessidad de la Revelacion, en Islam y en la Escolastica* (*Al-Andalus* III, 1935, pp. 345-389). He discusses the problem of revelation and reason in Jahiz, al-Ghazali and the *Falasifa* from Al-Farabi to Ibn Rushd, and in Ibn Hazm. He quotes *Tahsil* 41.12 to the effect that "Philosophy precedes religion in time." Before knowing this study I had been puzzled by this passage for a long time until I discussed quite recently this whole argument of Al-Farabi's about demonstrative proofs versus persuasion and imagination with Prof. D.H. Baneth of the Hebrew University in Jerusalem. As a result I am inclined to think that in the phrase *al-falsafa tataqaddamu biz-zamani-l-millata* the last word, *religion*, is a misprint of *al-malaka, hexis*. So it is 41.1 as is clear from the context, from 40.11 ff. where *malaka* is used and meant, and from 44.7. If this correction is sound, the above quoted passage 41.12 cannot be used as an argument in the prolonged discussion on the question of revelation and reason. Here is one of many examples which shows how necessary critical editions of Al-Farabi's writings are. See also *PIR* 273.†

Greeks and Syrians until it came to the Arabs. After singing the praises of philosophy, Al-Farabi remarks that 'there is no difference between the philosopher and the first ruler.'[1] He possesses first all the theoretical and then all the practical virtues with certain insight, and has afterwards the power to bring them all into being in nations and City-States, in proportion to the possibilities of every one of their citizens. The political significance of philosophy could not be emphasized more clearly.

Whether the fact that Al-Farabi makes no mention of revelation and prophecy in the *Tahsil* has a special meaning or not can perhaps best be answered in the negative by the following consideration: it may be conjectured that the *Madina Fadila* was written first, since it contains the most elaborate superstructure to politics proper, as stated in the beginning of this article. The *Siyasa* has a much shorter account of revelation in which the term 'prophet' does not occur, since the imaginative faculty is not acted upon in the process of emanation. But imagination is essential and indispensible for prophecy, as is clear from the *Madina Fadila*. The only conclusion to be drawn from the treatment of *wahy* in the *Siyasa* is therefore, that Al-Farabi considered a full exposition unnecessary, unless we assume a gap in the text of the *Siyasa*. On the other hand, one might take the opposite view and assume that the shorter version is the first attempt and the fuller the more mature, later development. But against this view, I would point to the greater precision, concentration and more concisely argued presentation of the problem of happiness in the *Tahsil*. Unlike the two other treatises it does not follow so closely the pattern of Plato's *Republic*, but has a plan and arrangement of its own. The problem of happiness attainable in the State has occupied Al-Farabi throughout his literary work. Without referring to other of his writings, he may well have allowed himself more brevity in the *Tahsil* in the conviction of having dealt with certain topics fully in his earlier works, if we are justified in assuming that the *Tahsil* is in fact the latest of the three, for the reasons I have advanced. The way in which the term 'first ruler' is mentioned without introduction and definition, unlike *imam*, king and lawgiver, points, I believe, to my assumption. In the *Siyasa* the term 'first ruler' is still defined when introduced.

Conversely, Al-Farabi speaks in the *Tahsil* of the lawgiver (*wadi'u-l-nawamis*) whom he identifies with the *imam* and the philosopher, previously equated with the first ruler. A lawgiver in this sense is not mentioned in the two other treatises. That a revealed law, brought by a prophetic messenger to mankind, is meant can only be inferred by implication, that is, if the Al-Farabi of the *Tahsil* understands by 'first ruler'

1. *Tahsil* 39.13. Averroes expresses himself in similar words about philosophy as a natural gift to be met with among the peoples of Spain, Syria, Iraq and Egypt, all countries near to Greece, on the basis of *Republic* 435e 436a. His claim thus opposes Plato's view of the Greeks as the people most gifted for speculation.

what the Al-Farabi of the *Madina Fadila* has explicitly stipulated, namely, the philosopher-prophet. In the *Tahsil* the lawgiver is described as a philosopher first and foremost. He 'has the power, by the excellence of his reflection, to bring about the conditions by which the laws actually exist (effectively), and thus utmost happiness is attained.' Before he can lay down laws he must be skilled 'in philosophy and possess a nature of mastery, not of service. He must possess the speculative virtues and be capable of producing the states and conditions for the volitional intelligibles by which actual existence comes about. He must also possess the intellectual and practical virtues and the capacity for excellent persuasion and imagination.'[1] 'Philosophy is with the lawgiver what habit (*hexis*) is with the masses; what in his knowledge is certain insight, is with them persuasion and imagination.'[2]

That 'the meaning of *imam*, philosopher and lawgiver is one and the same'[3] is, thus, obvious.

'King' indicates dominion and power with utmost knowledge, reflection....'! 'He is in his essence a philosopher and lawgiver.'[4] With the statement that 'the meaning of philosopher, first ruler, king, lawgiver and *imam* is the same'[5] the adaptation of the philosopher-king of Plato to Islam is complete. This blending of Platonic and Islamic qualifications required of the ruler of the Ideal State is Al-Farabi's outstanding contribution to political philosophy in Islam and, as far as Maimonides is concerned, also in medieval Judaism. As I have stated elsewhere, the concept of Law provided the common ground necessary for the fusion of formative ideas between the two civilizations. But it has to be borne in mind that the *Shari'a* as prophetically revealed law is superior to the *Nomos* of Hellas, because only its fulfilment guarantees man the twofold perfection: happiness in this and in the next life. Philosophy is the best guide to the understanding of the deeper meaning of the *Shari'a* for the faithful.[6]

Al-Farabi devotes the last pages of the *Tahsil,* as we have it, to a discussion of the nature of true and false philosophers in connection with the philosopher-lawgiver-*imam*-king. He says: 'one whose way it is to delve into speculation must be prepared by (natural) disposition for the speculative sciences; the following are the conditions which Plato mentions in his book on *Politics* .....'[7]

He proceeds to summarize *Republic* VI, 484a-487a. This summary agrees in every essential point with the twelve conditions stipulated for

1. *Tahsil* 41.17-42.11
2. *Ibid.* 44.7 ff.
3. *Ibid.* 42.11
4. *Ibid.* 42.19-43.8
5. *Ibid.* 43.18
6. See my *M* 197 ff; *SAIPT* 6 ff.; *PIB* 193 f. and especially *PIR* 261 f.; 273 ff.
7. *Tahsil* 44.16 f. *Siyasa* is the term used for the *Republic*. Similarly *Republic* 487b–497b serves Al-Farabi as model for his description of the false philosophers.

the first ruler of the Ideal State in the *Madina Fadila*. This is not surprising since both descriptions are based upon the just-quoted passage in the *Republic*. Such superficial adaptations as 'love of *dirhams* and *dinars*' for Plato's 'love of money', or the naming of the pleasures of the body and the inclusion of 'gambling' for clarification, no doubt go back to the Arabic translation of the *Republic* (or of its Alexandrian Summary) and to Al-Farabi; they do not constitute any real adaptation to Islamic conditions, such as the seven qualifications demanded of the *imam* according to Al-Mawardi. That some of them are identical or similar, like *'adala*, *'ilm* and *salama*, is accidental and simply the result of the same political realism in both cases in the interests of good government. There is no blending of Platonic with Islamic conditions, much less a replacement of the *Republic* by *Fiqh* or by Al-Farabi's own ideas, as far as the twelve conditions are concerned.[1]

We find in the *Tahsil*, however, an important and significant addition. The true philosopher must have sound religious convictions: 'he shall have perfect faith in the opinions of the religion in which he was reared, seizing the virtuous actions which (are enjoined) in his religion.[2] Al-Qifti mentions of Al-Farabi's books on Political Science only the *Siyasa* and the *Madina Fadila* (as *al-sira al-Fadila*) and states in the course of a brief characterisation that Al-Farabi "described the various kinds of perfect and imperfect States and the need of the (Ideal?) State for royal ways of life and prophetic laws."[3]

The *Tahsil* concentrates on the nature and meaning of happiness of the citizens living in the State, and stresses the part the ruler has to play as the highest authority in the education and guidance of the citizens towards their attainment of the goal: happiness as the Highest Good, the aim and purpose of Political Science. The theoretical and practical virtues and arts which the Head of State must possess in order to rule the ideal political association for the attainment of the happiness and perfection of all its members, in accordance with their natural disposition, can only be acquired by the study of philosophy. For Al-Farabi philosophy means the philosophy of Plato and Aristotle which, he avers, is in essence one philosophy with one aim. Therefore he announces at the end of the *Tahsil* his intention to describe first the philosophy of Plato and then the philosophy of Aristotle from beginning to end. Hence his stress on the political nature of Plato's *Dialogues* in his treatise *De Platonis Philosophia*. (The companion treatise *De Aristotelis*

1. See *Mad. Fad.* 59.14-60.11. In other words, he describes Plato's philosopher-king as such, following the *Republic*, having previously established the identity between first ruler, *imam*, philosopher and *prophet* (*ibid.* 57.17-59.13). This ideal ruler is *'aql bi-l-fi'l wama'qul bi-l-fi'l* (58.1)
2. *Tahsil* 45.6 f. Plato also demands right beliefs and convictions, but especially Knowledge of Reality which is superior to Belief (*Republic* 474a-480.)
3. Ta'rikh al-hukama, ed. Lippert, 116.

Philosophia has not yet been made available).†

We must therefore look in the two other treatises, the *Madina Fadila* and the *Siyasa*, for a discussion of the perfect and imperfect rulers and their States. We now turn to a summary treatment of the relevant parts in both.

As stated before, Al-Farabi enumerates twelve requirements in the 'first ruler' of the Ideal State. He was aware that it would be difficult to find such an ideal man and is, therefore, content to admit as ruler the man who combines five or six of the twelve qualities in his person.[1] The second ruler must also fulfil six conditions; in the first place, he must be wise, that is a philosopher; next he must know and keep the laws and rules of conduct of the first rulers and observe them all in his own actions as an example and an obligation; then he must be able to decide points of law which have not arisen before by following the example set by the first *imams*. He must further possess insight and knowledge to cope with entirely new problems unforeseen by the first rulers, guided by the best interests of the State, and give guidance and direction to the laws of the first *imams* and to his deductions from these laws. Finally he must master the subordinate and leading art of war. There is here much more affinity with the conditions which the *Khalifa* has to fulfil, in content and in terminology. But it should be noted that, in stipulating skill in the art of war, Al-Farabi does not speak of *jihad*.[2] He speaks of the ruler in general, including that of the Muslim State.

Besides, he leads back to Plato's pattern by his statement that if the necessary conditions are not found in one man but in two of whom one is *hakim*, a philosopher, while the other is endowed with the remaining qualities, both together shall be the rulers. If the qualities are dispersed among six different men, all six together rule as "the most excellent rulers," that is, Plato's *aristoi*.

But if wisdom (or, philosophy— *hikma*—) is absent from the government, the State is without a king, even if the other conditions are fulfilled. It will gradually perish, if no philosopher is attached to the ruler in charge of the State.[3]

This means that the philosopher alone guarantees the survival of the Ideal State which was founded by the first ruler who, to repeat, was philosopher, prophet, king, lawgiver and *imam* in one.

---

1. The following summary is based upon *Mad. Fad.* 60.11—61.15. There is nothing corresponding in the *Siyasa*.
2. But see Dunlop, *op. cit.* § 53 C "that he should be able to go on the holy war". The *Fusul* say nothing about the combined rule of two men, but deal in A with the first ruler, in B with a group of *aristoi* and in C with our 'second ruler', but stripped of his first qualification, that of philosopher. It appears that the ruler in the *Fusul* is modelled less on the Platonic than on the Muslim pattern. These passages in the *Fusul* will be commented on in connection with Averroes in the final section.
3. *Mad. Fad.* 61.11-15.

The States in opposition to the ideal State are discussed in the *Madina Fadila* and more fully in the *Siyasa*. Since I have dealt elsewhere with these constitutions based on Plato's *Republic*,[1] I shall review them here only very briefly. It is again to be noted that Al-Farabi judges these imperfect States by their ideas of the human end: happiness. He is not interested in their constitutions as such. As far as their numbers go, Al-Farabi differentiates more than Plato, and their designations are partly derived from Plato and partly represent Islamic notions. They are called by a collective name 'ignorant States'[2] which are, then, subdivided into a number of States or associations, much in the way of Plato's subdivisions, although with him they are not all separate constitutions, as will be seen later.

'Ignorance' as opposed to knowledge is used by Al-Farabi in the same sense as by Plato in the *Republic*,[3] but may well have in addition the meaning which *jahiliya* has in Islam. The inhabitants of the 'ignorant' State do not know happiness as it is understood in the Ideal State. They aim only at external goods, like health, wealth, the pleasures of the senses, desires or honour. This State is divided into an association of States according to the various aims just mentioned.

The first is the *State of Necessity* (*daruriya*); its inhabitants aim at the necessities of life, like food, drink, clothing, dwelling, carnal gratification, and they assist each other in securing their object.[4]

Next comes the State called in the *Siyasa the vile State* (*nadhala*) whose citizens aim at wealth and riches for their own sake.[5] 'The base and despised State' receives its designation from the aim of its citizens: the pleasures of the senses, games and other pleasantries.[6]

Al-Farabi next mentions *Timocracy*[7] whose citizens assist each other in their striving for honour, glory and fame. Honour is of two kinds, the honour between the one worthy of honour because of some virtue in him, and the other who, in honouring the first, recognizes in him his

1. In *PIB* and in the Notes to my edition of Averroes' Commentary on Plato's "*Republic*" which is in the press and will appear in the *Cambridge Oriental Publications* (Cambridge University Press).†
2. *Madina jahiliya* or *ahl al-jahiliya* in the *Mad. Fad.* (*jahila in the Siyasa*).
3. See *Mad. Fad.* 61; *Siyasa* 58.7 ff.
4. See *Mad. Fad.* 62.4 ff.; *Siyasa* 58.11-59.2 with a detailed description of the means whereby the necessities of life can be acquired (agriculture, hunting etc.)
5. Siyasa 59.3-12, including a characterisation of its ruler. Dieterici reads (*Mad. Fad.* 62.6) baddala which should be changed to na*dh*ala. In *PIB* I put the question whether na*dh*ala was perhaps corrupted from baddala, in view of mubaddala and mutabaddala which are both meaningful. In fact, baddala is simply a misreading of na*dh*ala which is correct.
6. *Mad. Fad.* 62.8 ff. *khissa wa-shaqwa*; *Siyasa* 59.12-19 *khasisa*. Averroes uses the term *himud* in his Commentary, just as the Hebrew translation of the *Siyasa* renders *khasisa* by *hamudah*.
7. *Mad. Fad.* 62.10-14 *madina karama*; *Siyasa* 59.20-60.15. The various kinds of honour are fully discussed *ibid.* 60.16-64.2.

superior. The other kind of honour is accorded to men because of wealth, victory, authority and the like. This honour-loving State is the best of the ignorant States. Al-Farabi may be influenced by Aristotle[1] in his attitude to Timocracy, as is also Averroes whose treatment of the 'ignorant States' closely follows that in the *Siyasa,* though not in the same order as here.

Tyranny (*taghallub*) is so called because the citizens aim in their co-operation to be victorious over others, but refuse to be vanquished by them. Absolute mastery and the pleasure resulting from 'victory' is the purpose of their effort.[2] Al-Farabi dilates in the *Siyasa* upon the various kinds of tyranny, surpassing in number the honour-loving States in accordance with the desire of the tyrant whose will rules supreme. This is a differentiation within the broad distinction between tyranny, exercised within the State by the tyrant and his helpers as master over the citizens, and tyranny of one State over others outside.

Democracy (*jama'iya*) is characterized by the freedom of its citizens to do as and what they please; they are equals and nobody exercises dominion over another. The one who governs them does so only with the consent of the governed.[3]

The 'States' discussed so far by Al-Farabi correspond to Plato's four imperfect States: timocracy, oligarchy, democracy and tyranny. The Arabic terms used correspond to the Greek terms with the exception of na*dh*ala and its near-equivalents *khissa* (*khasisa*) and *shaqwa.* It is clear from Averroes' Commentary on Plato's *Republic* that they represent oligarchy and plutocracy, its equivalent.[4] Averroes uses Al-Farabi's three terms to characterize the viciousness of "the rule of the few" or "the plutocratic association"; the former is Platonic and the latter goes back to Xenophon. Averroes calls this State also hedonistic.[5] On the other hand, Al-Farabi distinguishes between the State aiming at wealth (*nadhala*) and the State aiming at pleasure (*khissa wa-shaqwa*).

To these four States Al-Farabi adds three more 'ignorant States':[6] the vicious (*fasiqa*), the transformed (*mubaddala*) and the erring (*dalla*) States. The opinions of the *madina fasiqa* are those of the Ideal State, that is, its inhabitants have the right beliefs and convictions and know what happiness is; but in their actions they are like the citizens of the

1. *NE.* VIII. 10, 1160b.
2. *Mad. Fad.* 62.14 ff.; *Siyasa* 64.3-69.3.
3. *Mad. Fad.* 62.16 ff.; *Siyasa* 69.4-71.5.
4. Averroes calls it "the constitution of the vicious", "the plutocratic association based on money", "the rule of the few", and characterizes it as "a vile, despicable and base rule."
5. It is the seventh of his eight constitutions: "..the government of the pleasure-seeker. This is that constitution in which the rulers aim at pleasure alone."
6. *Mad. Fad.* 61.17 f. *fasiqa, mutabbadala* (*mubaddala* 63.1) and *dalla*; as well as *saqita* (80.5); *Siyasa* mentions and describes only *fasiqa* and *dalla.*

States of ignorance.[1] They can, therefore, not reach happiness at all.

The *madina mubaddala* is only mentioned in the *Madina Fadila*.[2] Originally its opinions and actions were those of the Ideal State, but later on other opinions found an entry into it whereby its right opinions were transformed and its actions changed.

The State in error (*dalla*)[3] is to all appearances like the Ideal State; but its inhabitants, though imagining to hold right beliefs about God, the Active Intellect and happiness, in fact hold corrupt beliefs. Similarly their 'first ruler' sometimes imagined to have received a revelation which, however, was fraudulent. True happiness is unattainable for them, since false opinions and wrong actions had been prescribed by their ruler on account of his error.

It is significant that all three terms occur in the Qur'an and must have had a quite definite meaning for every believer. The same applies to *jahiliya* and to *saqita*, if this term is correct in the *Madina Fadila* 80.5. Bearing their Qur'anic context in mind, it is more than likely that Al-Farabi used them intentionally in order to effect an assimilation of Plato's four vicious, imperfect States to Islam and Muslim notions. It appears probable that right beliefs and convictions and their contrast are understood by the Muslim philosopher both in their Platonic and in their Islamic meaning; the more so since he follows up the description of these ignorant States by a statement in the *Madina Fadila* of the knowledge required of the citizens of the Ideal State, in terms similar to the detailed discussion in the *Tahsil*, which has been summarised earlier. The philosophers of the Ideal State acquire their knowledge by means of demonstration and insight and teach it to their followers. But all others must be taught by allegories. The aim of the Ideal State is true happiness, whereas the aim of the different kinds of ignorant States is merely the happiness of their respective kings. The vicious States arise because their religion is based on corrupt opinions.[4]

Al-Farabi includes among the ignorant States yet another category whom he calls *nawabit*.[5] They live as isolated individuals in States and are for that reason debarred from reaching true happiness, although at least one of the six kinds distinguished by Al-Farabi 'are not opposed to the Ideal State, but follow the right road and seek after truth.' These individuals play an important part in Ibn Bajja, who understands them

1. *Mad. Fad.* 62.21 ff; *Siyasa* 73.16—74.3.
2. 63.1 ff.
3. *Mad. Fad.* 63.3—16; *Siyasa* 74.4—7, much shorter.
4. This is of course a Platonic notion. See *Mad. Fad.* 69.6—73.16; *Siyasa* 71.6—73.15 in much greater detail.
5. See *Mad. Fad.* 61.18; *Siyasa* 57.11 ff. and at great length 74.8—end of this treatise. I have dealt with the *nawabit* in my *PIB* and must forgo a repetition here. Cp. *PIB* 203 ff. with ns. 55—59.

in an entirely positive sense and identifies them with the *strangers*[1] and with his *mutawahhid.*

That this is not the only point of contact between Ibn Bajja and Al-Farabi I hope to have shown on a previous occasion.

The *strangers,* whom Ibn Bajja rightly traced to the Sufis, thus not only form a link between Al-Farabi and Sufism, but also supply corroborative evidence for the view that happiness and highest perfection are possible only for those citizens who play an active part in the Ideal State ruled over by the prophetic philosopher king. Those who are 'the excellent, best and happy men' in the Ideal nation or State are only 'most excellent strangers' if they are dispersed over a number of different places which are not under such an Ideal government. Averroes endorses Al-Farabi's view which is the view of Plato and Aristotle, but not that of Ibn Bajja whose *mutawahhid* can reach happiness in isolation even in imperfect States.[2]

Of the great importance of Al-Farabi's political thought for Averroes evidence has been given on more than one occasion.[3] It will, therefore, suffice if this point is here touched upon only briefly.

There is broad agreement between the two thinkers about the human end, happiness, and how to attain it. The four-fold perfection, consisting in the possession of speculative, intellectual and ethical virtues and practical arts, is demanded by both; Averroes found them mentioned together by Al-Farabi while they go back to Aristotle's *Nicomachean Ethics.*[4] The two methods of teaching: the elect by demonstrative proofs, and the masses by persuasion, are not only differentiated by Al-Farabi and Averroes, but by all *Falasifa,* as well as by Jahiz and Al-Ghazali.[5] Since both thinkers are Muslims it is only natural that they should insist on the true philosopher's need for strong and sound religious beliefs and convictions. That Averroes is more concerned with the *Shari'a,* and that he establishes a claim for the philosopher to be the only competent interpreter of the inner meaning of the prophetic law is no doubt due to the circumstances of his own time, and to his life and activity under the Almohads. This more conscious Muslim attitude runs through the whole discussion of happiness and the opinions held by various people by which the character of the various States is determined. For Averroes insists on the overriding claim of the *Shari'a* as the repository of the will of God

1. *Al-ghuraba* (*Siyasa* 50.12). See L. Massignon, *La Passion d'Al Hallaj,* Paris 1914/21 pp. 740 and 751 on *ghuraba* and also H. Corbin, *as-Suhrawardi's Opera Metaphysica et Mystica* II, Teheran 1952, p. 86 and 97 f. (*Qissat al-Ghurbat al-Gharbiya*).
2. See *PIB,* 205 with *n.* 63.
3. See my *M, SAIPT, PIB, PIR* and the Notes of my edition of Averroes' Commentary on Plato's *Republic.*
4. *NE* I. vii, 1098a; I. xiii, 1103a (intellectual and moral virtues); X. vii, 1177a (contemplation); 1177b (practical virtues).
5. It need not necessarily go back to Cicero, as Madkour *op. cit.*, p. 22 suggests.

which is made known by prophecy. This Islamic attitude is reinforced by Averroes' political realism which is responsible for his continued application of the teachings of the *Republic* to contemporary Muslim States. This is a feature entirely absent in Al-Farabi.[1]

Where Averroes agrees with Al-Farabi in detail, a distinction must be drawn between Al-Farabi's own contribution and his reproduction of his sources, in the first place Plato's *Republic* and Aristotle's *Nicomachean Ethics*. This must be borne in mind in the case of a common terminology which goes back, as a rule, to the Arabic versions of the Greek originals or their summaries. That Averroes is usually closer to his source is due to the different type of books they are writing; Al-Farabi writes a book of his own, based on Plato's *Republic*; whereas Averroes writes a Commentary in the course of which he often reproduces literally Plato's argument.

But he frequently follows Al-Farabis's interpretation and adaptation, especially in his introductions which sum up in advance Plato's argument; he then comments on it in detail. This applies also to his many theoretical digressions, though to a lesser degree. These digressions are usually based on Aristotle's *Physics, Metaphysics, De Anima* and particularly the *Nicomachean Ethics*, and are mainly Averroes' own work, except for passages which agree so closely with similar discussions in the political treatises under review that borrowing can be assumed. Such an assumption seems justified since Averroes refers to the *Siyasa* and to the Commentary on the *Nicomachean Ethics*, which has so far not been unearthed.

The definition of Political Science and the division of the arts into master arts and subsidiary arts, common to both authors, may or may not go back to the *Nicomachean Ethics* and the *Politikos* in both. It is equally difficult to decide whether Averroes' definition of *ikhtiyar* is copied from *Siyasa* 42.7 or from *Nicomachean Ethics* VI, 2, 1139b (*proairesis.*) But on the other hand, Averroes' statement that the Good is attainable by choice and free will first in the City-State as the smallest unit originates in *Madina Fadila* 54.2f. Averroes exposition of the intellectual virtues reads like a terse summary of *Tahsil* 26.11–27 end. That in his description of the 'Ignorant States' Averroes follows closely Al-Farabi has been stated before. But it must be remembered that Averroes never copies slavishly in such a case, but shortens and modifies in the light of his better understanding of Plato' argument and its topicality, and on the basis of his penetrating analysis of Aristotle. He is more concise and realizes the significance of Plato's constitutions and their transformations. In this, he shows not only remarkable insight into Greek political thinking, but is, moreover, convinced that Plato's and Aristotle's political philosophy is relevant to Islam in his own time.

---

1. See *PIR*, 247 ff,; 270 ff.

Earlier in this paper an example was given in connection with oligarchy, a term which is not used by Al-Farabi. On the other hand, Averroes adopts terms coined by Al-Farabi which, though based on the *Republic* were not used by Plato as constitutional designations, namely 'States of Necessity' and 'Ignorant States in Error'. But he does not speak of *madina fasiqa, madina mubaddala* and *madina dalla* because they are not directly related to Plato.

A few examples may illustrate the handling of his material as he found it in Plato and Al-Farabi.

Tyranny is for Al-Farabi a mixed rather than a simple, imperfect State. It contains elements of timocracy and oligarchy which latter Averroes further defines as plutocracy or the hedonistic State. Al-Farabi already combines honour and pleasure including wealth, but he accomodates in the tyrannical State those who look upon wealth, games or the pleasures of the senses as a kind of honour to be aimed at.[1] Without transition he then treats of democracy.

Averroes follows Plato's discussion of the transition from timocracy to oligarchy but adds to his description of the oligarchical man the hedonistic. He says: 'Love of honour will be driven out of the soul of him who prefers the acquisition of money, and for this he will throw away all desires........ In general, the transformation of the timocratic into the hedonistic man is obvious, whether he takes delight in money or in the other remaining pleasures. The same seems to apply to the timocratic and the hedonistic State. For the plutocratic and the hedonistic State belong to the same category'.

Then follows the application of Plato's argument:

'We often see kings becoming corrupted into such men. Similarly there is in our time the kingdom of men known as the Almoravids. At first they were imitating the constitution based on the Law—this under the first of them—then they changed (it) under his son into the timocratic (constitution), while there was in him also an admixture of the love of money. Further, it changed under his grandson into the hedonistic (constitution) with all the paraphernalia of the hedonists; and it perished in his time. The reason was that the constitution which was opposed to it at that time resembled the constitution based on the Law.'

We note that he attributes the downfall of the Almoravids to moral corruption and the consequent inability to resist the Almohads, who were animated by religious zeal for obedience to the *Shari'a* of Islam and for the restoration of its purity.

A comparison of Averroes' treatment of tyranny, correctly reproducing Plato's argument, with Al-Farabi's rather involved description of a hybrid State which he calls *madina taghallub,* reveals Averroes' clarity of mind and precision of diction. Al-Farabi's description only faintly

1. See *Siyasa* 62. 5,9 ff., 16; 68.2—69.3.

echoes the *Republic,* and what follows in the *Siyasa* is his own exposition; whereas Averroes the Commentator follows Plato to 587, with which he considers the theoretical arguments at an end and his task fulfilled. He ignores what cannot be proved, but what can be proved is valid and applicable to political reality.

This being so, there is still a large area not only of agreement with, but of actual borrowing from Al-Farabi, as the few examples quoted at the beginning of this section show. Thus, Averroes accepts Al-Farabi's definition of king, lawgiver and *imam,* and his identification of philosopher with these three, making a reservation with regard to the necessity of prophecy in the Ideal Ruler. Again, both thinkers agree in the view that without philosophy there can be no Ideal State.

An interesting instance of adaptation is Averroes' modified acceptance of Al-Farabi's intermediate stage between monarchy and aristocracy, as understood by Plato, namely, the joint rule of the philosopher and the man who possesses "the other qualifications" demanded of the second ruler.[1] Significantly, Averroes does not insist, as Al-Farabi does in the *Madina Fadila,* on the philosophic qualification, but follows Al-Farabi's exposition in the *Fusul al-Madani.*[2] Averroes introduces the third treatise of his commentary with a summary of the imperfect States. He combines Plato with Al-Farabi, as we often find in his introductions to a detailed commentary on a section of the *Republic,* and in his digressions. The Hebrew text is difficult and can only be understood by comparison with Al-Farabi, in this case with the *Fusul.* The relevant passages follow here in translation. This will enable us to see Averroes at work and to observe one of the characteristic features of his Commentary: his judicious use and adaptation of material borrowed from Al-Farabi. After enumerating Plato's five constitutions Averroes remarks that if we divide the first, ideal leadership into that of the king and the best (*aristoi*), there are six. He goes on:

(A) "For if there is placed over this administration one in whom five conditions are combined, namely, wisdom, perfect intelligence, good persuasion, good imagination, capacity for (waging) *holy war,* and no physical impediment to the performance of actions *in connection with holy war,* then he is absolutely king, and his government will be a truly royal government."

(B) "But when these qualities exist only separately in a group (of people) so that the first contributes to the end (of the State) through his wisdom, the second contributes that which leads to the (same) end through his intelligence, the third possesses good persuasion, the fourth a good imagination and the fifth a capacity for (waging) *holy war*, but

1. *Mad. Fad.* 61.8.
2. See Dunlop, *op. cit.* § 53 C. I am indebted to Mr. Dunlop for giving me the Arabic terms relevant to my argument.

they help each other to bring about and preserve this constitution, then they will be called the elect princes (that is, Plato's *aristoi*), and their rule will be called the exalted and choice rule (that is, aristocracy)."

(C) "It also happens sometimes that the ruler of this State will be one who does not attain this status, that is, the dignity of king, yet he is expert in the laws which the first (lawgiver) laid down, and possesses a good (power of) conjecture, so as to deduce from them what the first did not expound, for every single legal decision (?) and every single law case. To this category of knowledge belongs the science called among us the art of jurisprudence. In addition he has the capacity for (waging) *holy war*, and he is called king of the laws."

A, *B* and *C* correspond closely to $53 A, B and C in Dunlop's English translation. The six conditions in the *Fusul* are reduced to five by Averroes who treats, quite logically, as one, Al-Farabi's "(*e*) power to fight the holy war in person; and (*f*), that there should be nothing in his person to prevent him attending to matters which belong to the holy war." The end of *A* in Averroes is a well-defined, concise summary of Al-Farabi's "He in whom all these are united is the model to be imitated in his ways and actions, and his words and counsels are to be accepted. It is his prerogative to rule all he comes to, and as he wills."

B is practically identical with B, except that Averroes is again more specific with regard to the first two conditions, where the *Fusul* have: "........one of them provides the end, a second provides what leads to the end."

In *C* Averroes is more precise and to the point, and actually combines the passage in the *Fusul* with that in the *Madina Fadila* (60.19-61.6), the description of the second ruler; but like C, he leaves out the first of the six conditions: "he shall be a philosopher," and seems to follow C in the use of *jihad*, since the *harb* of the *Madina Fadila* should have been translated by *milhamah*, and not by *sheqidah* in our *C*. Apart from the compression of the corresponding passages in the two treatises which not only simplifies but greatly clarifies Al-Farabi's description, Averroes adds the sentence about jurisprudence. This enables him to express the legal qualifications of the ruler in one term *dayyan* which stands for (*a*)–(*e*) of *Fusul* §53 C and for the second to fifth conditions of the passage referred to in the *Madina Fadila*.

He says: *D* "However, it may not happen that both these (qualifications) are found in one man, rather the one (capable of) waging *holy war* being another than the *legal expert*.[1] Yet of necessity both will share in the rule, as is the case with many of the Muslim kings."

1. Mr. Dunlop informs me that the MS. on which he based his translation reads *jihad* and *umur jihadiya* for the Hebrew *sheqidah* and *shoqedim*. *Shoqed* presumably goes back to *mujahid* in the lost Arabic original of Averroes.

Before interpreting these passages in Al-Farabi and Averroes, we must briefly discuss the meaning of the terms *holy war* and *legal expert*. On the basis of the *Fusul* and in view of the almost word for word agreement of Averroes's text with it, we must assume that Averroes used the term *jihad*. The Hebrew translator was unaware of its technical meaning and legal connotation and simply translated the basic meaning of the root *jhd* by the corresponding Hebrew root *shaqad*, hence *sheqidah*, 'assiduity' and, derived from it, perhaps also 'perseverance'. The same applies to his translation of *umur jihadiya* by *ma'asim shoqedim*. It is interesting, as has been remarked earlier,[1] that Al-Farabi avoids the use of *jihad* and *jihadiya* in the *Madina Fadila*, but uses instead *harb* in the combinations *a'mal al-harb* and *sina'a harbiya* (61. 5f.). This may be explained by the difference in purpose of the two treatises. The *Madina Fadila* was intended to convey Al-Farabi's political philosophy and is for that purpose provided with its elaborate philosophical superstructure, as stated before. Al-Farabi develops his political ideas against this background and gives them a general application. Although the Muslim ruler is naturally included, non-Muslim rulers, especially the Ideal Ruler of the Ideal Universal State, are by no means excluded. Moreover, Al-Farabi speaks both as a Muslim affirming the claim of Islam to universality and as a philosopher on the basis of the Hellenistic *Oikoumene*.

On the other hand, the *Fusul* are more narrowly conceived, as far as one can judge by the translation of a fragment. It is possible that Al-Farabi had his patron Saif al-Dawla in mind when writing them. This would, at any rate, explain why he included the duty of *jihad* among the conditions of the ruler. Saif al-Dawla certainly excelled in matters of *jihad*.

As far as Averroes is concerned we cannot be certain, in the absence of the Arabic original of his Commentary, whether our explanation of *sheqidah* as meaning *jihad* is correct. But it seems at least probable.

The translation *legal expert* for the Hebrew *dayyan* is a little more conjectural, because there is no exactly corresponding passage to *D* in Al-Farabi. But the juxtaposition of *dayyan*, which literally means "judge," and *shoqed* which means "capable of waging *jihad*" makes it very probable that the Arabic term rendered by *dayyan* must reflect the legal qualifications demanded of Al-Farabi's ruler. The context makes this very plausible. We have already remarked on Averroes' adaptation of the statement about the joint rule in the *Madina Fadila* in the light of the *Fusul*. In the *Madina Fadila* the second ruler is replaced by two men, the philosopher and the man who possesses the other necessary qualifications, namely expert legal knowledge and independent decision as

1. See above, p. 167—with *n* 2.

well as ability to wage holy war. Averroes replaces the second ruler by the 'king of the laws' of the *Fusul*. He thus drops the philosophic qualfication of the *Madina Fadila* and divides the remaining qualifications—of the 'king of laws'—into legal expertness in one man and ability to wage *jihad* in the other. The *Fusul* do not have this division. Averroes' combination of the *Madina Fadila* and the *Fusul*[1] must, therefore, be recognised as a deliberate adaptation to Islamic conditions, as his additional remark about the frequency of this joint rule among Muslim kings clearly shows. It may also be recalled that in the *Fusul* it is only the first, Ideal Ruler who must be a philosopher.

We know that both these qualifications, power of independent decision on the basis of erudition in *Fiqh*, and power to wage *jihad*, are required of the *Khalifa*. Moreover, the right to and the duty of *ijtihad*, the rejection of and struggle against *taqlid* —the unquestioning submission to authority-holds an important place in Muslim theology[2] from the earliest times.

On these grounds it appears probable that Al-Farabi has a Muslim ruler in mind, at any rate in the *Fusul*. The case is somewhat different in the *Madina Fadila* for the reasons I have stated before.

But even there the qualification of *ijtihad* is demanded although *hikma* is throughout the first and quite indispensable condition for a perfect State and its maintenance. Here Al-Farabi is true to the Platonic ideal of the philosopher-king.

The combination of *ijtihad* with *jihad* guarantees the Islamic character of the State and its ruler, only that without philosophy neither State nor ruler can be considered perfect in the meaning of the term in the *Republic*. That the *Politikos* is one of the sources for the *Fusul* is not im-

---

1. Whether this means that Al-Farabi himself has modified his views and that the *Fusul* are later than the *Mad. Fad.* can, if at all, be decided when the whole text of the *Fusul* is available. For the moment, the discrepancy between the second ruler of the *Mad. Fad.* who is philosopher *and* 'king of the law(s)', and the third stage in the *Fusul*, namely, the 'king of law(s)', may simply be due to the different purpose and reading public of the two treatises.
When looking at the *Mad. Fad.* alone, I was at first inclined to assume that the Hebrew translator might have misread *hākim* for *hakīm*—provided Averroes reproduced the passage of the *Mad. Fad.* But *hākim* would hardly be used to denote a judge since it means 'governor' as well. It is more likely that the Hebrew translator found *faqih* in the Arabic text of Averroes. Plato's 'judges' of *Republic* 405a are rendered by *shofetim*, presumably translating *qudat* in Averroes' comments. Moreover, if *shoqed* translates mujahid, as I assume, *dayyan* would presumably represent *faqih* most likely.

2. See I. Goldziher *Streitschrift des Gazali gegen die Batinijja-Sekte*, Leiden 1916, *Einleitung*, esp. pp. 1—22.

possible, directly or indirectly.[1] But before we assume its influence on Al-Farabi's definitions and formulations we must remember that he, like the other *Falasifa,* especially Averroes, was first and foremost an educated Muslim. That means that *Fiqh* was an integral part of the education of the *Falasifa* and shaped their outlook. They approached Graeco-Hellenistic philosophy as Muslims and took what was akin to their own way of thought and life, from Plato and Aristotle, as they were presented to them in their writings, summaries and commentaries. It is that common ground based on the concept of Law which must be taken into consideration if we want to understand the attitude of the *Falasifa* to Plato and Aristotle. It is the conviction that good government depends on just laws, and that man can reach true happiness only in such a good State.[2]

Averroes' treatment of his sources in Al-Farabi is similarly determined by his Islamic outlook, only even more so, as I have tried to show. He was strongly opposed to *taqlid* in the wake of Ibn Hazm by whom he seems to be influenced in his theology generally.[3]

In conclusion, it can be said that Al-Farabi's political thought represents a blend of Platonic, Aristotelian and Islamic notions, on the basis of that common ground of which I have repeatedly spoken.

Averroes, building on strong Al-Farabian foundations, brings precision, clarity and system to the theories of his great predecessor. More importantly still, he brings his practical experience to bear on these theories and their Platonic-Aristotelian sources, and applies his political realism to the contemporary Muslim States in the form of a critique which has its roots in and takes its principles from Plato's ideas on Politics.

---

1. Mr. Dunlop, in a conversation, expressed the opinion that the *Fusul* were connected with the *Politikos.* He thinks that 297e of this treatise may be the likely source for Al-Farabi's 'king of the laws'. It has, however, to be borne in mind that Al-Farabi commented on Plato's *Laws* as well which, no doubt, contributed to the formulation of his own ideas, as they did in the case of Averroes.
   A much closer parallel is provided by *Laws* 710, especially 710d, the combination of legislator and autocrat, cp. also Al-Farabi's summary of 709c–711b in his *Talkis,* ed. Gabrieli (see p. 157, n. 3), p. 22 of Arabic text, especially line 19 (divine laws). As for Averroes, the Islamic character of his joint rule is even more apparent by contrast, no doubt under the influence of the *Fusul* and *Al-Madinatal-Fadila.*
2. See above, p. 165—with n. 6, to which the following references may be added: *M* 192 ff., 204 ff.; *SAIPT* 6; *PIR* 255, 259 ff.
3. See *PIR* 257 ff.

6

IBN JALDŪN'S ATTITUDE TO THE 'FALĀSIFA'[1]

IBN Jaldūn's attitude to movements, institutions, groups or individuals in the Islamic world and outside is determined by two considerations. The one springs from his empiricism which has led him to formulate his New Science of History. This embraces mankind in one society and its civilisation, *ᶜumrān*, which he sets out to describe in its various, inter-related manifestations. The other consideration is that acute observation and deduction are made by one who thinks and writes as a Muslim, who has received a traditional education and has been a *mālikī qāḍī*. He is convinced that Islam as a system of life and thought is the perfect example of the Highest Good and ideally supplies a complete answer to his empirical inquiry into the laws and practice of human association. His method is new and has opened for him new insights into the working of political and social organisation and into the connection which exists between the several factors of human life: political, social, economic, religious and cultural. Howewer far removed from the ideal *Šarᶜ* the results of his investigation may at times be, it is this *Šarᶜ* to which as the norm he relates them [2].

1 Paper read to the XXIIIrd International Congress of Orientalists at Cambridge, August 1954. An inquiry into Ibn Jaldūn's sources is called for in order to assess his contribution to Muslim historiography and political thought. This short paper is a modest beginning in the field of Politics.

2 I am not now concerned with his sincerity or otherwise. It is very difficult to see into another man's soul, especially into such a complex character as Ibn Jaldūn. He can only be understood in the political and spiritual setting of the Maghreb of his day, and it must be remembered that medieval man, Muslim,

Ibn Jaldūn's attitude to the *falāsifa* is thus determined by and must be related to his empiricism and to his traditionalism.

He studied the philosophical sciences alongside with the traditional Muslim disciplines. The rational sciences, he says, are natural to man, are found among all civilised nations, and are called *ʿulūm al-falsafa wa-l-ḥikma* [1]. They are listed in this order: logic, physics, metaphysics and mathematics. They form an integral part of *ʿumrān* and have their uses for all men, particularly for historians; but the pursuit of philosophy has also its dangers. It cannot and does not reach its objective: the perception of all Existing Things; besides, it teaches doctrines contrary to the divinely revealed laws and their plain sense. He warns against indulging in speculation unless mastery of the religious sciences has first been achieved, and thus right beliefs and convictions have been firmly established in the student of philosophy [2].

In a chapter 'On the uselessness of *falsafa* and the corrupting influence of its doctrine' he sees its only advantage in the skill it imparts in debate and understanding. Yet, at the beginning of his *Muqaddima*, he stresses no less the value of philosophical method in historical research and claims for the Science of History a place among the philosophical disciplines. He criticises the historians for neglecting philosophy which would give them indispensable knowledge of the physical world. They would not depart from truth in their description and evaluation of events if they took speculation as arbiter *(taḥkīm al-naẓar)* [3]. To some extent, his approval of philosophy may be due to his desire for justifying his superiority over the Muslim historians whom he has so freely and often indiscriminately used. It rem-

Jewish or Christian, rarely if ever possessed that consistency which we moderns demand of him, but often are lacking ourselves. Ibn Jaldūn's pronouncements must be seen against the purpose he had in mind in a given place within his work and cannot be pressed into a system which encloses the whole *Muqaddima* from beginning to end.

[1] See *Muqaddima*, ed. *Q*(atremère) III. 87 ff. / ed. *B*(eyrout) 478.

[2] See *ibid. Q* III. 219 / *B* 519.

[3] See *Q* I. 69 / *B* 9 f.

inds us also of al-Gazālī's qualified and limited acceptance of philosophy in his *Iḥyā'* [1]. No reservation is placed on logic and mathematics; physics is innocuous as long as the *falāsifa* conform to the teachings of the *Qur'ān;* but metaphysics is dangerous.

In his dual capacity of political scientist and post-Ghazalian Muslim he sharply attacks certain views and theories of the *falāsifa*, and I now turn to a brief summary of *some* of his criticisms, as far as the time at my disposal allows.

D. B. Macdonald called him a «convinced Ghazzalian» [2]. This is true of his general line of attack and of his opposition to the explanation of prophecy advanced by some philosophers of Islam, from the point of view of orthodoxy. Ibn Jaldūn explicitly recommends al-Gazālī's books, particularly his refutation of the *falāsifa* [3]. He asserts that the prophetic lawgiver *(al-šāriᶜ)* possesses a comprehension *(idrāk)* superior to that obtained by means of speculation — which it actually includes —, because he draws his perceptions directly from 'the divine lights'. His knowledge is not bound by the canons of speculation, and we must prefer the comprehension to which he has led us to our inadequate rational perception. We have to accept religious conviction and knowledge commanded by the divine Law; what we cannot understand we should not attempt to examine rationally. We must trust in the prophetic lawgiver. It is not for us to verify and justify by demonstration the truth of revelation [4]. There could be no clearer distinction between the compulsion of revealed truth and the rational inquiry into physical

[1] Discussed by Louis Gardet, *Raison et Foi en Islâm* in: *Revue Thomiste*, xliii, 1, 1937, p. 157. This series of articles, the same author's *Introduction à la Théologie Musulmane* (together with P. Anawati) and, particularly, his *La Pensée Religieuse d'Avicenne*, Paris 1951, chs. IV-VI, are fundamental for the understanding of the *falāsifa*.

[2] In *The Religious Attitude and Life in Islam*, Chicago 1909, p. 131.

[3] See *Q* III. 63 / *B* 467.

[4] Ibn Jaldūn goes further than the *Kalām* and al-Gazālī in excluding philosophy from theology; he would not even tolerate the former as handmaid to the latter. See *Q* III. 121 ff. / *B* 496 f.

and metaphysical problems in order to discover truth by our own effort.

From this traditionalist position Ibn Jaldūn launches his attack upon *falsafa*. He emphasizes the importance of this special chapter, referred to above, 'because these sciences are <natural> concomitants of civilisation, occur frequently in the cities and do much damage to religion *(dīn)*' [1].

He rejects the claim that all Existing Things can be perceived rationally and denies that *naẓar* is competent and sufficient to verify religious beliefs and convictions *(ʿaqā'id imāniyya)*. This can alone be effected by tradition based on revelation *(samʿ)* [2].

His contention that philosophy does harm to religion must be understood in relation to the great importance he assigns to religion in the State, for its founding as well as for its successful maintenance [3]. The weakening of religion inevitably leads to the weakening of the State. Political scientist and believer are at one in condemning philosophy in this respect.

Convinced of the inadequacy of human reason, Ibn Jaldūn next challenges the opinion of the *falāsifa* that Happiness *(saʿāda)* consists in the perception of all Existing Things. In the first place, they derive them from the First Intelligence and not, as Muslims ought to do, from the Necessary Being, God (*al-wāŷib*). Then the empiricist objects to their method since the correspondence between their premisses and Reality cannot be proved by demonstration, but only by experience. Even if the *falāsifa* were right in respect of the first Intelligibles, a Muslim must abstain from speculating on them, for physical problems are not important for his religion or for his subsistence. As for the spiritual beings *(al-rūḥāniyyāt)*, it is impossible for us, he says, to attain knowledge of them, since their essence is alto-

[1] See *Q* III. 210 / *B* 514.

[2] See *ibid*.

[3] See my *Ibn Khaldūn's Gedanken über den Staat* (Beiheft 25 d. Historischen Zeitschrift) Berlin/München 1932, chapter *Staat und Religion*, for a fuller treatment; also my *Ibn Khaldun: A North African Muslim Thinker of the Fourteenth Century* in: John Rylands Library Bulletin, XXIV, 2, oct. 1940, p. 319.

gether unknown to us; their existence cannot be established by certain proof *(burhān yaqīnī)* [1].

Ibn Jaldūn's own concept of perception is very close to that of Ibn Sīnā, modified by al-Gazālī, and to Ṣūfism. It deserves a special study [2]. Here a few remarks must suffice.

Man's nature is composite; body and soul have perceptions peculiar to themselves. Only the spiritual part in man can obtain physical and spiritual perceptions. It perceives the physical ones with the help of bodily tools: the brain and the senses. The spiritual realm is perceived in its essence without intermediary. So perceiving, the spiritual soul experiences joy and delight as the result of the withdrawal of the veil of the senses and the abandonment of sense-perception, not by *naẓar* and *ʿilm*. Since demonstration depends on the faculties of the brain, namely imagination, reflection and memory, it is absurd to contend, as the *falāsifa* do acording to Ibn Jaldūn, that joy and delight of the soul can be attained in this way, that is, by intellectual perception by means of demonstration. He says: 'the first thing we have at heart in order to obtain this perception <of the spiritual world> is the mortification of all these faculties of the brain'. Hence, those are wrong who follow Aristotle, al-Fārābī, Ibn Sīnā's *Šifā'*, *Naŷāt* and *Išārāt* and Ibn Rušd's Commenta-

1 See *Q* III. 212 ff. / *B* 515 ff.

2 In order to assign Ibn Jaldūn's epistemology and psychology their place within Muslim thinking a detailed comparison between Ibn Sīnā, al-Gazālī and the relevant sections of the *Muqaddima* is essential. The three last chapters of the *Išārāt* are most important, as Mehren has already seen (see his *Traités Mystiques d'Avicenne, ... Al-Ishārāt, etc.*, Leyden 1891, p. 19, n. 1). Such a study will reveal interesting adaptations and modifications; for example, Ibn Sīnā's *ʿārif* is very close to Ibn Jaldūn's second of the three kinds of soul he distinguishes (*Q* I. 178 ff. / *B* 98 ff.). But Ibn Jaldūn is not only heir to a long and varied, by no means uniform, tradition, he must also be seen against the background of thought in the Maghreb since the death of Ibn Rušd, and we know as yet insufficiently the views of philosophers, theologians and mystics of that time. As stated on p. 75, n. 2, we cannot expect consistency in Ibn Jaldūn any more than in al-Gazālī. *Cf.* also al-Kalābāḏī's *K. al-Taʿarruf li-maḏhab ahl al-taṣawwuf*, ed. A. J. Arberry, on the Ṣūfī doctrine of angels and messengers; and I. Goldziher, *Vorlesungen ü. d. Islam*[2], pp. 169 and 172 ff.

ries on Aristotle's works [1], and assert that the contact *(ittiṣāl)* with the Active Intelligence brings us our share of happiness, and that the resulting joy is the essence of that blessedness which the Lawgiver has promised us. Reality is too vast to be perceived by human reason. Besides, we do not know whether the philosophers' happiness *is* the promised blessedness which we shall experience in the future life. It cannot be perceived, it can only be obtained by obedience to the commandments of the prophetic Law [2].

A special target for his criticism of the *falāsifa* is their theory of prophecy as evolved by al-Fārābī and developed by Ibn Sīnā. His own explanation combines various elements which exist side by side and are not integrated into a consistent whole [3]. Naturally, he upholds the Qur'anic concept of *tanzīl*, that is, that the word of God 'descends' on to the chosen prophet/messenger by means of an angel. He opposes the contention of the *falāsifa* that the prophet performs miracles by his own power. Prophecy has also an important part in his psychology [4].

Although he mentions al-Fārābī and Ibn Bāŷŷa he does not seem to have read their writings. But he certainly knew those of Ibn Sīnā's works already mentioned and actually gives the meaning of a passage from the *Kitāb al-mabda' wa-l-maʿād* [5]. He objects to the *mutakallimūn* because they mix theology *(kalām)* with philosophy as if they were one science *(fann)* [6],

[1] The text reads: *wa-talājīṣ Ibn Rušd lil-faṣṣ min ta'līf Arisṭu*. De Slane says *faṣṣ* means Aristotle's *Organon*, but I do not know on what he bases this identification. According to Dozy, *Suppl.*, *faṣṣ* can mean «texte d'un livre». Should we perhaps read *naṣṣ?*

[2] See *Q* III. 214 ff. / *B* 517 ff.

[3] See p. 79, n. 2.

[4] See *Q* I. 165 ff. and 178 ff. / *B* 92 ff. and 98 ff.

[5] I have traced this passage to Alpagus' *Avicenna De Almahad*, Venice 1546, p. 61. According to Louis Gardet, *La Pensée Religieuse d'Avicenne*, Errata et Addenda, p. 99, n. 1 Alpagus' Latin version has been compared with Ibn Sīnā's *Risāla aḍḥawiyya fī amr al-maʿād*, ed. Cairo 1949 by Dr. Georges Vajda and found to be an exact translation of this treatise. I was unable to consult the Arabic text.

[6] Ibn Jaldūn singles out *Imām Ibn al-Jaṭīb fī al-mabāḥiṯ al-mašriqiyya*, that is Fajr al-dīn Rāzī.

and he levels the same accusation against the Ṣūfis towards whom he is otherwise very sympathetic [1]. In the manner of Ibn Rušd he attacks the *mutakallimūn* because they deal with metaphysical problems which are outside their province and because they use philosophical arguments in their exposition of religious beliefs and convictions. They ought to be content with guarding pure Islam and refuting heresy [2]. But there is no evidence that Ibn Jaldūn knew the *Tahāfut al-tahāfut*, the *Faṣl al-maqāl* or the *Kašf ᶜan manāhiŷ al-adilla*.

Ibn Jaldūn's opposition to the explanation of prophecy advanced by the *falāsifa* [3] is also, and probably mainly, grounded in his political thought. In this respect his criticism is much more telling and convincing, and serves to underline his originality as a political thinker.

He accepts the philosophers' statement that 'man is a political being *(madanī)* by nature'. From it he derives his concept of *ᶜumran*. 'Human association is necessary which is the City-State *(madīna)* in their terminology, and this is the meaning of *ᶜumrān*' [4]. Significantly, he adds that experience forces man to associate with others of his kind in order to ensure life and existence. Experience and reflection enable man to manage his affairs [5].

He refutes the proof of the *falāsifa* that prophecy is nec-

1 He shares their view of immediate, transcendental perception of the spiritual world, without the help of *naẓar*, *ᶜilm* or *naql*.

2 See *Q* III. 122 f. / *B* 495 ff.

3 But not by Ibn Rušd, as I have tried to show in my *The Place of Politics in the Philosophy of Ibn Rushd* in: BSOAS, XV, 2, 1953, pp. 258 ff.

4 See *Q* I. 69 / *B* 41. Ibn Jaldūn means here by *ḥukamā'* the Greek philosophers as well as the *falāsifa*. If he aims exclusively at the latter, as in his attack on their theory of prophecy, he uses the term *falāsifa*. It is interesting to note that when al-Fārābī speaks of human association in his *Madīna fāḍila* he speaks of the largest political association as extending over the whole inhabited (or cultivated) earth, *maᶜmūra* (p. 53. 18). This term is derived from the same root *ᶜmr* as Ibn Jaldūn's *ᶜumrān*.

5 See *Q* II. 371 / *B* missing. In this context Ibn Jaldūn has yet another threefold division of human Reason: *ᶜaql tamyīzī*, *taŷrībī* and *naẓarī*. The last named is described by the *ahl al-ᶜulūm* < *al-ᶜaqliyya* >. He goes beyond Ibn Sīnā, *Naŷāt* 498 f., though he follows Ibn Sīnā's description of the necessity of human association which, in turn, goes back to al-Fārābī.

essary and peculiar to man's nature, and that the restraining authority *(ḥukm wāziᶜ*, or *wāziᶜ wa-ḥākim*, or simply *wāziᶜ)* which man needs, is based on a law imposed by God. His source for the opinion of the *falāsifa* is, no doubt, the chapter *fī iṯbāt al-nubuwwa* in Ibn Sīnā's *Naǧāt* [1]. Against it, he points to the existence of ordered human life before or without prophecy. The majority of mankind has no revelation *(kitāb)* and does not obey prophets, but their rulers derive their authority from the power they exercise, or from the *ᶜaṣabiyya* uniting their supporters [2]. Observation and experience, gained by the study of history and of contemporary States in whose administration he took a leading part, disprove an argument based on Reason. As often, he has recourse to the opinion of the *salaf*, the early Muslims. The *Šarᶜ* is the authority for prophecy, and not Reason.

Further, he emphatically denies that the *Šarᶜ* prescribes a *wāziᶜ*. The Lawgiver knew what was best for man, both in this world and in the next, and only the Divine Law provides for man's needs to gain eternal life. The believer whose life is guided by the *Šarīᶜa,* has, therefore, the *wāziᶜ* in himself. Only when religion declined, man had to be coerced by restraining statutes *(aḥkām wāziᶜa)*; the *Šarᶜ* became a science and art which had to be acquired by study and education [3]. We are here not concerned with the bad effect of this decline on man's courage in conjunction with his change-over to settled life, but rather with the superiority of the *Šarᶜ* as a source of authority. Ibn Jaldūn stresses against the *falāsifa* that the *wāziᶜ* is inherent in the very nature of the *Šarᶜ (fī-hā ḏātī)*. Given the comprehensive realm of this Law, authority based on it is superior to that rooted in government based on Reason *(siyāsa ᶜaqliyya)*. The advantage of the latter is confined to this world [4], and the subjects

1 See *Naǧāt* 499 f. Ibn Sīnā does not use the terms *ḥukm wāziᶜ*, etc., but instead *sānin, muᶜaddil, an yuṭāᶜa amruhu*, etc. He thus clearly invests the Lawgiver with executive power.

2 See *Q* I. 72 / *B* 43 f.

3 See *Q* I. 232 / *B* 126 f.

4 Maimonides (*Dalālāt al-ḥā'irīn* II, ch. xxxix) and Ibn Rušd (see *loc. cit.*

expect a reward from the earthly ruler in proportion to their usefulness to him and to their contribution to the general welfare. Ibn Jaldūn distinguishes two kinds of *siyāsa ᶜaqliyya:* in the one the advantage of the ruler is the primary purpose, in the other the general welfare [1]. The emphatic denial that the *Šarᶜ* prescribes a *wāziᶜ* as something external, namely a political authority, a ruler, points to Ibn Jaldūn's rejection of the political interpretation of prophecy advanced by the *falāsifa*. For him, the prophet is in the first place the *ṣāḥib al-šarīᶜa* or the *šāriᶜ*. He is *not* the ruler; this is his *jalīfa*. The *Šarīᶜa* bound the *umma*, that is the *ŷamāᶜa*, together and ruled supreme in the time of the four *julafā' rāšidūn* and Muḥammad's Companions generally. The decline of religion — to repeat — coincided with the transition to *ḥaḍāra* and with the transformation of the *jilāfa* as effective religious-political power into the *mulk*. He defines the government of the Muslim kings as *siyāsa ᶜaqliyya* even if the primary, though not the only source, of their laws is the *Šarīᶜa*.

His concept of prophecy and prophetic Law shares with his empiricism the responsibility for excluding from detailed description yet a third kind of government; this he terms *siyāsa madaniyya*, the administration of the *madīna fāḍila*. He says: 'The community of its citizens has altogether no need of governors *(ḥukkām)* [2]. They do not aim at a *siyāsa* of a kind which society is urged to follow in the interests of the public good *(maṣāliḥ ᶜāmma)*, for this <siyāsa> is not <the same as> the other. This *madīna fāḍila* is in their <that is, the philosophers'> opinion rare or unlikely to come into being, and they discuss it only hypothetically' [3].

273 ff.) make the same distinction between divine and human laws, and the governments based on them.

[1] See *Q* II. 126 ff. / *B* 302 ff.

[2] Whether this meaning is Ibn Jaldūn's own interpretation or was already in his Arabic source I cannot decide, but it seems to fit the context better than the meaning 'judges, magistrates' corresponding to Plato's *dikastēs* in *Republic* 405a.

[3] See *Q* II. 127 / *B* 303.

His treatment of the philosophers' Ideal State is summary, superficial, even condescending. If he had known al-Fārābī's political writings, especially his *Kitāb taḥṣīl al-saᶜāda*, he would hardly have failed to object to the identification of prophet with philosopher, king, lawgiwer and *imām*. Ibn Rušd's Commentary on Plato's *Republic* must also have been unknown to him, or he would not have said that the *falāsifa* looked upon the Ideal State as a 'hypothesis and supposition'. He would have recognized in Ibn Rušd's criticism of views and institutions of contemporary States in the Maghreb a certain political realism akin to his own to some extent, even if it did not find expression in an independent political theory. The same applies to Ibn Rušd's political evaluation of religion [1]. Ibn Jaldūn did not deem worthy of consideration what appeared to him merely as a theoretical exercise of philosophers. For the Ideal State of the philosophers is for Ibn Jaldūn not in the same category as the Ideal State represented by the rule of the *Šarᶜ*. That was, indeed, once a political reality, and he set himself the task to investigate human society as it was and is, not as it should or might be in theory. In his political thought there is no room for 'hypothesis and supposition'. Only observation and experience count in the sphere of practical politics. Not the metaphysician rules the State, but the man who, supported by religion and/or *ᶜaṣabiyya*, wields power and enforces the obedience of his subjects.

In this sense he criticises Ibn Rušd's attribution of *ḥasab* to 'long establishment of a family in a city <State>' in place of the true reason, namely *ᶜaṣabiyya*. But he excuses him because Ibn Rušd had not grown up in a city where there was *ᶜaṣabiyya* [2]. That means, what we do not experience we cannot know.

[1] Cf. my article, *loc cit.*, p. 265 f. I deal fully with this topic in my Notes to the edition of Averroes' Commentary on Plato's *Republic*, which is in the press (Cambridge University Press).†

[2] De Slane in his translation, *Prolégomènes*, I, 282 f., n. 2, refers to Aristotle's *Rhetoric*, I. c. 5. The passage is I. v, 5/1360 b. I was as unsuccessful as De Slane in tracing Ibn Jaldūn's reference to the Latin version of Ibn Rušd's Commentary on the *K. al-jiṭāba*, Venice 1550, and I am inclined to assume a lacu-

Or, the philosophers claim that the equatorial regions are uninhabited. This claim is disproved by the testimony of eye-witnesses.

The State is built on and maintained by power. Its life is governed by the law of causality. This is the conclusion to which Ibn Jaldūn's study of Politics has led him. The *falāsifa* are concerned with the Highest Good and with individual happiness in the Ideal State of philosophical Reason. This contrast is at the root of Ibn Jaldūn's opposition to them in the realm of Politics.

na with De Slane. The passage should be found on *f.* 34 b r., 11. 15 ff. and before 1. 18 end. See *Q* I. 244 f. / *B* 135.

7

THE CONCEPT OF 'EUDAIMONIA' IN MEDIEVAL ISLAMIC AND JEWISH PHILOSOPHY

A consideration of the concept of *eudaimonia* in the religious philosophy of Islam and Judaism is instructive in that it illustrates how an originally purely philosophical concept was taken over, adapted and transformed by thinkers bound to and by a different religious outlook and tradition. That it could be naturalized in medieval philosophy and could even become its central theme is due to the common ground which existed between Greek-Hellenistic philosophy and the three monotheistic systems. It is the idea of law, with justice as its guiding principle and as the foremost civic virtue. As the highest good *eudaimonia* is aim and object of practical philosophy. It is also the end and purpose of the religious person and community.

It is well known that Stoic, Neo-platonic, Neo-pythagorean, Gnostic and Hermetic ideas — singly or combined in late Neo-platonism — have deeply influenced Islamic and, mainly through it, also Jewish religious philosophy. Their religious bent no doubt paved the way for the acceptance of Platonic and Aristotelian ideas. The monism of a Plotinus, a Proclus and a Porphyry was more akin to a Jew, Christian or Muslim. It is important to remember, therefore, that original Platonic and Aristotelian notions have been accepted and adapted by Muslim and Jewish thinkers, though often in Stoic or Neo-platonic modification. It is with these that I am here concerned, rather with the source than with the actual text from which they are taken. The constituent elements of the concept of beatitude or true happiness such as contemplation, love, pleasure, immortality and the hereafter-culminating in the *homoiosis theou*– go all back to Plato's Dialogues. It is less important to determine whether the Muslim philosophers, the *Falasifa,* have found the idea of ' becoming like God in our actions ' in the *Theaetetus* or in Plotinus' *Enneads* or in a Hellenistic summary of Plato's philosophy which Farabi used for his own treatise *On Plato's Philosophy.* What matters is that Plato assigns the philosopher this duty and this aim and that he explains it as ' becoming just, holy and wise '. For Farabi it constitutes man's highest perfection, his ultimate beatitude. Maimonides equates it with the love of God arising out of the knowledge and perception of God, the goal of a religious person. He introduces this idea in his *Guide to the Perplexed* with the statement that God's actions — his thirteen attributes — are necessary for the government of states. His proof-text is naturally neither Plato nor Plotinus, but a *Midrash.* Yet to look upon *homoiosis theou* as a political duty and necessity is a Greek idea, and Maimonides may well have accepted it from Farabi who defines it as self-improvement to be followed by improving others in house or state. This example illustrates the attraction which Greek philosophy exercised for Muslim and Jewish thinkers, although their concept of God was so different from a Plato or Aristotle. For it is difficult to see how the God of Abraham could at the same time be the god of Aristotle, as Judah Hallewi pointed out and Pascal so well formulated in his reply to Descartes. The personal God of Bible and Koran, the God of the covenant with man, the God of love, mercy and compassion, the demanding God cannot be a mere abstraction, the First Cause, the Demiourgos, the One, the Good, the Beautiful. And yet, the knowledge and perception of God as a religious duty has been interpreted as a philosophical duty to perceive Reality, to ascend from the sensible to the intelligible world, from the physical to the spiritual. This gradual ascent is only possible with the help of the philosophical sciences, chief among them metaphysics. The possession of ethical and intellectual virtues to perfection alone enables man to reach ultimate happiness. Metaphysical truth is contained in the prophetically revealed divine law. But it can only be understood after the study and with the help of philosophy. True happiness is thus accessible only to the metaphysician, as long as the perception of God is man's aim and purpose. But the love of God, though in its highest form necessarily preceded by the knowledge of God, can be won by serving him with our whole being. Some of the later medieval thinkers, especially among the Jews, hold that one need not be a philosopher in order to be a devout servant of God. The love of God can thus bestow beatitude on every sincere believer, even if he is not capable of intellectual perfection. But even the intellectualism of the stricter Aristotelians among Muslims and Jews did not hinder them from granting the humble, naive believer who observes the divine law his share in beatitude in accordance with his capacity.

Eudaimonia, sa'āda in its Arabic and *haṣlaḥah* in its Hebrew form, naturally does not mean the same thing for all religious thinkers. This is not surprising since Plato himself has discovered and stressed different aspects of *eudaimonia* at various stages of his career, as reflected in his Dialogues (*Phaedo, Phaedrus, Philebus, Republic, Laws*); see Festugière, Hackforth). The earlier Dialogues stress the individual beatitude *per se,* the later ones, especially the *Republic* and the *Laws,* attach great importance to the civic responsibilities of the philosopher-ruler. The various aspects are reflected among his medieval disciples, Aristotelians and Neo-platonists alike. It is clear from the apparent conflict between contemplation and action, that is, whether ultimate beatitude is a state of the soul or, in the words of Aristotle, an activity in conformity with virtue, when he stresses in his *E. N.* the priority of active contemplation as the exercise of the highest, the intellectual virtue of wisdom. This agrees with Plato's view that *theoria* must fulfil itself in action: we must not only contemplate the Good, but do it as the result of our intellectual endeavour. It is this interpretation of true happiness as the result of action born of knowledge or intelligence (*phronesis*) which appealed to those Muslims and Jews who saw in the joyous fulfilment of the commandments of the divine law the only sure way to the attainment of beatitude in the perception and love of God. Those who strive after it are happy in this world and blessed in the after-life. Stoic influence — mainly indirectly through later Neo-platonism — and indigenous religious tradition combined account for this emphasis on moral action. Plato is largely preoccupied with the philosopher and sees in his beatific vision the necessary condition for his just and wise government of the city. Thus he says in the *Republic* that the philosopher 'draws nigh unto, and is united with that which truly is' (490 B). The same vision, intensified and for ever, is granted to the purified soul after death, free from the prison of the body and its impurities. Purification, *katharsis*, is an important element on the journey of the soul to its happy destination. Farabi defines true happiness (in his *Madīna fāḍila*) as a stâte ȍf the soul, in which it exists free from matter and tends towards pure substances — Plato's Ideas or Forms — entirely free from corporeality. Such true happiness is only attainable in the ideal state. Avempace (Ibn Bajja), who is exclusively interested in the beatitude of the philosopher, knows that the ideal state makes this beatitude possible. But following the *Phaedo* and not the later *Republic* he allows the metaphysician to withdraw from society in order to concentrate on the perception of reality by rational speculation, which he identifies with the future life. [He is the only Muslim philosopher who rigorously and boldly applies the figurative interpretation of Scripture to gain its hidden, inner meaning]. He has openly abandoned the traditional explanation of the after-life. Whether Farabi and Avicenna have gone so far is at least doubtful, but Averroes certainly adhered to the definition given in the revealed law. Avicenna explicitly states that Muhammad has given the Muslims a clear idea of happiness or misery as concerns the body; the after-life is a religious notion and must be accepted at its face-value. At the same time he stipulates a spiritual happiness for the metaphysician: his rational soul becomes a microcosm which reproduces the order, justice and beauty of the macrocosm. By contemplating the absolute Good and true Beauty, the divine Essence, the rational soul achieves union with the Divine in love and thus gains supreme beatitude. It can only leave the body after having purified the other parts of the soul. This idea is Platonic and developed in Neo-platonism and by its Muslim and Jewish adherents. It is easy to understand how the philosophical eschatology of Plato with its mystical undertones could be appreciated by Muslims and Jews and was adapted with the help of Neo-platonism to their religious eschatology. Plato and his Neo-Platonic continuators enabled these medieval thinkers to give to important tenets of their faith an esoteric, philosophical meaning while at the same time insisting that the masses, incapable of following a demonstrative argument, had to be satisfied with the literal meaning of the metaphors and allegories of Scripture. The teachings of the divine law were binding on all believers, and obedience to the law and all its commandments secured a share in the world-to-come to all — to use a Rabbinic phrase. The philosophers had to conform to authoritative tradition by observing the regulations of the law, by fulfilling the duties of the members (ceremonial) as well as the duties of the heart (the seat of the intellect), that is, the ethical and intellectual precepts, to speak with Bachya, the foremost medieval ascetic pietist thinker. Just as the duties of the heart — foremost the perception of God in his unity — were more important for God-centred beatitude, so was the intelligent profession of right beliefs and convictions the inescapable duty of the religious thinker within his community. This is also Plato's demand for his ideal state.

Only philosophy could satisfy their intellectual zeal and desire to perceive and love God. They were at pains to stress that the aim of philosophy was identical with that of religion, namely to secure happiness and perfection. Truth is one and indivisible. But while religion teaches it in a form accessible to all, philosophy enables the elect intellects to pass beyond the hints contained in the divine law and penetrate to the real meaning of such concepts as providence, retribution, that is, reward and punishment or happiness and misery in the after-life. It would be hazardous to dogmatize on the beliefs and opinions held by the religious thinkers of Islam and Judaism by isolating or by trying to harmonize apparently conflicting statements. The ambiguity of their use of certain terms is of the very essence of their thought. This ambiguity arises from their use of such terms now in a traditional religious sense, in another place in a philosophical connotation. E. g. did they believe in the resurrection of the body and the Day of Judgement as Bible and Koran teach them or rather in the sense in which Plato employs these concepts of the immortal soul in the *Phaedo* (81-82 D) or in the *Laws* (959 AB)? Some, like Avicenna held both views; we need only think of his description of the after-life, quoted before. Avempace is explicit: his seeker after God relies on the unremitting exercise of his intellect, unaided by the prophetic teaching of Muslim law. For him, human perfection consists in the union of the human with the active intellect. It necessarily precedes the consummation of beatitude in the perception of the divine essence.

Ghazali's attack on philosophy has forced the Muslim philosophers on the defensive. Hence Averroes avers that philosophy and divine law share identity of purpose, but he claims that only the metaphysician can, with the help of demonstrative proof, explain the theoretical knowledge which is contained in this law together with practical knowledge, the knowledge of happiness and misery in the future world. Abstract knowledge concerns God and reality; the law commands us to know God, which is the business of philosophy. « True practice », he says, consists in adopting the actions which promote happiness and in avoiding those which lead to misery. They are divided into two; external, physical action — the science concerning them is called jurisprudence (*fiqh*); and the actions of the soul like gratitude, patience and other virtues which the *Shari'a* (Muslim prophetic law) recommends or prohibits — the science concerning them is called asceticism (*zuhd*). He maintains that the prophets issue « religious laws which conform to the truth and impart a knowledge of those actions by which the happiness of the whole of creation is guaranteed ». Philosophy, on the other hand, is concerned with the happiness of the few elect intellects, but only the religious law teaches the masses and leads them to happiness. Right beliefs and convictions, together with moral conduct, secure the happiness of all, philosophers and masses alike. He deliberately excludes from comment Book X of the *Republic*, in particular Plato's rhetorical or dialectical argument about the immortality of the soul and his tale about « the bliss and delight which the happy, just souls attain, and also what the tormented souls reap ». He dismisses these tales as of no consequence. « For the virtues that result from them, are not true virtues ». These tales and myths cannot be proved, but the Koran is true because it is revealed. Only divine law can guarantee the twofold happiness to the believer: earthly well-being and eternal bliss in the hereafter.

It contains certain truth as opposed to Plato's myths. Yet

for Averroes as for his predecessors beatitude is a relative term; it means one thing for the philosophers and another for the masses. The philosopher's happiness depends on his perfection in the practical arts, the ethical, intellectual and speculative virtues, an Aristotelian demand in his *E. N.* Only thus equipped can he reach his human destiny: beatitude in the perception of God.

In general the Jewish medieval thinkers follow their Muslim teachers in their blending of Greek philosophical with traditional-religious features of the originally alien concept of *eudaimonia.* But after Maimonides, towards the end of the creative period of Jewish religious philosophy, a more thorough transformation and even a restoration of the traditional position took place. God and his law are their starting-point and the knowledge and love of God are the end, leading to that communion with God which is ultimate happiness. It is only attainable in the ideal state whose constitution is the law of Moses who is superior to all other prophets. Maimonides distinguishes, with Farabi, between true and alleged beatitude. The former exclusively depends on the revealed law. The latter belongs to the human state based on the *nomos* (in this he goes further than Farabi). Even so, he insists that only intellectual perfection enables man to perceive God as commanded in the divine law and to proceed from the perception to the love of God by imitating his ways. Highest human perfection, active contemplation in the Greek meaning of the term, makes man truly human and is his very own. It corresponds to Aristotle's 'goods of the soul' and brings him immortality.

Again and again, Maimonides claims that man-made law only cares for the physical welfare of the citizens, regulates inter-human relations and prevents injustice and oppression. Yet it neglects man's spiritual side, that which makes him truly human. Only the divine law provides for the soul by its demand of the perception and love of God which philosophy explains as far as human reason can grasp metaphysical truth. In this he is at one with his contemporary Averroes. Both agree that highest perfection, true beatitude must be reserved for the metaphysician who is an intelligent believer. But all believers are enjoined and obliged to fulfil the law. Their joyful obedience enables them to gain its blessings, that is, their share of beatitude. The study of the law is incumbent on all, it leads to the knowledge of God. Yet the true perception of reality, of God and his Universe which he created in his free will out of love for mankind, is an additional duty falling on the philosopher. Insight and full comprehension are his reward.

Other Jewish thinkers, like their Muslim teachers and contemporaries, both Aristotelians and Neo-platonist followers, balance ethical against intellectual perfection, or even give precedence to moral action as a primary religious duty. For them the divine law is a guide to ethics and not to *theoria*. The improvement of morals is a necessary preparation for the attainment of happiness. They add to Plato's cardinal virtues others which have their seat in their religious tradition; these are love of neighbour, humility, devotion, asceticism, a spirit of conciliation, charity (Abraham ibn Daud). Highest perfection and supreme happiness are only assured if the rational soul is in unchallenged command over the other parts, a well known Platonic idea, blended with Aristotle's psychology.

A deliberate turning away from the intellectualism of the Aristotelians has been brought about by Crescas. He has developed Maimonides' concept of the love of God by separating it from the intellectual perception of God as a necessary prelude. He has thus broken the hold which philosophy had over the religious thinkers in respect of man's highest good. The philosophical justification of religious truth is no longer necessary and philosophy is deprived of its position of authority and of its dominant role in the process of attaining supreme happiness. Every believer who fulfils spontaneously the commandments of God's perfect law can rise to the love of him who loves his creatures. Philosophy is not condemned and banished: it is still a legitimate way to God, but no longer the only one. It is definitely subordinated to the self-sufficiency of revelation which guarantees happiness to all who live under God's law.

8

SOME OBSERVATIONS ON THE PHILOSOPHICAL THEORY OF PROPHECY IN ISLAM[1]

It is generally agreed that the theory of prophecy as developed by the *Falâsifa* is influenced by Greek-Hellenistic ideas about divination. Recently two important contributions to the difficult question of the precise origin of that theory appeared which have greatly advanced our understanding of it. R. Walzer(2) has shown that Al-Fârâbî's application of *mimesis* to prophecy goes back to Middle Platonism, whereas F. Rahman(3) claims the Stoic Panaitius as the source of the whole theory. It may, therefore, not be out of place to offer here a few critical observations.

The first consideration must be that the *Falâsifa* in their philo-

1. I am indebted to my publishers W. Kohlhammer Verlag, Stuttgart for their permission to use Exkurs II: *Bemerkungen zur Theorie der Prophetie bei den mittelalterlichen islamischen und jüdischen Philosophen* of my book on *Griechisches Erbe in der jüdischen Religionsphilosophie des Mittelalters* (1960) for this contribution. I am here only concerned with the *Falâsifa* and Islam and not with the Jewish religious thinkers and Judaism. For a fuller discussion of the concept of prophecy the reader is referred to chapter 4 of this book, entitled *Sendungsprophetie und natürliche Prophetie,* and to my earlier studies, published in *Islamic Culture* (The Place of Politics in the Philosophy of Al-Fârâbî, xxix. 3, 1955; The Place of Politics in the Philosophy of Ibn Bâjja, xxv. 1, 1951) and in *BSOAS* (The Place of Politics in the Philosophy of Ibn Rushd, xv, 2, 1953); and my book *Political Thought in Medieval Islam,*[3] Cambridge 1968.
2. In his contribution to *Hellenic Studies* 1957, entitled "Al-Fârâbî's Theory of Prophecy and Divination".
3. In his important book *Prophecy in Islam,* London 1958

sophical explanation of a fundamental religious concept started from inescapable presuppositions of their faith as Muslims: the prophetic revelation of the divine will in form of an all-embracing law announced by the messenger of God. This recognition conditioned their attitude to Greek-Hellenistic ideas about the nature of dreams and their interpretation, about divination and soothsaying. It demanded a religious transformation and adaptation of the concept of law in Plato and Aristotle. It determined their explanation of the prophecy of Muḥammad, of his activity as a lawgiver and worker of miracles. In this connection it is noteworthy that both Ibn Sînâ and Ibn Rushd do not apply the theory of emanation to Muḥammad, just as the Jews exempt Moses from the operation of natural prophecy(1).

It is irrelevant whether their adherence to a traditional tenet was their inmost conviction or a concession to orthodoxy. It has, at any rate, imposed severe restrictions and limitations on their freedom to apply philosophical concepts to their exposition of traditional beliefs and convictions.

In the realm of practical philosophy, it has necessiated an essential transformation of Plato's concept of the ideal ruler. The philosopher-king and lawgiver had also to be a prophet in the ideal-religious-state. The prophet must be a philosopher, but he must be more than that to fulfil the basic demands of the religious law. Only Ibn Sînâ and Ibn Rushd among the *Falâsifa* have succeeded in overcoming the rational incompatibility implied in this "more": they draw a fundamental distinction between divine and human law in origin, scope and competence. Ibn Sînâ is not so consistent and unequivocal as Ibn Rushd who had, moreover, to take note of Al-Ghazâlî. This emerges from Ibn Sînâ's use of the terms prophets, prophetic lawgiver who promulgates divinely inspired laws in his own formulation, and the prophet *par excellence* who simply announces the divine law. In all

1. Cf. my *Averroes' Commentary on Plato's "Republic"* [3], Cambridge 1969, II. 1.7 (p. 61/177); *Political Thought in Medieval Islam*, pp. 57 f. 127 ff., 144 f., 151, 183 ff.

probability it was only Ibn Rushd who adhered strictly to the traditional concept of *tanzîl*. The other *Falâsifa* have identified the angel with the Active Intellect and thus largely emptied *tanzîl* of its traditional content and substituted the philosophical theory of the intellect for it.

Be that as it may two facts stand out in this encounter of Islam with the philosophy of Plato: one is the correlation between the Law and the philosophical qualification of the ruler, and the other is the *Falâsifa's* recognition of the political significance of the divinely revealed law brought by the prophet to the community of believers, a law that is alone capable of ensuring the twofold happiness of body and soul in this world and in the hereafter. The *Falâsifa* in so far as one can treat them as a group took their stand on Islam and its law and attempted a philosophical justification and explanation of their faith; they did not make out of Islam a philosophical abstraction for the few elect and did not leave the masses with Islam as a popular religion. Moreover, there is a deep significance in the fact that the impetus to a deliberate political interpretation of the *Sharî'a* came from Plato and Aristotle and not from Neoplatonism or the Stoa, no matter how much the *Falâsifa* looked at them through the eyes of their later commentators.

Nor should we forget that the ideal Islamic state, the *khilâfa*, is understood by the *Falâsifa* no less than by the jurists as a religious and political unity. Classical Islamic political theory has formulated this essential, characteristic unity. Acquaintance with the practical philosophy of the Greeks–in particular with Plato's political philosophy–made the *Falâsifa* see more clearly the political significance of the *Sharî'a*. It also conditioned their philosophical interpretation of the political thought expressed by the jurists in constitutional law.

The Muslims are not only citizens of the Islamic state, they are also and perhaps even more so members of the *umma*. Hence, prophecy as the transmitter of the divine law gains the ascendancy over all other qualifications of the ideal ruler. Only this *Sharî'a* bridges and eliminates in the religious realm proper the gulf that naturally exists on the intellectual plane, between the few elect philosophers and the broad masses. The *nomos* of the Greeks keeps this gulf open: it only secures the metaphysician's highest perfection, his ultimate happiness by his intellectual exertion.

On the other hand, the prophetically revealed divine law guarantees to all its adherents–through the wholehearted fulfilment of its commandments–such happiness as is appropriate to each individual believer. That is to say that the distinction on the intellectual plane between the philosophers and the masses is not blurred, let alone eliminated. But all believers are linked together as the *umma* in a higher unity of faith (1). The metaphors and images of the divine law enable all believers without exception to gain true convictions and right opinions. But their deeper meaning is only open to the seeker after truth through demonstrative argument. But since religion and philosophy teach one and the same truth, prophecy ensures the happiness of all even though the degree of intellectual perception may differ from person to person.

These general observations were necessary for a critical appreciation of F. Rahman's penetrating exposition of the theory of prophecy in Islam; for he underestimates the Islamic origin and basis of the views of Al-Fârabî and Ibn Sînâ on the political character of prophecy (2). This is evident from his neglect to take into account the two formative concepts of *umma* and *khilâfa*, just discussed. The idealisa-

---

1. Asín Palacios, *La Tesis de la Necessidad de la Revelacion en Islam y en la Escolastica* in: *Al-Andalus,* III, 1935, pp 345 ff.; my *Political Thought...* pp. 129, 151, 179, f., 184, especially 205 with n. 92 (p. 298) which discusses S. van den Bergh's view that the three classes of Ibn Rushd are derived from Aristotle (*Metaphysica* A. 3. 995a. 6), cf. Averroes' *Tahâfut al-Tahâfut* II, p. 98)
2. Cf. the passages adduced in n. 1, p. 344; a; so L. Gardet's profound *La Pensée religieuse d'Avicenne,* Paris 1951.

tion of the first four successors of Muḥammad, the *khulafâ râshidûn*, by the historians of early Islam has not only been accepted by the jurists who formulated constitutional theory and law, but also by the *Falâsifa*. It is in these concepts and institutions, it seems to me, that we see the source for the political evaluation of prophecy and of its principal function, the promulgation of an all-embracing law on the part of the *Falâsifa*, and not in the threefold theology of Panaitius, as Rahman claims(1). This legislative function constitutes the link with the philosopher-king of Plato. Rahman rightly observes that "there is nothing specifically religious" in Plato's conception, no revelation is required. He, therefore, looks for and finds the origin of the Islamic combination of revelation and legislative activity of the ruler in the hero- and king-worship of early antiquity and their later rationalisation(2). This seems highly improbable; for monotheists reared on the fundamental concept of revelation and revealed law would not be influenced by mythology, even if rationalized by Stoic philosophers. But Rahman interprets Al-Fârâbî and Ibn Sînâ on the basis of this assumption, without paying attention to different interpretations put forward by other scholars over a number of years(3). One is justified in doubting Rahman's claim that the Stoic doctrine of three kinds of divine worship is reflected in the *Falâsifa*'s differentiation of three aspects of prophecy. He is of the opinion that natural philosophical worship corresponds to the philosophical interpretation of prophecy as revelation influencing the intellect; mythical worship taught by poets to revelation influencing the imagination; and legally decreed worship

1. In his *op. cit.*, pp. 52 ff. and particularly the notes, p. 80 ff.
2. *Ibid.*, p. 56f.
3. Cf. e. g. Leo Strauss, *Philosophie und Gesetz*, Berlin 1935; L. Gardet, *op. cit.* especially chapters iv and v which present his convincingly argued opinion that Ibn Sînâ's concept of prophecy stems from Islam and not from Greek philosophy. Cf. also my already quoted studies, in particular the study on Al-Fârâbî and *Griechisches Erbe* Exkurs II, n. 13.

(the *theologia civilis*) to the *Sharî'a*(1). It is true, he modifies this analogy by the word "broadly" and, moreover, admits that the *Falâsifa* as monotheists in their allegorizing interpretation do not so sharply reject Islam as the Greek rationalists have done with regard to the popular religion of their age. Islam and Judaism, he grants, approach in their symbolism as nearly "the higher truth" of philosophy as possible.

Rahman finds the key to this close approximation in Muslim eclecticism "where prophetic revelation, the intellectual consummation of a philosopher and the poetic art of imaginative creativity were all combined in one ideal personality". Thus "it becomes still easier to ground the law in a religious basis of revelation", thanks to the "actual image of the Prophet Muḥammad as it was developed in the mind of the Muslim Community..." In fact, the author does not attach any importance to this vital fact; indeed, he thinks the idea of Muḥammad as a philosopher as forced as the corresponding one of Moses in Philo. The comparison with Philo is rather unfortunate, for the intellectual perception of God is a fundamental Biblical command. The intellectualism of the medieval Jewish thinkers who are so strongly influenced by the *Falâsifa* finds its justification precisely in this commandment. It has actually made "the natural" explanation prophecy possible. Surely, it is no different in Islam.

Turning very briefly to Ibn Sînâ, we must remember that he clearly distinguished between the prophet and the philosopher, as Rahman states himself. This is not the place to follow Rahman's exemplary discussion of the theory of the intellect in Al-Fârâbî and Ibn Sînâ. Nobody can in future ignore the first chapter of his book. The difficulties in our way of understanding Ibn Sînâ's theory in itself and in relation to Al-Fârâbî's are fully set out there. But a further complication must be added: Ibn Sînâ assumes different degrees of prophecy, even different kinds, for he could not possibly put on the

1. In *op. cit.*, p. 56 with n. 86 (p. 87 f.).

same level Greek "prophets" like Pythagoras, Socrates and Plato with the messenger of Allah, the Prophet Muḥammad who made known the law of God to his countrymen. When Al-Fârâbî demands moral and intellectual preparation to gain certain knowledge through the study of philosophy, Ibn Sînâ insists that the prophet is distinguished from the philosopher precisely through a trait peculiar to himself alone, that is, that he is capable of spontaneous intuitive perception and that he can perform miracles. The prophet being above the grade of the philosopher, is prepared to hear the word of God and to see the angels, through the intermediacy of the Holy Spirit, i.e. the Active Intellect(1). Rahman traces Ibn Sînâ's theory to Aristotle's *anchinoia*,(2) but in its development he is indebted to Plotin and the Stoa(3). Yet, he finds that Ibn Sînâ shrinks from following his philosophical guides all the way. For he is inclined to see the source of revelation outside man, as a transcendental force(4). To my mind, this transcendental principle is no other than God, namely God who revealed the Qur'an. Ibn Sînâ distinguishes, as Rahman also states, between the prophecy of the prophets and the prophetic activity of the mystics(5). This is surely a pointer in the same religious direction. But Rahman does not admit that a conscious religious attitude and, resulting from it, honest scruples to draw the final logical deductions from a strictly philosophical approach and perception, are responsible for this distinction and for the obligatory axiom of religious faith.

The same applies to Ibn Rushd even more, he is_I think

---

1. Cf. my *Political Thought*, pp. 144 ff. with notes which give the relevant passages in Ibn Sînâ.
2. Cf. Rahman, *op. cit.*, p. 31 and his *Avicenna's Psychology*, Oxford 1952, pp. 93 ff. and my *Political Thought*, p. 283. n. 8.
3. Cf. Rahman, *Prophecy in Islam*, pp. 28f. (n. 32) and p. 66 (ns. 3, 8, 9).
4. Cf. *ibid.*, p. 33.
5. Cf. *ibid.*, p. 39 and my *Political Thought*, pp. 156 f.

significantly only mentioned in a number of notes (perhaps because he did not accept the philosophical theory of prophecy?). To my mind, Ibn Sînâ wanted to separate Muḥammad from the other prophets, in particular from the aforementioned Greek "prophets". He did not aim at the difference between the prophet worthy to receive *waḥy*, revelation, and the mystic whose *ilhâm*, inspiration, enabled him to prophetic action. Moreover, I am convinced that the *Falâsifa* were compelled, as Muslims, to modify the strictly philosophical explanation of the human intellect in relation to the Active Intellect. Only through such a modification were they able to safeguard the extraordinary character of the prophet *par excellence*, even though perfect imagination differentiates the natural prophet from the philosopher.

One further point: Ibn Sînâ holds that prophecy is necessary to preserve mankind and to attain ultimate happiness. He says: "When such a man does exist, it is necessary that he should promulgate law among people by the command and permission of God, through His revelation and His sending down upon him the Holy Spirit"(1). It follows from this quotation that God is not free: He *must* send a prophetic lawgiver. A possible explanation is that Ibn Sînâ was concerned to justify the religious law and its divine-prophetic origin *vis-à-vis* the philosophical lawgiver of Plato. Ibn Sînâ did this at the price of getting involved in theological difficulties the consequences of which were in all likelihood not apparent to him. For what mattered to him before all was the character and purpose of this law: knowledge of the Creator, of the Hereafter, Reward and Punishment and obedience through worship of God and justice in human relations(2).

It is curious that Rahman should see the true aim of the state and its laws in spreading philosophy among men as far as

1. Cf. Rahman, p. 87 (n. 81), a quotation from Ibn Sînâ's *K. al-najât.*
2. Cf. Ibn Sînâ, *K. al-ishârât,* p. 200 and also *K. al-najât,* pp. 498 ff., quoted in my *Political Thought* pp. 149, 283 f. (n. 10).

possible, for he quotes a similar passage. I do not know where Ibn Sînâ says so, but Rahman rightly continues "and bringing them near unto God". Yet he discovers in this aim the Greek doctrine of "the interdependence of theory and practice which has produced the amalgam of Muḥammad cum Plato-Aristotle"(1).

In view of Rahman's tendency to trace the origin of the theory of prophecy to the philosophy of antiquity and to place philosophy above jurisprudence I should like to end this brief birthday tribute with two quotations from Ibn Rushd. The first comes from his *Commentary on Plato's "Republic"* and concerns the end of man: "What the religious laws in our own time think of this matter is what God wills. The only way to know what it is that God wills in respect of them is (through) prophecy. If you investigate the laws, this law is divided into abstract knowledge alone such as our religious law commands regarding the perception of God_and into practice_such as the ethical virtues it enjoins. Its intention as regards this purpose is essentially the same as that of philosophy. . ."(2) The second stands in Ibn Rushd's *Faṣl al -maqâl*. The passage states the identity of purpose of philosophy and religious law in similar terms thus: "the aim of the law is only to teach true knowledge and true practice, and true knowledge is the knowledge of God and the other "Existing Things" in their reality, in particular the *Sharî'a*, and the knowledge of happiness and misery in the future world. True practice consists in adopting the actions which promote happiness and in avoiding those which promote misery. The knowledge of these actions is called practical science; they are divided into two: external, physical action, and the science concerning them is called *Fiqh*; and the actions of the soul like gratitude, patience and other virtues which the *Sharî'a* recommends or prohibits and the science concerning them is called

1. Cf. Rahman, *op. cit.*, p. 58 and my *Griechisches Erbe*, Exkurs I: Begriff and Bedeutungswandel der Eudämonie, pp. 73 f. (on *'ilm wa-'amal*)
2. Cf. my *Averroes' Commentary on Plato's "Republic"*, p. 66/185.

Zuhd and the sciences of the hereafter" (1).

1. Cf. ed. Müller, pp. 22 f., also quoted in my *Political Thought*, pp. 179, 293 (n. 13); and cf. my *The Place of Politics in the Philosophy of Ibn Rushd*, pp. 258 ff., section "The Supremacy of the *Sharī'a* and the Place of Prophecy in the Philosophy of Averroes".

PART II

RELIGION AND POLITICS IN MODERN ISLAM

9

THE ROLE OF ISLAM IN THE MODERN NATIONAL STATE

THE visitor to contemporary Muslim States in South East Asia and the Middle East is struck by the complexity of a situation which, viewed with the eyes of a student of classical Islam, is at once familiar and disturbing.[1] It is familiar in so far as he expects to find unresolved tensions and inner conflicts caused by the impact of Western political, social and legal ideas and institutions upon a way of life at once comprehensive and essentially static, medieval and unfavourably placed in the face of rapid change and desperate need for adaptation and adjustment. It is disturbing because the masses are largely inarticulate owing to a low literacy-rate, and a standard of living which at its best is just above the poverty line and at its worst near starvation level, with consequent dangerous inertia. Naturally, the situation varies considerably from country to country, but on the whole the difference is rather one of degree than of substance.

The most frustrating aspect of a confused situation in Pakistan is the uncertainty of many of the intellectuals. There is a notable absence of purposeful direction, of clear thinking, and of a broadly based, concerted effort at translating into political action the aspirations of a young nation with a long history of significant cultural achievement. One gets the impression that much of the drive, energy and determination is, at the moment at any rate, concentrated in the

[1] A generous grant made by the Rockefeller Foundation to the University of Cambridge to enable me to study the problem of constitutional theory and law in contemporary Islam has been used to visit Muslim countries like Pakistan Malaya, Iran and Turkey. This study tour will be continued in North Africa. The present short article tries to sum up the situation in Pakistan and Malaya in particular. The conclusions are necessarily provisional.

President, his Ministers and a devoted band of civil servants. This is not to belittle the considerable achievements made under appalling difficulties since the formation of the State in 1947. We need only think of the transformation of Karachi into a large modern city and port. But one sadly misses the initial enthusiasm among the people at large to redeem the pledge of the Muslim League before partition to set up a separate State for the Muslims so that they might live a life of freedom, dignity and well-being as Muslims. The government is making a tremendous effort to raise the standard of living, and especially of education, surely a long-term job. The role of Islam in the process of rousing the people to a great national effort and to a sense of civic responsibility has been a serious problem from the beginning of the young State. It is for this reason that much of the present article deals with Islam as an issue in the constitutional field. Constitution-making was a prolonged business until it—temporarily—culminated in the 1956 Constitution which was, however, suspended when Field-Marshal Ayub Khan seized power in 1958. We are here concerned with views and attitudes of Pakistanis in all walks of life, not with the debates of the former Constituent Assembly nor with books and pamphlets about an Islamic constitution. The same applies to Malaya.†

Tensions and Conflicts

Before the Western observer may presume to pass even the most guarded and provisional judgment, he must remember that Muslims in Malaya and in the subcontinent of India have only quite recently attained independent Statehood. He must also take into serious consideration the human situation and its background before independence.

While we could hardly imagine a greater temperamental divergence than exists between Pakistani and Malay Muslims, they have some fundamental factors in common which go a long way towards helping us to understand their attitudes when faced with problems of modern State- and nationhood in a rapidly changing and essentially unstable world. What

European nations were able to evolve and develop gradually over centuries, newly independent States in Asia and Africa must achieve in a matter of a few years, or at best decades. Adjustments to modern science and technology are not the most burning and difficult issue; to attune their inherited culture and traditions to modern ways of thinking is a grave problem. It is not a matter of acquiring skills, but of adopting different attitudes, and perhaps even values.

It is human factors and problems of the political organisation resulting from liberation from foreign rule and tutelage which present Muslims today (and the Western student) with baffling and rather intractable problems. On the human side, we must recognise that the impact of Western " ideology " is strongest upon those intellectual circles which, educated in Europe or America, are often considerably less imbued than their anti-Western traditionalist fellow-citizens with a sound knowledge of Islam as a religious way of life founded on an all-embracing law for which the believer claims divine origin and prophetic perfection as well as complete adequacy to solve all problems at all times. They live, so to speak, on two levels simultaneously: intellectually they are " modern," with a Western academic training and a scientific outlook which is, as far as traditional law and, to a much lesser degree, beliefs and convictions, are concerned, historical-critical. But emotionally they are deeply attached to Islamic culture, civilisation and history, and, however vague their knowledge of it may be, are proud of their spiritual heritage. Far too rarely are far too few Western students aware of this parallel existence today. They expect and demand, without any justification in present circumstances, a fully integrated personality acting rationally in the context of a modern national State and society.

Nationalism, Indian Islam and British Rule

The human situation is closely linked with the political factor, an intense nationalism. This lack of Islamic knowledge and understanding is often explained as the negative result of education under British rule. The British favoured and furthered a Western education of a type designed to produce suitable candidates for the lower cadres of the Indian Civil Service. The same applies to British possessions in South East Asia. In Pakistan, no doubt, it is an important contributory factor to the widespread ignorance of Islam among the educated classes, as distinct from the largely illiterate rural population and urban " proletariat " still naïvely believing and practising a popular Islam influenced by Hinduism. But it is not the whole explanation, for it is at least matched by the internal Muslim neglect of customary traditional training and religious learning which was in the past one of the most characteristic and positive features of classical Islam. This neglect dates back to the later Mughal period and the low ebb of the position of Indian Muslims after the mutiny of 1857. This, coupled with anti-Westernism and the rejection of the education which the British provided in India, led to the large-scale exclusion of the Muslims from the professions and the civil service. It is part of the irony of the situation that those Pakistanis who no longer subscribe to the unalterable, eternally valid and obligatory Islamic law, draw their inspiration from their own history in India under Mughal rule, both for a modernised Islam built into the fabric of the State and for a separation of " religion " from " politics," reducing Islam to a religion of and for the individual citizen—a matter of his own conscience and choice.

It is noteworthy that many intelligent, patriotic Pakistanis conveniently blame British imperialism for the unsatisfactory state of Muslim education. This sometimes, especially among the younger generation, leads to the peculiar symptom that an emotional attachment to Islam constitutes the answer to " colonialism " and " imperialism," the twin roots of all evil. The result is often a rather confused, barren thinking that moves relentlessly in a vicious circle. Such a combination is unfortunately not at all conducive to a calm assessment of the relative value and significance of both Islamic and Western components of Pakistani State and society. It shows itself in the first place in a dangerous confusion of an Islamic with a Muslim State, and results in ambiguity, indecision and even apathy which every well-wisher of Pakistan must deplore. There are many people who value Islamic ethics and believe that it could be an important formative influence on a viable and vigorous State playing its full part in the world today. It is to be hoped that the new system of education, now being implemented, will rapidly remedy this malaise.

The Islamic State

An Islamic State—at least in classical theory, though rarely in practice—is based without equivocation on the Law of Islam as it has crystallised in the four orthodox schools in a historical situation vastly different from the contemporary scene. Hence, its wholesale application to modern social and economic life is extremely difficult, if not impossible, without radical adjustments and modifications amounting to considerable reforms of legal concepts and injunctions. At the same time it must seek to preserve the spirit of the primary root of the prophetically revealed law, the Qur'an. Yet, the traditionalist orthodox elements are naturally not prepared even to contemplate this, let alone carry it out. Such a reform would affect in the first place the position of women (marriage and divorce, inheritance, etc.) and banking and insurance (interest, etc.).

" Modernists " who genuinely want to harmonise the ideals and ideas of Islam with a democratic State, particularly through the social ethics of Islam, underrate the complexity of the task of bridging the gap which has arisen over the last two or three centuries, when Islamic law has largely lost its flexibility in a world whose attitudes and institutions have been continually subjected to revolutionary changes.

Islam never had a reform and, apart from Turkey, no Muslim—certainly not in Pakistan or Malaya—would ever use the word " reform " or admit that any modification that may be necessary constitutes a reform.

Paradoxically enough, however, the much deplored and resented British rule has, in fact, provided a means in the law in force during the British occupation that can be used to effect such a blending of tradition and modernity and that can, with certain amendments, be taken over and applied in the sovereign State of Pakistan. However, it is hardly sufficient that a law is not repugnant to Qur'an and Sunnah, to borrow a phrase from the defunct Constitution of 1956. In order to be the effective law of the land Islamic law must be positive; it must provide the legal framework for an Islamic State in our time; it must rule supreme in the spheres of public and private law; it must provide for criminal and civil legislation. Nothing else would constitute an Islamic State, and this is precisely what its champions, foremost among them Abul A'la Maududi, advocate with more logic than political realism and accurate assessment of the needs of contemporary society. Muhammad Asad, another advocate of an Islamic State, reduces the minimum requirements of Islamic law to what Qur'an and Sunnah have commanded or forbidden, thus excluding the whole corpus of *Fiqh* (codified Islamic Law). This is a much more reasonable and practicable proposition, but it may be seriously doubted whether the outcome could be rightly called an Islamic State in the apostolic succession of the medieval jurists.

Mr. Parwez similarly would build an Islamic State solely on the principles of the Qur'an and the example of the prophet Muhammad. He would recognise of the Sunnah (the exemplary life, practices and sayings of Muhammad) only that which is clearly in agreement with the Qur'an interpreting the Qur'an itself in the wake of the rationalist Sir Sayyid Ahmad Khan; he would build on his liberal interpretation an Islamic State fully consonant with Qur'anic principles on the one hand and with the spirit and practice of parliamentary democracy, as we understand it, on the other. The majority of the members of the legislature must decide what he calls the by-laws, *i.e.*, detailed laws based on the immutable principles of the Qur'an. The 'ulamā (the learned in Islamic Law) should be represented and able to argue their case, but decision must rest with a majority naturally composed largely of laymen, including non-Muslims.

Many distinguished judges and lawyers hold similar views. They are convinced that the existing (British) law can easily be brought into line with Qur'anic requirements. It is true that the Qur'an is today, as it has always been, a guide to a life of justice and righteousness providing sound principles upon which a polity can be built. Its actual legal stipulations are few, but very precise. Much, therefore, hinges upon their interpretation if the pressing needs of social and economic life of a struggling nation are to be met. It is only by ignoring historical precedent, as Mr. Muhammad Asad does, *i.e.*, the whole development of medieval Islamic Law, and of historical continuity, that the unfettered exercise of *ijtihād* (independent legal decision based on a rational interpretation of Qur'an (and Sunnah)) can lead to a new law. While the result may be some kind of an Islamic State, it will be vastly different from what the jurists of Islam understand by a State based on traditional Islamic law. A procedure such as this would amount to a radical reform. It would require a historical-critical approach to Qur'an and Sunnah, upon which alone the law should be based—a far-reaching departure from the time-hallowed practice of considering the whole range of previous decisions by the jurists throughout the generations right back to the early Caliphate. I can see little likelihood that this will be attempted without first agreeing on the meaning of an Islamic State and what the correct interpretation of the Qur'an is. Besides, what will be the criteria for determining what is and what is not authentic Sunnah?

The Muslim State

There are many thoughtful Pakistanis who oppose an Islamic State of any kind because they are convinced that religion should be kept out of politics. This applies in particular to personally devout, practising Muslims who consider Islam the private concern of the citizen, and who want to create a Pakistani State and nation in which Muslims, Hindus and

Christians enjoy equal rights and owe equal duties as citizens. The founder of the State, Muhammad Ali Jinnah, strove after the realisation of this ideal.

Apart from the minorities, there are also " secularised " Muslims who would consider an Islamic State, especially one of the orthodox pattern, a grave infringement of their freedom of conscience. The prophet of Islam himself declared that there must be no compulsion in religion, and while he, no doubt, had in mind non-Muslims who must not be forced into conversion, there is nothing to prevent us from applying his saying to Muslims.

This is where new attitudes come in and different values have to be recognised. One vital difference (compared with the medieval position) lies in the modern attitude to religion and faith. In the Middle Ages, faith was a universally accepted element of human nature, and the generality of men were believers. In the case of Islam, the Middle Ages have never ended; the term is meaningless, as far as traditional Islam is concerned. Hence, the very basis of Islamic law, faith, is being denied or at best seriously questioned by many today. Those devout Muslims who insist on its rule must squarely face the present human situation. It is not enough to equate agnosticism and atheism with Western " ideology," and to condemn it out of hand as alien to everything Islam stands for. It is too facile a deflection from the real universal crisis besetting religion all over the world today. Immorality, sexual promiscuity and rank materialism may, and to my mind do, have a good deal to do with the absence of a sincerely-held religious faith and its moral discipline. But they are symptoms of a disease which has not been caused by " the West " and its " ideology." While it is easy for us Westerners to point this out to our Muslim friends, it takes more than logical argument to free the minds of men in newly-independent States from suspicion and hostility. For the memory of a very recent colonial past is all too fresh in their minds. We have bequeathed the theory and practice of law and order, a tradition of an efficient, honest civil service, as well as good roads and military installations. But we did very little to solve the social problems of poverty, overcrowding and disease on the Indian subcontinent. The governments of India and Pakistan are therefore faced with a big problem which, in spite of generous aid and five-year plans, is far from being easy and quick to solve, especially as long as population growth cannot be checked effectively. Nor should we forget that even the most humane and benevolent foreign rule tends to breed resentment and a feeling of inferiority which only time can assuage. Real co-operation between us, urgently needed if independent statehood is to have any meaning and is to be used to solve economic and social problems, can only begin when mutual trust and confidence have been established on the basis of a true equality of minds.

A further, not unimportant difficulty is created by past misunderstanding, both conscious and unconscious, and misrepresentation of Islam by Western Orientalists. Where Western presentation of Islamic culture and civilisation (religion, ethics, law and institutions) has erred, it is easily mistaken for a manifestation of " imperialism."

While our legacy of law and order and of a clean administration is highly appreciated, the parlous state of education and the lack of a sound knowledge and understanding of traditional Islam is strongly resented. Hence, the West is saddled by the traditionalists with the responsibility for a widespread ignorance of traditional values and institutions among the intellectual *élite* who enjoyed a Western education. No wonder, then, that any " reform " of that tradition designed to make it blend with a modern outlook and to facilitate the inevitable changes which a modern economy and a society based on it require, has to contend with strong opposition. This opposition is very complex and by no means confined to the guardians of orthodoxy and to fanatics. For it is charged with emotion as well as with intellectual conviction. We, who witness the crumbling of " Western " values in our own house and do very little about it, should view the sustained effort in Pakistan to build a modern State in which Islam must, by definition, play its part, with sympathy and patient understanding. This is especially needed when we want to assess the tortuous process of constitution-making, an issue in the public life of the young nation which has assumed an importance quite out of proportion when seen in the context of the struggle for mere physical survival and growth. Its significance derives from the undeniable fact that it reflects the long-drawn-out battle between those who look back to the glory of early Islam and its astounding flowering and imposing achievement, imagining it can simply be revived here and now, and those who, while emotionally attached to Islam, desire a modern State which combines the best the West can offer with the principles and values of Islam, without accepting its timebound elements and institutions.

The sympathetic observer—if I may speak personally—goes away after months of friendly discussion puzzled by the confusion between the concepts of an Islamic State—as described—and a Muslim State, *i.e.*, a secular State the majority of whose citizens are Muslims of varying degrees of observance or non-observance, but attached to Islamic culture and history, to the ethics of the Qur'an and the many considerable achievements in all fields of human endeavour. The student of classical Islam especially cannot escape a feeling of frustration; surveying the scene he becomes aware of the painful process of searching for an ideal which can and must inspire the nation to find fulfilment, an ideal that at the same time combines the values of Islamic culture with those of Western civilisation. Reluctantly he will arrive at the conclusion that no formal constitutional document, be it imposed by the government or arrived at through free discussion ending in a majority vote, can determine the character of the State and the spiritual basis of national life. The battle of the mind has still to be fought to a reasonable conclusion allowing State and society to develop organically towards a modern Islam. For it seems obvious that the only alternative attractive enough to rally the people to a common effort and achievement is communism. To Asia and Africa communism appears as an ideal unsullied by " imperialism " and " colonialism." Though it has not achieved a classless society or led to the withering of the State, it does tackle the material side of life which is of paramount, often of exclusive, importance for the millions of undernourished men and women whose newly-won freedom can mean little to them in these conditions.

Education for Citizenship

Yet Islam, with its doctrine of social justice and equality, can supply all the needs, physical and spiritual, of people who have lived under it for centuries, provided it is brought home and demonstrated to them as a good, workable system.

This is a long-term business seriously begun by a government bent on eradicating illiteracy. The government's new education plan provides for instruction in the tenets of Islam, its history and institutions. Naturally enough, Islamic instruction can only be a part of a whole. The larger part should be devoted to training citizens able to contribute towards the stability and growing well-being of the State which, on slender natural resources, must establish industries in order to achieve a viable economy and a flourishing society. Everywhere today the stress is on technology and science. Where there is a sound humanistic tradition, such as exists in the West, a balance will, we hope, be struck, and personal as well as collective happiness result eventually. However, where an underdeveloped country emerges from foreign domination, the stress is necessarily placed on subjects of instruction which lead to the rapid training of technologists and civil servants. The requirements of strong physical foundations of the State and of an economy which adequately supports a population growing far too quickly are no doubt responsible for the fact that Islamic subjects are only optional in the upper forms. This is unfortunate, because the adolescent needs most the ethical training which religion can best provide during the formative stage of his character-building. One can only hope that the compulsory stage of Islamic instruction will not only lay a sound and lasting foundation, but will be such as to make the pupil of the upper forms wish to use the optional stage to good advantage. When beset by the problems of growing maturity he needs guidance most;

when assailed by doubts, he requires the guidance of enlightened teachers in his critical examination of faith, doctrine and morals.

Here one comes up against the practical difficulties inherent in a system of integrated education with Islam at the centre. There are neither suitable textbooks nor teachers capable of using them for the dissemination of Islamic ideals and ideas. Hence, the present government has implemented the provision, made in the 1956 Constitution, to establish centres of Islamic research whose primary task it is to make use of the tools of critical scholarship in order to present Islam in terms intelligible to a modern generation. This is a sound move, but it is obvious that it will take a long time until Muslim scholars have produced this new presentation of Islam so that it can then be popularised in textbooks for teachers and, finally, for schools. Even then, formal education can merely teach the values and principles of Islam. It cannot endow them with life. The home must be the testing ground for their application in daily life.

With the gradual emancipation of women, an end towards which the All-Pakistan Women's Association is striving hard and successfully, much of the responsibility for a home in which Islam is a living force and guiding principle will devolve on the mother. APWA has been pressing for greater safeguards for the married woman as regards marriage and divorce, and the President's recent Ordinance on Marriage and Family Laws goes a long way towards bringing the status of married women in line with that in Western society. Polygamy is severely restricted, and divorce can be sought by the wife under certain conditions, in particular if the husband has taken a second wife contrary to the provisions of their marriage. But because polygamy is permitted in the Qur'an, provided the husband is willing and able to accord equal justice to all his wives (he may have four), the President's measure has met with protests claiming it was un-Islamic. This shows that reform of any part of Islamic law is apt to arouse strong opposition in orthodox circles.

It makes one wonder whether modern social conditions can be created so long as traditional Islam is actively associated with political life. Perhaps those who plead for a secular State in which religion is the private concern of the citizen are right. One is inclined to agree with them at this juncture. Reform does not seem feasible until and unless knowledge and understanding of Islam, its teachings and institutions, has become the property of the young and coming generations.

Yet, one cannot but ask with concern and apprehension what is to happen in the meantime. The pace of life is such that the time-factor is very important. The fear that unless Islam is firmly anchored in the fabric of the State it will go by default is real. Perhaps to declare Islam the State religion, with proper safeguards for religious minorities such as were incorporated in the defunct Constitution, would at least temporarily stabilise the position of Islam in the modern State of Pakistan in the way in which this has been done in Malaya.

"Secular" Islam

There also exists an attitude which can, paradoxically enough, only be termed "secular" Islam. While to the student of classical Islam this must appear a contradiction in terms, it is to be seen less against the medieval background and more in the context of the present situation, with its widespread agnosticism finding its political expression in the modern nation State guaranteeing freedom of conscience, of religion and worship to all its citizens.

Whether we consider the partition of the sub-continent of India as a human tragedy or hail it as a triumph of self-determination—albeit achieved at the cost of much human blood, cruelty and anguish—it has come to stay, at least in our time. The student of Indian history may find good and valid reasons for the parting of the ways of the two communities. Nevertheless, they have much in common, having for many decisive years striven together for national independence and freedom from foreign rule.

Islam is the one world religion which has emerged from its period of "imperialism" unscathed in that it knows no distinction of race and colour. Its universalism is pure, its spirituality unsullied. Islamic ethics, like Jewish and Christian ethics, firmly rooted in the idea of one moral God, is, in its social aspect, eminently suited for playing an active role in the movement towards one world.

The unfortunate corollary of the tragedy of partition is that Islam has had to be turned into an "ideology" of a nationalism alien to the very spirit of a community of believers in one God who knows no geographical or national boundaries. Polemical and apologetic defence of the compatibility of nationalism with religious universalism apart, the fact remains that Pakistan originated at a moment in the history of the human mind when the very basis of religion—faith in God—is being seriously questioned and undermined for a variety of reasons. Yet, the Muslims of India had to rally round the banner of Islam—even if it were only as an afterthought, as some hold—to secure that economic and social position to which they consider themselves entitled against a feared Hindu majority. The two-nation theory developed by Sir Sayyid Ahmed Khan, the founder of the Muslim University of Aligarh, has a solid basis of historical fact; but as long as universal concepts are kept in the background and the particularist features of Hinduism and Islam are allowed to predominate, it is difficult to see how the two nations could be welded into a harmonious whole. For we must not forget that today there are many millions of Muslims living in India, and millions of Hindus in Pakistan.

It is, therefore, only natural that Muslims who have stayed in India should, in so far as they are believers, see in Islam a matter of the individual conscience. Among them, there are some of the foremost fighters for a free India inside the Congress Party. These men sincerely hold that as Muslim citizens of India they have a specific contribution to make stemming from the ethics of their religion. In so far as they are "secularists" they work actively for a social revolution which would sweep away distinctions of religious belief and caste as outmoded forms hindering the emergence of a progressive modern Indian State and society.

The latter group is just as much attached to its cultural heritage from Mughal India as its religious fellow-Muslims. These Indian Muslims want to preserve it in their personal lives. Thus, we see emerging in India a " secular " Islam, an essential element in the personality of the Indian Muslim, distinguishing him from his Hindu or Sikh fellow-citizens. It is a compound of ethical and social concepts, a consciousness of a common history and a distinctive culture with a rich literature, art and architecture.

The circumstances in which the new Muslim State of Pakistan has come into being are not favourable for the growth of this somewhat emaciated " secular " Islam. Islam as a way of life, not only for the individual but also for the group, constitutes, if not the principal, at any rate a very important link between the various groups in West Pakistan (Sindis, Punjabis, Pathans, etc.) and their Muslim brothers in East Pakistan so different in language, cultural tradition and outlook.

Whatever Islam means to the individual Muslim today, it is an essential factor in the political thought and life of the Pakistanis. To the outside observer it appears that this has its disadvantages and its dangers as is clearly realised and admitted by many thoughtful Pakistanis. It is again the irony of history that Western influence should be most evident and effective in the growing emphasis among the Western-educated classes on Islam as the religion of the individual in the Western sense of the term. The same Western outlook is evident in the stress on " ideology "—surely a political concept—that is, on the State- and nation-building Islamic virtues of social justice, equality, brotherhood of man, etc. All these concepts are, after all, the common possession of the whole civilised world. Hence, one asks oneself in all seriousness whether the answer to the problem of the existence of Islam in a modern national State is not a modern form of Islam expressing itself in the specific character and quality of the law of the Muslim State.

Islam in Malaya

In Malaya the situation is very different from that in Pakistan. It is similar merely in so far as it has also emerged from British rule and administration into independent nation- and statehood. Even in this respect it was more fortunate than Pakistan, for the transition from foreign rule to independence was orderly, and the machinery of government continued to function without break or hindrance. Many British civil servants stayed on in their posts. The complete Malayanisation of the administration is now not far off. By contrast, the machinery of government in Pakistan had to be created overnight under the shadow of Muslim-Hindu war. There were hardly any trained civil servants available, especially for the higher grades. This is often forgotten when the situation in Pakistan is being studied.

In another respect Malaya was also more fortunate: it succeeded in adopting a Constitution for the Federation which declared Islam the State religion.[2] Since only just over half of the citizens of the Federation of Malaya are Muslims (comprising all the Malays) the setting up of an Islamic State was out of the question. But the Pan-Malayan Islamic Party aims at an Islamic State under traditional Islamic law; it was actually in power at the time of my visit in two States on the East Coast, in Kelantan and Trengganu, and hard at work bringing existing law into line with Islamic law, *e.g.*, in the matter of interest. The State neither pays nor receives interest in its banking operations. Both States are almost entirely Malay and Muslim.

Among fundamental liberties the Constitution guarantees freedom of religion and the grant of definite rights to its various communities in the field of education, that is, to the Malays, the Chinese, both Buddhist and Christian, and the Indians. Except in Malacca and Penang, former British governorates as distinct from States ruled by a Malay sultan, the ruler of every

[2] See *Constitution of the Federation of Malaya*, supplement to Federation of Malaya, *Government Gazette*, December 11, 1957, p. 509.

State of the Federation is also, within his sphere, the Head of the Muslim religion. These two territories have now Malay governors, but the Head of the Muslim religion is the King of Malaya who is elected for a period of five years from among the Malay rulers. The king, as Supreme Head of the Federation, cannot be impeached during his term of office.[3] This is in accordance with modern usage, but hardly compatible with Islamic law where the Head of State is subordinate to the law in all circumstances. The Malay Supreme Head swears by Allah that he will protect the Muslim religion. But non-Muslim Malayan citizens are free to establish their own educational institutions and teach their own religion. They neither contribute to corresponding Muslim educational establishments nor pay any Islamic dues and taxes. They are entitled to send their children to State schools in which primary education is free for all. No pupil must attend a religious ceremony of a religion other than his own or receive instruction except in his own religion.

Separation of "Church" and State

Naturally, there are separate Federal and State laws. Among the latter are included "Muslim law and personal and family law of persons professing the Muslim religion."[4] It is the responsibility of the Supreme Head "to safeguard the special position of the Malays and the legitimate interests of other communities."[5] There exists, as far as I could see, in fact no discrimination whatsoever on account of religion. Every State has a Department of Religious Affairs whose rights and duties are defined by a law passed by the Legislative Assembly, and the Head of the Muslim religion in every State is advised by a "Council of Muslim Law" in matters of the Muslim religion. He, the ruling chiefs and the Legislative Assembly of the State, enact Muslim law. The "Council of Muslim Law" consists of a Chairman who is a member of the State

[3] *Ibid.*, p. 522.
[4] *Ibid.*, p. 622.
[5] *Ibid.*, para. 153 (1).

Executive Council, the President of the Religious Affairs Department, the Mufti (expert in Islamic law which he interprets and on which he bases his decisions), the Chief Kathi (judge according to religious law), the Inspector of Religious Schools and members of the State Legislative Assembly and other members. The number of the members in these two groups varies in the several States. In Negri Sembilan, for example, there are four members of the S.L.A. and five others of whom one must be a non-Malay Muslim. Here the Chairman and the nine members are to be appointed by H.H. the Sultan with the concurrence of the other Rulers. The Council is responsible for the administration of Muslim law. The Mufti is appointed by the Sultan on the recommendation of the Public Services Commission or another body authorised by State law to make such recommendations. Before making the appointment H.H. is to consider the advice of the Chief Minister of the State. The Mufti is, in addition to his duties, described above, to give advice on request to any civil court in questions affecting Muslim law. He also presides over a Legal Committee of the " Council." [6]

Ordinarily, justice has to be done in accordance with " the orthodox tenets of the Shafeite sect," [7] unless this conflicts with public interest. Then the Chief Kathi's Court is to follow the less orthodox tenets of the Shafeite rite. If these also offend against the public interest the court has to follow the tenets of any of the three other orthodox rites. In this last case, the special sanction of H.H. as the Head of the Muslim religion is required.

The religious court has jurisdiction over any civil or criminal matter in the State; it can " try any criminal offence committed by a Muslim and punishable under this Enactment and may impose any punishment therefor provided." In its civil jurisdiction this court is competent to " hear and determine all actions and proceedings of Muslims in matters of betrothal, marriage, divorce, nullity of marriage, or judicial

[6] See *Administration of Muslim Law Enactment, 1960*, paras. 11, 35, 36.
[7] *Ibid.*, para. 38.

separation." [8] Witness and evidence must be in accordance with Muslim law.[9]

What is interesting in this connection is that the procedure of the religious court follows that of the (civil) State court. The enforcement is actually handed over to the State, a person sentenced to a term of imprisonment being sent to prison " in the custody of a police-officer." [10] The judgment is sent to a magistrate's court for execution,[11] and in certain cases recourse is had to a civil court procedure.[12]

The conclusion to be drawn from this procedure is clearly that although State and Religion are separate, the authority of the State must be invoked for the execution of punishment. This also includes the enforcement of payment of fines for such strictly religious offences as repeated non-attendance at the public prayer in the Mosque on Fridays, the breaking of rules of fasting during the month of Ramadhan in public and the refusal to pay *Zakat* (prescribed charitable tax).

As far as the laws governing marriage and divorce are concerned Muslim law is in force in place of " The Married Women and Children (Maintenance) Ordinance, 1950," except in respect of the maintenance of illegitimate children. Maintenance of legitimate children in case of divorce, for example, is governed by Muslim law.[13] Non-payment is punishable by a term of imprisonment, and it seems that this constitutes an extension of Muslim law in accordance with State law.

Other States in which customary law is strongly entrenched, for instance, Malacca, Pahang and Trengganu, include in their legal provisions both Islamic and Malay customary law. This is in accordance with classical Islamic doctrine. But an attempt is being made to bring customary law in line with Islamic law where possible and, in fact, to replace the former by the latter. But in Negri Sembilan landed property is exclusively

[8] *Ibid.*, para. 41 (3).
[9] *Ibid.*, para. 50.
[10] *Ibid.*, para. 63.
[11] *Ibid.*, para. 81.
[12] *Ibid.*, para. 88.
[13] *Ibid.*, par. 132.

reserved for matriarchal succession, except what was acquired during married life which is shared equally by both sides.

While the basic provisions regarding the application of " Muslim law " are the same throughout the Federation of Malaya, the terminology shows interesting variations, as does the constitution of the " Court of Muslim Law." Thus, in the State of Trengganu, H.H. the Sultan as Head of State and of the Muslim religion appoints a " Committee of Ulamas " three of whose numbers at least serve on what other States call the Legal Committee within the " Council." The President of the Department of Religious Affairs is here called " Commissioner " and the " Council " is termed " Council of Religion and Malay Custom." Besides this, an Appeal Court is functioning, called " The Shariah Appeal Court." The " Council " is to " take notice of and act upon all written laws in force in the State, the provisions of the *Hukom Shara'* (*Sharī'ah* or Islamic law), and the ancient custom of the State or Malay customary law." [14] Requests for a ruling are to be sent by the Commissioner to the Mufti where a point of Islamic law is at stake, but to the " Council " where it concerns Malay customary law.

Again it can be observed that the separation of State and Religion works better in theory than in practice. For we find a very important ordinance stating explicitly that " nothing . . . shall affect the jurisdiction of any Civil Court and, in the event of any difference or conflict arising between the decision of a Court of the Chief *Kadzi* or a *Kadzi* and the decision of a Civil Court acting within its jurisdiction, the decision of the Civil Court shall prevail." [15]

It is also stipulated that the Chairman of the abovementioned Shariah Appeal Court is required " to hold or have held the office of Magistrate." [16]

On the other hand, the Qur'anic prohibition of *riba*, understood to mean interest—a very controversial matter in contemporary Islam—is being taken at its face value: from the

[14] See *The Administration of Islamic Law Enactment*, *1955*, supplement to Federation of Malaya, *Government Gazette*, March 29, 1956, p. 8, par. 18.
[15] *Ibid.*, p. 11, par. 25 (4).
[16] *Ibid.*, p. 12, par. 26 (2).

General Endowment Fund of the Corporation (the name for the Department of Religious Affairs in other States) there is excluded " the interest on all deposits left by the Corporation in the State Treasury as long as they remain in the custody of the State Treasury "; also every use made of it " for charitable purposes for the support and promotion of the Religion of Islam or for the benefit of Muslims in the State in accordance with Islamic law. . . . Monies arising from (this subsection) shall be paid by the Corporation to the State Treasurer for the benefit of the State." [17]

The close co-operation between State and Religion can also be seen from the regulation concerning illegitimate children: a claim for maintenance must be brought in the Magistrates' court against the putative father.[18]

In the State of Perlis both the Chief Minister and the State Secretary who is the principal administrative officer must be male Muslims. But it is explicitly stated that Estimates of Expenditure must " not include any sums received by way of Zakat, Fitrah (rice or money equivalent payable at the end of Ramadhan) and Bait-ul-Mal (treasury of the Corporation) or similar Muslim revenue. . . ." [19]

Education and the Future of Islam

Public interest is paramount and determines the degree of orthodoxy to be practised in the application of Islamic law. The religious leaders, in particular the Muftis and Qadhis (or, as the enactments spell Kathis or Kadzis), are very conservative and not prepared to change or even to admit that changes are needed. Some modifications are practised where customary law is prevailing, as in the case of succession to landed property, mentioned before. But the widow's share of one eighth in the estate of her deceased husband is maintained. Yet, this can be circumvented by the husband settling during married life property on his wife. Such property is excluded from the estate on his decease. This is not considered contrary to Muslim law

[17] *Ibid.*, p. 23, par. 57 (1, c-2). [18] *Ibid.*, p. 44, par. 120.
[19] See *The Laws of the Constitution of Perlis*, 1959, p. 20, par. 66 (3).

as long as the widow does not receive more than one-third of the estate. But it can easily be envisaged that in present circumstances when the position of a Malay wife among the educated classes is one of complete equality, succession will one day be completely regulated by private arrangement between husband and wife, so as to render Muslim law inoperative.

Such a contingency is, however, not contemplated by the conservative religious leaders in Malaya today. They are usually trained in either Mecca or Cairo. The liberalism claimed for the Muslim University of Al-Azhar does not appear to animate those trained there who are now administering justice and teaching in Malaya. The vast changes in economic and social life do not seem to affect the outlook of at least the older religious leaders. Whether the younger generation of teachers training the children in traditional Islamic sciences will effect any change in outlook remains to be seen. There are some hopeful signs; the Ehya Sherif Institution Gunong Semanggol, for instance, has introduced in its curriculum introductory courses to both sociology and economics; secular subjects are taught alongside with traditional ones. The pupils are to be fitted for the teaching of Islam; for Higher Studies they proceed to the Muslim College at Klang, which is under the influence of Al-Azhar. Since much will depend on the intellectual equipment of the future religious leaders and teachers, it is not easy to make any prophecies. The traditional teaching in Arabic, which is widespread, is being pursued with enthusiasm and energy. Balanced by a thorough schooling in secular subjects, its effect should be beneficial. Much is expected from the Muslim College at Klang, and there is widespread hope among civil servants and educators that a new generation of religious leaders with a modern outlook will be trained there. The Department of Islamic Studies in the University of Malaya at Kuala Lumpur could make a vital contribution to a consciousness of Islamic values developed on academic lines, and do much to foster knowledge of and interest in Islam among the academic youth of the country.

It is clear, therefore, that reform is as little contemplated here as in Pakistan. But several Muftis are prepared to decide new cases on the basis of *ijtihād*, *i.e.*, by going back to Qur'an and Sunnah and by using their own judgment. They will not touch existing Islamic law. Yet, a change must come to keep pace with the economic and social revolution now in progress in a young country vigorously pursuing the development of its economy. The government is doing all in its power to raise the standard of living of the Malay rural population by development schemes and education. While the Malays have political power, economic power is largely concentrated in Chinese and British hands. Increase in population may easily upset the balance between the two major groups, the Malays and the Chinese. The present plans of the Malayan Prime Minister Tunku Abdul Rahman for a larger Malayan Federation must, no doubt, be seen in this context.

Insurance for a bright future is to be largely seen in improved education. In this field the British come in again for censure. They are held responsible for the economic backwardness of the Malay masses. The same criticism can be levelled against the British in Malaya as in the Indian subcontinent, namely, that they educate their subjects mainly for the lower cadres of the civil service, with English serving as the principal language of instruction, and ignoring Muslim education. Far from being confined to the orthodox groups, this criticism is widespread among the Western-educated classes as well. Here, too, the legacy of foreign rule must be liquidated in the educational field by a tremendous effort. The Ministry of Education is energetically engaged in implementing an Education Plan which secures free primary education for every child, Malay, Chinese and Indian; attempts to provide a balanced secondary education which, though not free, will grant scholarships for the gifted children of parents unable to pay fees; and furthers the rapid expansion of the University of Malaya. In this scheme Islamic instruction is not neglected.

By and large Islam plays an important part in the lives of the rural population, but is of less significance among the

Western-educated classes, at least in their private lives. As in Pakistan, stress is laid on Islamic " ideology," but with the exception of the advocates of an Islamic State, " politics " is kept free from " religion." One can only hope that the raising of the standard of living among the rural Malays goes hand in hand with a strengthening of the moral and intellectual values of Islam. Otherwise communist ideology will win a speedy, easy victory here, as possibly elsewhere in Asia and Africa where Islam is in transition, with the exception of Turkey and North Africa.

10

SOME REFLECTIONS ON THE SEPARATION OF RELIGION AND POLITICS IN MODERN ISLAM

I

The great question in contemporary Islam is really *what* is Islam and not what is usually debated today, namely, how much or how little of the *Sharī'ah* should be reactivated or modified or discarded. Hence, the answer to the actual questions Muslims ask themselves today depends on their basic attitude to and understanding of classical Islam and its relevance to the practical problems they are called upon to solve in their national sovereign states.

The Western student of Islam has certainly no business to give his, an outsider's, answer to that basic question. But as a sympathetic observer he is interested in what his fellow human beings, who profess Islam, are thinking, because on their conclusions the future of Islam depends. Naturally, much more than that future is at stake in the contemporary world which, though riven by nationalism, is forced by the facts of human existence today to become one world despite distinctions of creed and colour. That creed is put before colour indicates that the overriding problem is a spiritual one. It also means that the much discussed crisis of Islam is only a part, though a large and crucially important part, of the general crisis of modern man. The fact that the Muslim part of the world is in a state of transition only obscures the struggle of the mind, the malaise of the spirit. Political survival, economic viability and growth, the emergence of a new society on an equal footing with its former 'imperialist' and 'colonialist' masters, the specific contribution which the newly independent nations and states should make to the comity of nations in an—ideally—

undivided world, all these urgent tasks ultimately hinge on the solution of the spiritual crisis of all men of all creeds and colours.

In the following pages a pointer to an answer is offered not to the basic question "What is Islam ?" but to a subsidiary, historical question : "Why and how has a situation arisen which forces the Muslims of today to seek and find a solution to that basic question?"

The roots of the problem are to be found in two movements which despite appearances to the contrary are interrelated, one external and the other internal. It is well known that the modern national state with its separation of religion and politics—or, to give these two wider terms their proper names in their European context, the separation of state and church—is the legitimate child of the French revolution. The movement that culminated in the French revolution and the modern national state did not make itself felt in Muslim countries of Asia and Africa until well into the nineteenth century, in the wake of colonial expansion and empire-building. The inner-Islamic movement is usually called modernism and is traced to al-Afghānī and Muḥammad 'Abduh ; it was continued by Rashīd Riḍā.† What has been written in the last thirty years offers hardly anything new when considered in the context of Islam.

The two movements were brought into contact by the Turkish revolution and its result, a lay republic which rigorously excluded Islam from the public life. Contemporary Turkey has not yet succeeded in solving the problem of Islam which, although Islam is the private affair of the Turkish citizen, is today still a political issue of vital importance. This cannot concern us here. But, since Islam is not only an internal Turkish problem, it is worth remembering that the very fact of the existence of a Muslim lay state, successor to the Ottoman empire and caliphate, keeps the question of the separation of religion and politics in Islam continually to the fore. One compares other modern Muslim states with Turkey which is an example either to be followed or to be shunned, or at least a certain irritant.

Now, before Kemal Atatürk's revolutionary action, the 'modernists' were primarily concerned with restoring the purity of early Islam, a purity disturbed and threatened by European imperialism and internal decay. That this spiritual concern was politically linked with pan-Islamism of al-Afghānī's kind can at this point be bypassed. A more detailed examination of the writings of Rashīd Riḍā, 'Ālī 'Abd al-Rāziq and Muḥammad al-Ghazālī is intended to show two things before all : in the first place the fundamental opposition of modernists, and in their wake the Muslim Brotherhood in Egypt, for example, to a separation of religion and politics in principle, but not in practice, if I am not mistaken. Next, the strong religious colouring of Muslim traditionalist opposition to Western culture in so far as Western so-called neo-imperialism is accused of being anti-Islam, in other words of being actuated by activist Christian motives and trying to undermine, even to destroy Islam. The determined restoration of Islam as a religious and political unity, in short, of an Islamic state, is considered the unfailing remedy of the crisis. It will lead to the defeat of Western imperialism and the nefarious influence of its materialist culture. It is, in the view of Rashīd Riḍā and those who think like him, precisely the separation of religion and politics which is alien to the teachings of Islam, a fatal imitation of a moribund West and the principal obstacle to a fresh flowering of Islam as the saviour of mankind from materialism and atheism. Hence those Muslims who care so deeply for Islam participate in the nationalist movements of their countries—ambiguous as their attitude to separate nationhood is, when we take into account their insistence on the pre-eminence of the Arabs as Muslims.

Before going into detail, it must be said at the outset that the purification of Islam is envisaged by these men through elimination of impurities which have crept into Islam from the second century of its existence onwards, and through practical reforms here and there which are necessary for the restoration—not reformation in the Western sense—of the Islam of the *salaf*, the first Companions and Successors of the Prophet. The same applies to any and every deviation from pure Sunnī Islam, based on the Qur'ān and the *Sunnah*, and consequently the replacement of the four orthodox schools or rites by one universal orthodox pattern as the example to all professing Muslims is demanded. As is equally well known, this is to be achieved by the reinstatement of *ijtihād*. But, as every student of Muslim law and jurisprudence knows, this is much more complicated and difficult in practice than would appear from the way its protagonists use it—almost as a magic wand. The practice of *taqlīd* over a long period has not only made the 'ulumā' subservient to their rulers, Muslim as well as European, but—even worse—incapable of facing the modern world and meeting its challenge by the only legitimate means, namely, *ijtihād*. This, at least, is the considered opinion of Rashīd Riḍā.

Yet, in fact Rashīd Riḍā goes a long way towards a separation of religion from politics when he emphatically states the need for *ijtihād* in economic and social affairs not only but even in public and administrative law. What else is this but separation, even if it is disguised as *ijtihād*, which is to be exercised within the overall valid and obligatory *Sharī'ah* of Sunnī Islam? For the state is bound to be carried along by its own momentum primarily conditioned by political and economic necessity, quite apart from what the *'ulamā'* as the *ahl al-'hall wa'l-'aqd* desire and decide. Are the financial and administrative experts capable of running a modern national, i.e., largely nationalist, state?

It is no different with another concept freely used in order to show that Islam can and does supply everything needed in a modern state: *shūrā*. For can *shūrā*, confined to the *ahl al-'ḥall wa'l-'aqd*, be simply equated with parliamentary government acting on behalf of a sovereign people with full legislative power? As a traditionalist Rashīd Riḍā quite naturally and rightly grants them only consultant status. But consultation, listening to advice, is one thing, and legal power to force the administration to accept the assembly's advice and act upon it, i.e. implement the wishes of the elected representatives of the people as decisions binding on the government, something quite different. We are, naturally, used to considerable modifications and changes in the meaning of words; we need only think of the term "democracy". While the name is unimportant, the substance still matters, and it might be better to say simply that in Islam, according to the classical theory, it is the *Sharī'ah* to which highest authority belongs, and the decision consequently belongs to those learned in it, that is, the *'ulamā'*. Yet, it is a far cry from the legal experts to the freely elected representatives of the people who may or may not be experts in *fiqh*, and *mujtahids*, but are not necessarily elected for that reason.

Terms are expandable, certainly, but not beyond the point when their original meaning can no longer be discovered. This is not to say that parliamentary government is the universal remedy for all ills everywhere, nor that it is infallible and a realized ideal of government and administration. It may be doubted whether it is an article for export irrespective of the conditions prevailing in a given state and society. This is also not to deny that Islam, with the institutions it has developed and can still develop now and in the future, can be made flexible enough to accommodate itself to changing circumstances. But let us beware of the romanticism of those who think that in the past, even at the time of Islam's greatest power, reality was bent to the theory of its doctrines.

However, there is another factor which must be considered, and it may well constitute the most important and relevant difference between the past and the present. This is the undeniable fact that the ideal *Sh̲ari'ah* was accepted as obligatory by a community of *believers*, irrespective of what the political reality was like. The modern crisis consists precisely in this : there is no universal basis of faith any longer. Hence, the obligatory character of a revealed law regulating man's entire life will not be accepted by him who denies belief in God, who has revealed His will in the form of a law, though nominally he is still a Muslim. But for him Islam is rather a common culture and history to which he is heir.

The foregoing had to be said so that we can see the critical discussion of the views of several leading Muslim thinkers of the past and the present generation in proper perspective. At the same time, the relevance of their ideas and opinions to those of our contemporaries and to the acute crisis of Islam as an all-embracing religion in our day, will become apparent, beyond the purely academic aspect of this discussion.

II

RAS̲H̲ĪD RIḌĀ

First, let us consider the already quoted Ras̲h̲īd Riḍā in some detail. His important treatise *al-K̲h̲ilāfah aw al-Imāmah al-'uẓmā*[1] can be considered not only as the programme of the reformist party but also as the authoritative pronouncement on the attitude of modernism to politics. As the latter, it is a significant document which has lost nothing of its topical character. Its demand for the re-establishment of the caliphate has not been revived—after Ras̲h̲īd Riḍā's attempt, championed by the caliphate movement among Indian Muslims, had failed. The idea of the Islamic state—based on the *S̲h̲arī'ah* and brought into being and maintained by the courageous and determined exercise of *ijtihād*—has remained active in the hearts and minds of many traditionalist Muslim believers and has given stimulus and force to their political activities in many Muslim countries to the present day. This is largely due to Rashīd Riḍā's treatise and to his advocacy of Islamic revival in *al-Manār*. In both he shows himself as the continuator of the movement for purification and reactivation which was begun by al-Afghānī and Muḥammad 'Abduh, the *salafīyyah*.

In his exposition of the meaning and duties of the caliphate and the caliph he follows the classical exponents of the theory of the *khilāfah*. It interests us only as far as it affects Rashīd Riḍā's idea of an Islamic state. While making the usual distinction between the *Khulafā' Rāshidūn* and the Umayyad and 'Abbāsid caliphs, including the condemnation of Mu'āwiyah, Rashīd Riḍā acknowledges the signal services to the spread and growth of civilization which these 'temporal' caliphs rendered, but he denies that the principle which guided them is derived from the teachings of Islam. Membership of the Quraysh is essential for the caliph in order to preserve the link with 'the geographical cradle of Islam, the Ḥijāz'.[2] This view is noteworthy in that it not only places descent from the Quraysh immediately after the Qur'ān and *Sunnah* as the foundations of *khilāfah* and *khalīfah*, but also for the Syrian Rashīd Riḍā's strong attachment to the Arabs and Arabism.[3]

There is no need to stress that a return to the Qur'ān and the *Sunnah* is not as easy as it appears, and this for two reasons. In the first place, the modern legislator can derive little guidance in practical matters and in detail from them. For, apart from very few precise decisions and regulations, the Qur'ān only provides the general principles and religious and moral ideas as a guide to all generations of Muslims, despite its seventh century setting. But it is precisely this setting which demands of the present generation a radical re-interpretation in the light of modern attitudes and general no less than particular requirements. Historical and literary criticism may by some modernists be applied to the body of traditions, but not to the Qur'ān which as the word of God is outside the reach and realm of criticism, though open to fresh interpretation. In the second place, Western educated Muslims often lack the traditional training necessary to enable them to practise that *ijtihād* without which Rashīd Riḍā is convinced Islam cannot be purified and revived nor an Islamic state brought into effective existence. Nor do men and women so educated who form the core of modern Muslim administrations and are leading in education, willingly accept the interpretations offered by the traditionalists. The real difficulty, however, appears to lie with the very application of *ijtihād*. For, unless *ijithād* means an entirely fresh and new interpretation of the primary sources of Islamic law, irrespective of the development of *fiqh*, no effective answer can be found for the very different outlook and needs of our time, both spiritually and materially. As far as I can make out nobody possessing erudition and authority among the traditionalists is prepared to ignore the work and decisions of previous *mujtahids.* This is, indeed, a requirement which cannot easily be set aside if one wants to preserve continuity. In a matter so vital as this for the revival of Islam as a force in public life the practical difficulties can certainly not be overlooked. Ras͟hīd Riḍā never tires—in this book as well as frequently in his *al-Manār*—of pointing out the vital necessity of *ijtihād* and of creating the necessary machinery for its application.

Hence, he insists on the need to create a college for the training of the future *ahl al- ḥall wa'l-'aqd* who must all be capable of interpreting and applying the *S͟harī'ah* in the spirit of early, pure Islam and in conformity with the requirements of the age. He sees this education as the foremost task of his moderate reformist party which alone is in a position to implement his ideas. He divides his generation into three groups : (1) the servile imitators of the four different law schools ; (2) admirers of European laws and organizations and (3) the reformist party (al-Afg͟hānī, Muḥammad 'Abduh, Abū'l-Kalām Āzād, Zag͟hlūl Pas͟ha and others).[4] It is not without significance that Zag͟hlūl Pas͟ha was at the same time a convinced Egyptian nationalist who did much as leader of the Wafd to hasten Egyptian independence whereas Abū'l-Kalām Āzād as a staunch supporter of the Indian Congress Party opted for India at the time of partition, an exemplar of the patriotic Indian of the Muslim religion who looked upon Islam as a spiritual factor and force in the Indian subcontinent.

Ras͟hīd Riḍā believed that his party possessed sufficient independence of mind to appreciate at the same time the laws of Islam and the spirit of modern civilization, to make an end to the divisions in the Muslim community and restore the *imāmah.* To this end, he appealed to the Indian Muslims to supply money and men to carry through the reform and renewal of Islam. As is to be expected, he is at the same time strongly anti-Western ; *tafarnuj* and *mutafarnij* are terms of opprobrium for Europeanisation and Westernizers. He accuses the latter of trying 'to efface the last vestiges of Muslim law', and makes European education responsible for the opinion that religion was incompatible with contemporary politics, science and civilization and that a majority of them wanted a lay state, suppress the caliphate and weaken religion in the nation.[5] This is mainly directed against the Turks, but Rashīd Riḍā is obviously mixing up 'religion' with 'Islam', since these men are not against religion as such, but are convinced that Islam as it appears to them in their own country is incapable of creating an independent Turkish nation. For this reason, they wanted to exclude Islam from all influence on public affairs. He is, however, right when he says that they tried to replace the sense of Islamic solidarity by national and racial feeling.

His opposition to Europeanisation (*tafarnuj*) should, however, not be confused with out-and-out hostility towards what even he considered useful, even essential for the restoration of pure Islam in our time. Only he was convinced that what was good in the West has always been contained in Islam which is a spiritual principle, but also a social and political ideal.[6] He is so convinced of the excellence of Islam that he intends winning back those he terms "heretics" (presumably the Westernizers) by showing them that the laws of Islam 'are equal to the most developed civilizations and free from the imperfections and evils of the materialist civilizations'.[7] What he probably means is that Muslims have no need to ape the West, and what *looks* like imitation is nothing but a natural inner development or a return to Islamic sources. However, there is good reason to be in doubt about the real character of his attitude to the West, and the qualification just made may well not be justified, as will become apparent if we look at some of his suggested reforms and modifications, as they appear in his *fatwās*.

For him the Islamic state is the best, and this not only for the Muslims but for the whole of mankind, since it stands for justice, equality and legitimate aspirations and interests of everybody. But when he says that *zakāt* represents the Islamic solution of the social scourges which are inherent in materialist and atheist governments one begins to wonder whether this is really so and whether *zakāt* is an adequate answer to the economic and social needs of a modern state bound to secure freedom from want and hunger because all its citizens are free and equal and have a natural right to material sufficiency. This is not to deny that social justice is a fundamental demand of Islam, but so it is in Judaism and Christianity and among humanists. It is equally true that in all three world religions social justice is a religious commandment, yet it also forms a basic requirement in any modern state which does not appeal to the religious sanction for its moral values and its legislation based upon them. In any case, what matters is the realization in daily life *now* of this social justice.

His attitude to the new Turkey is equally ambivalent. On the one hand, he denies Kemal Atatürk the right to decide points of Muslim law, since this is and must remain the prerogative of the *'ulamā'* as the *ahl al- ḥall wa'l-'aqd* whom, surprisingly, he identifies with the *jamā'at al-Islām*. One of the examples he quotes deserves notice since it concerns the important question of women's rights. The Head of the Turkish government took a *fatwā* about women's right to do the work of men, but he is neither expert in the theory nor in the practice of Islamic law with all his courage, prowess and superb military and political leadership. As *al-Manār* has shown in matters of credit and interest, and of art and music through many *fatwās*, Islam contains in itself the means to an accommodation within strictly defined limits ! But this is the exclusive business of fully trained *'ulamā'* who issue canonically permissible decisions, arrived at through *ijtihād*. At the other end of the scale, there stands Rashīd Riḍā's conviction that the Turkish government having proved itself capable in war to preserve the integrity and freedom of its territory is well qualified to effect the needed reform of Islam. This view is the more surprising since Rashīd Riḍā is—fully in accord with tradition—only prepared to entrust the reform of Islam to the *'ulamā'* as the *ahl al- ḥall wa'l-'aqd*. He must, therefore, equate them with the members of the Grand National Assembly at Ankara who can hardly be considered experts in Islamic law and jurisprudence, except for a minority.[8] It would be easy to dismiss this view as inconsistency ; in fact, the matter goes far deeper for many strands, complementary and contradictory, are intertwined in Rashīd Riḍā's personality and work.

Undoubtedly, we must, therefore, start from his deeply-held conviction of the high excellence, even absolute superiority of Islamic law as 'the richest and most perfect of all the laws'. At the same time, he holds that Islam grants legislative power in political, military and financial matters, i.e. in all matters outside the cult in its widest connotation. This legislative power is entrusted to the community and is to be exercised through consultation by all those who possess knowledge and judgment.[9] We must, therefore, ask why did Rashīd Riḍā have such a high opinion of the Assembly at Ankara since he could hardly have endowed all or even a majority of its members with these necessary qualifications ? Perhaps an answer may be found in his firmly held opinion that the '*ulamā*' must be free and not mercenaries of the powers that be, Muslim or European.[10] Free the Turkish National Assembly certainly was ! But they were certainly not all *mujtahids*, a condition he imposes on the representatives of the whole community, nor was their knowledge of the Qur'ān and the *Sunnah* such as to enable them to exercise *ijtihād*. It must also be stated that while the principle, in case of discord, of going to arbitration to the Qur'ān and the *Sunnah* is sound,[11] cases are bound to occur where both primary sources of law are silent.

Strongly conscious of the subjugation of many Muslim lands to foreign domination, such as Egypt and India, Rashīd Riḍā could easily wax enthusiastic over the successful struggle of free Turkey. However, he managed to combine with this admiration for the Turks a sense of the importance of the Arabs and Arabic for Islam, as we heard earlier on. For him, the Arab nation is the vital principle of Islam ; without it there can be no unity of purpose and action among the Muslims.[12] Therefore, he first tries to rally the Arab princes by exhorting them to acquire scientific and technical knowledge as the precondition of efficient and effective rule and, then, to unite. Here his religious fervour is at one with his national feeling, yet he imagines that technical knowhow can be acquired without the principles and without the spirit of Western civilization which has produced it. The dilemma shows up clearly here : rationalisation of government, administration and economy goes hand in hand with a rational, progressive faith. But it cannot be simply grafted on to a medieval order of things. It can and does exist without faith in God, outside religion altogether !

In his view, Muslim civilization holds the right balance between the spirit of conservative immobility and the materialism of Western civilization which he thought was doomed to ruin in our time.[13] This idea of the *juste milieu* is no doubt borrowed from Ibn Taymīyah's concept of *wasaṭ* ; it is well known that this great Ḥanbalī jurist is the spiritual father of the modern *salafīyyah*. Rashīd Riḍā's concern about the necessity of instituting a strong caliphal government is understandable since his only hope, in the face of indecision and discord among the Arabs and between them and the Turks, was that a strong central government headed by a canonical caliph would be capable of bringing about the much needed revival of pure Islam. It is, therefore, surprising to see him state on one page that the caliph is a purely temporal ruler called upon to defend Islam *under* the *Sharī'ah*, but on another page, plead for a caliph who is the fountainhead of power, with the right and ability to legislate by *ijtihād*.[14]

Not having much confidence in either Turks or Arabs to set up a caliphate such as he envisages, he concentrates on the need to compose a work which should prove that Islam can adapt itself to modern civilization and culture. This plan is closely linked with his proposed Training College.[15]

Rashīd Riḍā combined to a remarkable degree tenacity of purpose—the restoration of Islam culminating in a powerful caliphate—with romantic enthusiasm and a healthy political realism. Thus, he could say that recent developments were the result of foreign oppression, not of a desire to return to their true religion or the consciousness of having lost the grandeur which it (Islam) once bestowed upon them when they observed it. He goes so far as to claim that if the Muslims had upheld their religion nobody could have surpassed them in technical knowledge and in the blessings of civilization. Nor would the renaissance he sees in progress have been 'secular' and 'nationalist', but, instead, in the spirit of Islam and inspired by it. He makes the absence of *ijtihād* responsible for the relapse into bedouinism or near-bedouinism no less than for europeanisation, heresy and atheism[16].

His own work in this direction is significant, but less for its actual results than for the spirit that animated it. As stated earlier, we owe to him a number of *fatwās*. But we may justifiably ask whether their scope and content really touch the fundamentals of modern life or whether his reforms—these they certainly constitute—are, in fact, rather confined to more peripheral matters? With the exception of his concession on credit and of his interpretation of *ribā* as compensation for service, following Muḥammad 'Abduh and Ibn Qayyim al-Jawzīyah, it is largely the latter, for his decision that art (music and painting) is canonically permissible hardly shows a sense of urgency in the face of pressing economic and social problems affecting the peace and stability of a modern state and nation, no matter how progressive such a *fatwā* is ; and its importance should not be belittled. What is needed are practical measures to raise the standard of living and of education, including education in the tenets and the history of Islam. Rashīd Riḍā is by no means unaware of this urgent need, as his plan for a college shows. But is it sufficient to train an *élite* of experts in Islamic law, no matter how important an investment for the future of an Islamic state this is ?

Let us look at his pronouncement on one of the most vital and controversial questions troubling modern Islam : the emancipation of women. Again, it is well to remind ourselves of his basic position : Islam is perfect, so is its law ; all that is needed is to give effect to it. Applied to the position of women in Islam, this means that 'the legal position of woman in Islam is certainly much the most elevated, just and best'.[17] He uses the arguments we can still hear today : women's natural sphere is the home, to be wife and mother ; it would lead to all kinds of depravity if we were to force a life of independence on woman. While insisting on the equality of the sexes, he, at the same time, points to the Qur'ān (II : 228 and IV : 38). His romantic idealism is evident in his view that women would never have wanted to earn their own living if the husbands had acted in strict application of the Qur'ānic injunctions. They would have been satisfied to manage and live on their husbands' earnings. He says that woman can add to the expenses of the household those of her personal requirements (dress, apparel, ornaments, etc.) and goes on : 'If there is trickery here it is, verily, the husband who is its victim'.[18]

There is much truth in what he writes about the policy of the 'temporal' caliphs and the behaviour of the '*ulamā*' and their joint responsibility for the neglect of Islamic law. The result, he rightly claims, was neglect of the just injunctions of the law, and it would be wrong to confuse this neglect with the unsuitability of Islam to meet any and every situation. Not the caliphate—canonically established and maintained—but the caliph is at fault and to blame. (This is, according to him, where the Young Turks went wrong.) The universal remedy—to this point he returns again and again—is, therefore, the reinstatement of *ijtihād*. In fact, the Muslim conception of state is much superior to any other doctrine for it permits '. . . to avoid evil, to guarantee the material interests, cause the law to be respected, and to propagate the virtues which perfect the dignity of man'.[19] All that is, therefore, needed today is an Islamic government strong and determined to implement the canonical law, suitably reinterpreted by *ijtihād* and applied in conformity with the traditional principle of *maṣlaḥah*, common weal, the welfare of the community. This principle—let us be clear—was formulated by the jurists to justify their *de facto* accommodation to the political power of amīrs and sultāns, and their recognition of political reality while upholding the ideal *khilāfah* or *imāmah* in theory.

Yet, it must be conceded, I fear, that good as this undoubtedly is in theory, the crucial test comes when the claim that Islam is able to meet any and every contingency out of its own principles and legal concepts is to be applied in practice. And here, it seems to me, Rashīd Riḍā is not prepared to go beyond Ibn Taymīyah and Ibn Qayyim al-Jawzīyah, as Henri Laoust has convincingly shown.[20] Rashīd Riḍā even thinks that there would actually be no need for modern socialism, since Islam teaches social justice which equals practical socialism. He has no doubt that if our modern socialists had known Islamic law properly they would have converted to Islam and become ardent defenders of their new faith.[21] He, therefore, fails to see how non-Muslims can reasonably object to the re-establishment of an Islamic state under Islamic law, based on the principles of the *Sharī'ah*. He suspects in such opposition a mixture of anti-Islamic Christian bias and imperialism.[22] The other enemy is internal ; the Westernizers who are heretics in his eyes. They would reduce Islam to a cultural and national bond, bereft of all religious meaning and obligation. Hence, he once again proclaims the necessity of an Islamic government, entirely free from European influence, its laws and traditions, except those which in matters of administrative organization agree with the religious law and are no different among the nations. The caliphate should have the right of organizing Muslim propaganda, apply legal sanctions, yet assure complete religious liberty.[23]

It is not immediately clear how the application of *ḥudūd* goes together with complete religious liberty. Nor can I see anything but a separation of religion and politics in two of his utterances : one applies to the caliph who in fact has authority only over education and personal status, that is, not over any of the matters usually under the authority of political governments. But in another place he is said to be a purely temporal ruler[24] and in a third place his spiritual guidance is compared to that of the Pope.[25] Yet, the caliph is the vicegerent of the Prophet, must be a *mujtahid*, defend Islam as religion and law and has coercive power to enforce the law of Islam. The other concerns his statement that the state should entrust all religious matters to free religious societies and to properly trained persons. To this end, an institute of propaganda and direction of conscience is to be set up which is divorced from politics.[26] It would appear that, while in theory Rashīd Riḍā upholds the religious and political unity of Islam, represented in the *khilāfah* or *imāmah*, in practice he advocates a separation of functions which is tantamount to a separation of religion and politics, once the religious basis and direction of government and administration is denied. In this connexion, it is relevant to recall his emphatic denial that Muḥammad was a ruler and a tyrant, and his insistence that the Muslim only owes obedience to the Prophet as the transmitter of the Divine message and in his application of the law, but not in temporal matters.[27] In this, he is very close to 'Ālī 'Abd al-Rāziq who draws the opposite conclusion by denying the necessity of the caliphate and by insisting on the separation of religion and politics, as we shall see presently.

It is by no means clear how Rashīd Riḍā could hold these divergent views at the same time unless we assume that terms like 'spiritual' and 'temporal' are introduced by him because he is aware of the dichotomy of the religious and the political spheres in the modern world while he himself is still firmly rooted in the Middle Ages and its assumptions. For it appears likely that as regards authority he wavered between the *Sharī'ah*, the *ahl al- ḥall wa'l-'aqd* (the *'ulamā'*) and the *ulu'l-'amr* ('those in command'). Yet a careful reading of his argument in the whole treatise and in his articles and *fatwās* published in *al-Manār* leads one to the conclusion that authority actually resides in the *Sharī'ah*, in other words, we see him adopt the classical theory. Says he: 'the authority of those in command is only established by God in the general interest in order to assure the application of the *Sharī'ah*.[28] Hence, he means by legislation always Islamic legislation, that is to say the laws issued by a Muslim government must be in conformity with the spirit of the *Sharī'ah* and must be arrived at with the help of the recognized principles of Muslim jurisprudence and those expert in them. *Ishtirā'*, nowadays usually called *tashrī'*, is there to establish the laws which the government needs in order to guarantee justice, protect the land, assure the interests of the nation and arrest the propagation of evil.[29] Though he avers that these laws vary with time and place and with the religious and temporal situation of the nations, there is no doubt that the *Sharī'ah* is the binding law for the Muslim at all times. New legislation is safeguarded through the principle of *ijtihād*, and he vigorously attacks *taqlīd* and its practitioners throughout the history of Islam. His insistence on *ijtihād* clearly points to his orthodox concept of Islam as 'at the same time a spiritual principle and a social and political ideal',[30] as we saw above.

So does his definition of religion : 'cult, care to avoid all bad and blameworthy actions, to respect right and justice in social relations, to purify one's soul and to prepare it for the future life, in one word, all the laws that aim at bringing man near to God'.[31]

He expressly states that certain prescriptions which concern social relations have also a religious significance, such as respect for life, honour and property of one's neighbour. It is precisely the neglect of the prescriptions of this law which has led to calamity, he points out repeatedly. Legislative activity is 'authorized by God and entrusted to the community ; it is exercised on condition of consultation (*shūrā*) by all those who possess knowledge and judgement,'[32] as stated earlier. Since power thus belongs to the community, the Muslim owes obedience to the law, not to the person of the caliph who is but 'the head of a constitutional government. He has neither authority nor control over the souls and the hearts and has no other mission than to apply the law'.[33] This is followed by the startling demand for the abolition of religious power in Islam. For, says Rashīd Riḍā, only God and His Prophet have the right to exercise authority over the faith and beliefs of every Muslim, hence no spiritual authority exists in Islam. But all the same, Islam is religion *and* law, and sulṭān and caliph have the duty and the power to enforce law and order.[34] The community, he maintains, has supreme authority over the caliph who is only a temporal sovereign. By contrast, the Pope is a spiritual sovereign.[35] Earlier on, we saw that he granted both, caliph and Pope, spiritual authority.

One might venture to suggest that Rashīd Riḍā, who recognized that 'one of the consequences of modern civilization has been the separation of the spiritual and the temporal,'[36] has not succeeded in harmonizing his strong, spontaneous attachment to Islam as an all-embracing religion and his great learning with the practical demands of modern civilization arising out of its principle of separation. The same ambivalence can be seen in his opposition to Ibn K͟haldūn,[37] many of whose conclusions pertaining to the Arabs and to the caliphate he nevertheless quotes with approval. He opposes the concept of *ʿaṣabīyah* because tribal bonds endanger the overriding loyalty to religion (Islam). It is a legitimate force in monarchies, but not applicable to prophets and their vicegerents (*k͟hulafāʾ*). He means naturally the theory of the *k͟hilāfah*, not the actual caliphate from Muʿāwiyah onwards. For, the adoption and application of the hereditary principle runs counter to Islam and to the intention of the Law, as does *ʿaṣabīyah* founded on force. Islam subordinates force to law, hence to restore Islam means to restore Islamic law whose writ is to run wherever Muslims live. It is precisely because law requires for its enforcement political authority, the state, that the application of this law depends on an *Islamic* state. It is for this reason that the inconsistencies and contradictions we felt obliged to record in his own words, cannot easily be resolved. It was certainly not my intention to belittle his personality and his work. I have discussed his ideas because they are fundamental to all subsequent thinking and writing to the present day, as will be clear from Muḥammad al-G͟hazālī later. Moreover, they illustrate—to my mind—the basic problem as one of incompatibility between a law based on revelation and its application in an age of doubt and unbelief. Ras͟hīd Riḍā forcefully demonstrates the conflict between an Islamic and a Muslim state, a religious law governing the community of believers and a political law securing individual freedom, life and property irrespective of belief and religious conviction. In this lies his importance, even today, as will be apparent in the subsequent discussion.

What is so interesting and important in his writings is the parallel existence of a religious and a lay state, despite the emphasis on the former and the condemnation of the latter. His exalted vision of pure and perfect Islam has probably made it impossible for him to realize his inconsistencies and contradictions. Otherwise, he would hardly have condemned the Muslims who 'have long spoken, like the others, of a spiritual caliphate, of the necessity to separate it from the temporal and political power' and would hardly have continued: 'we hope having shown, in this study, where truth lies'.[38] For he himself, as quoted earlier on, demanded an 'institute of propaganda and direction of conscience', surely suggesting spiritual or religious authority of a kind which is not only indistinguishable from the aspirations of those who are in favour of a separation of religion from politics in the interests of Islam, but incompatible with his own denial of the existence of spiritual authority in Islam, and with his championing of the Islamic state, convinced that the application of *ijtihād* will secure its viability in the modern world without impairing the validity of the *Sharīʿah*.

He would impose the legal penalties presumably on Muslims only, but would he restrict religious liberty to non-Muslims or would he interpret the concept in the modern sense as freedom to profess or not to profess religion, including Islam? This is an important point in view both of his own intention to direct conscience and of the modern demand for freedom of conscience which must mean freedom to contract out of established religion, to be an agnostic or an atheist. This is obviously a Western interpretation of freedom of conscience, but does not the Qur'ān forbid religious compulsion? Would Rashīd Riḍā and those who think like him today concede that where a Western idea is compatible with a Qur'ānic injunction it is permissible, hence any and every citizen in an Islamic state is free to profess or not to profess Islam? Or, are we to assume that 'Fight an unbeliever where you find him' abrogates the other injunction and is to be the guiding principle?

Besides, there is the positive demand that the *Sharīʿah* should be the law of the state—the *Sharīʿah* suitably interpreted to answer the needs of the day in matters not connected with religion in the strict, narrow sense of the term. Though there are many shades of opinion among the protagonists of this demand, they are all agreed on this in principle whether we label them 'orthodox' or 'liberal', 'traditionalist' or 'modernist'. On the other hand, we have the largely negative, purely defensive, attitude that no law should go against the principles of Islam. Surely, there is a world of difference between these two basic attitudes which is bound to show itself in the political, economic and social life of contemporary Muslim states. The label 'secularist' is rather inaccurate for this group which also shows a variety of shades of opinion. A better term would be 'lay' since a majority among those who insist on a clear demarcation of the two spheres of politics and religion are professing Muslims, a number of them very devout religious men.

It is evident that, although the dividing line between the two main groups is rather fluid, the yardstick to be applied to their respective positions is their attitude to the *Sharī'ah*. It is obvious that the 'lay' element envisage legislation decided upon by a legislature—elected under whatever franchise, or appointed—in the form of modern law codes and embodying modern legal principles and concepts. Yet, they are all agreed that no law must run counter to Islamic ideals and ideas.

III

'ĀLĪ 'ABD AL-RĀZIQ

In 'Ālī 'Abd al-Rāziq we meet for the first time with a consistent, unequivocal assertion of the purely and exclusively religious character of Islam. He asks and answers the question 'what is Islam ?' in order to define the place of Islam in our time as a universal religion, a religious call (*da'wah*), announced by an Arab in Arabic, but addressed to all men, not only the Arabs. Pre-eminence in Islam belongs to piety, not to any race or language, any nation or ethnic group. The religious community is the creation of Muḥammad ; the *imāmah* or *khilāfah* is neither a dogma in Islam nor demanded in the Qur'ān and the *Sunnah*. The theory of the *imāmah* or *khilāfah* is the work of theologians and jurists and is—in his thought—strictly separated from the *history* of the *khilāfah* which he views with critical eyes, guided by reason and experience. The application of Muḥammad's religious message has nothing whatever to do with politics which is exclusively man's rational task. From the start, the *khulafā'* betray the pure *da'wah* that is Islam ; Abū Bakr was the first *malik* or temporal ruler and this in spite of his 'religious' behaviour in his imitation of the Prophet in private and public life. For 'Ālī 'Abd al-Rāziq there is nothing specifically 'Islamic' in the caliphate, hence, since Islam has nothing to do with politics, he rejects the religious and political unity of Islam claimed by jurists and Ibn Khaldūn by whom he is clearly strongly influenced otherwise. Thus, the way is free for him to demand uncompromising separation of religion and politics as the basis for a modern state and for the permanence of Islam as a religion.

This has far-reaching consequences inasmuch as his attitude enables him to apply historical criticism to the caliphate from its inception without having to exclude the *Khulafā' Rāshidūn* and without letting deviation from the ideal, pure Islamic state only begin with the *mulk* of Mu'āwiyah. For, he confines pure Islam to the Prophet whom he exempts from the usual political categories, as we shall see presently. Muḥammad is the undisputed religious leader and example, his 'political' activity is not only accidental to his *da'wah*, in fact it shares with political activity nothing but the name. Muḥammad has not delegated his religious pre-eminence to the *khalīfah* in the original signification of this term—the vicegerent of the *Rasūl Allāh*—no, creative and normative religious 'mission' has ceased with the Prophet's death. The unity of the Arab nation is religious, not political, thanks to the message of the Prophet.

Whether one agrees with 'Abd al-Rāziq's reading of the Qur'ān and the *Sunnah* and of the history of the Islamic empire or not, it is undeniable that he adopts a definite position which leads him to assign Islam a momentous role in the life of the Muslim believer, but apart from politics. The strength of this attitude is that it starts from first principles and, by taking Islam as a religious *da'wah* out of national and nationalist politics, safeguards that purity of Islam as a universal faith which Rashīd Riḍā strove to recover. But, whereas for Rashīd Riḍā this purity was represented by the *imāmah* of the *Khulafā' Rāshidūn* which he wanted to restore in the twentieth century, 'Ālī 'Abd al-Rāziq rejected the canonical necessity of the *imāmah*, together with the actual caliphate, as contrary to the nature and intention of the original Islam of the Prophet Muḥammad.

From his basic supposition, we can assume that he approved of the Turkish 'solution': a lay state that guarantees the freedom of religion to his citizens who want to practise Islam, but excludes Islam from playing any part in public life, in government and administration.

That his interpretation of Islam aroused the violent opposition of the guardians of the traditional understanding and interpretation of classical Islam and led to his public disgrace is natural. Yet, their rejection does not necessarily imply that his interpretation is untenable and wrong. That his ideas fly in the face of a tradition continuously cultivated does not automatically rule them out of court. His interpretation rests on the soundness of his distinction between the political actions accompanying and consolidating the Prophet's *da'wah* which, he claims, are not political in the accepted sense of the term, and the political actions of the caliphs as rulers of a state. If he is right then the whole theory of the *khilāfah* not only, but also the more fundamental one of the *siyāsah sharʻiyyah* of Ibn Taymīyah and also of his modern disciple Rashīd Riḍā is untenable. Then also the position of the *Sharīʻah* is thoroughly undermined and its claim to be or become the law of the state falls to the ground. The lay state is then the inescapable consequence, and no conflict need arise between the demands of Islam and the exigencies of a modern national state. If the Qur'ān does not lay down political laws and rules of behaviour it is no longer the first and foremost of the principles of *state*-law. Moreover, the legislative function and activity of the state can and must be based on political considerations—anchored in right and justice, whatever their origin, divine or human—without reference to or regard for the *Sharīʻah* of Islam. It is significant that in ʻĀlī ʻAbd al-Rāziq's treatise, written soon after Rashīd Riḍā's, the *Sharīʻah* is not discussed at all. Admittedly, the treatise is primarily concerned with the theory of government, its origin and especially the source of its authority.[39] By a critical examination of the theory and practice of the *khilāfah* the author sets out to disprove and reject the claim that the *khilāfah* was the foundation of all authority in Islam. Yet, nobody can comprehend and evaluate the nature and function of the *imāmah* or *khilāfah* without determining the place of Islamic law in it.

For, the student of Islam from its origin to the threshold of the modern age knows that the question of a religious or a lay state hinges on the place of the *Sharīʻah* in a state created by and for the Muslims. The source (divine or human) and the extent of the law of such a state determine its character. The law in force makes it a religious or a lay state. This truism is sometimes lost sight of in discussion and debate. By definition, then, a state whose criminal and private law is not based on the *Sharīʻah* is not an Islamic state even where Islam is the state religion and personal status law is the *Sharīʻah*-law, be it entirely traditional or modernized in varying degree, and whether this personal status law is administered by judges under religious or state authority.

With this proviso, ʻĀlī ʻAbd al-Rāziq's ideas put forward in his treatise *al-Islām wa-uṣūl al-ḥukm* may now be briefly reviewed. For it would appear that this treatise is or could be the theoretical basis for a Muslim as distinct from an Islamic state. In such a state Muḥammad and his religious *daʻwah* would be the pattern rather than the caliphate of the *Khulafāʼ Rāshidūn* with Islamic law on the basis of the Qur'ān and the *Sunnah* interpreted afresh with the help of *ijtihād*.

As is well known, al-Māwardī insists on the necessity of the caliphate which he derives from the Qur'ān (IV : 62): not reason, but the Shar' demand it ; it 'is established to replace prophecy in the defence of the faith and the administration of the world'.[40] 'Alī 'Abd al-Rāziq who states the case for the traditional concept of the *imāmah*, quoting, moreover, Ibn Khaldūn's definition of the *khilāfah*,[41] denies that the doctors of Islam proved the necessity of having an *imām* from the Qur'ān. It can, therefore, only be justified by *ijmā'* or reason. We know, again from al-Māwardī, that *ijmā'* is necessary to make the contract between the *Ummah* and the *Imām* binding. What the Qur'ān (IV : 62 and 85) says—this is 'Abd al-Rāziq's view—is merely that some Muslims have responsibility for public affairs. In his support he refers to T. W. Arnold's *The Caliphate*. He quotes *al-Mawāqif*, II : 464, that *ijmā'* has no authority in tradition. Against Rashīd Riḍā he maintains that there is no basis for the institution of the caliphate in the *Sunnah*. Not only is Rashīd Riḍā wrong, but he was anticipated by Ibn Ḥazm. Though undoubtedly authentic, these *aḥādīth* do not constitute, he avers, a valid argument for the *imāmah* as a religious obligation, but simply speak of *imāmah*, *bay'ah*, *jamā'at al-Muslimīn* as existing in fact. He puts these statements on a par with Jesus' saying 'Render unto Caesar. . .' and concludes that we must obey rebels who rule us by force, but we do not thereby recognize rebellion nor authorize revolt against constituted authority. Does not the Shar' command us to respect the poor, but it certainly does not command us to create them, or slavery.[42] As a student of Ibn Khaldūn, the author appreciated the paramount role military force and personal power, based on the active support of family, clan or tribe, play in politics. His study of the caliphate convinced him that in theory it rested on the power of those who have the right to decide, yet, he is no less convinced that in practice it is based on force : 'we do not at all doubt that brute force has always been the support of the institution of the caliphate'.[43] He claims that the Muslim historians clearly demonstrate that there was always opposition to the caliph, for the Muslims only submit to Allāh voluntarily, but accept the rule of the caliph—supported as it is by force—under duress. Thus, he concludes, the caliphate rests on force and proves it by quoting many examples from the history of the Umayyads, ʿAbbāsids, Mamlūks and other dynasties. Even Abū Bakr had already to contend with opposition. He approvingly quotes Ibn Khaldūn to the effect that the *khilāfah* disappears with the *ʿaṣabiyyah.*[44] Power is the motif force of the caliph and of him who aspires to the caliphal power, as the murder of Ḥusayn by Yazīd b. Muʿāwiyah shows.[45] In fact, Allāh does not want His religion to be subjected to a specific form of government nor to a particular group of rulers.[46] Religious observance is independent of the caliphate.[47] This observation is important inasmuch as it clearly shows political power and authority to be unnecessary for the practice of religion. And yet, he admits that Islam has not only theoretically formulated laws, but has obliged its adherents to practise them. These laws are founded on brotherhood and equality.[48]

The question arises at once, who enforces these religious laws and sees that they are applied to everyday life? Can everyday life be lived in isolation? Naturally, the organization of a religious community is inextricably bound up with politics. ʿĀlī ʿAbd al-Rāziq is fully aware of this. For this reason he distinguishes between the pre-eminence of the Prophet and the political government of the caliph and 'those in authority',[49] between a religious authority deriving from revelation, and political power based on force.

He is at pains to show the fundamental difference between the Prophet as the *Rasūl Allah* and a governor (*ḥākim*), be he a *malik* or a *sulṭān*. Steeped as an *ʿālim* in traditional law and lore he uses the whole traditional terminology of constitutional theory and law to demonstrate that—applied to Muḥammad—authority and power which these terms express, stand on a different level, decidedly on a higher plane, than when applied to an ordinary monarch or ruler whose authority and power are invariably founded on brute force and can only be maintained and handed on to his successor by just this force. The Prophet's authority is spiritual, his power and influence extend to the heart and mind of the community of believers. Undoubtedly, the *risālah* or messengership of the Prophet demands of the *rasūl* a kind of force (*quwwah*) so that he can fulfil the Divine command (*qawl*) and see that his *daʿwah* (call) be followed. In this ʿĀlī ʿAbd al-Rāziq agrees with Ibn Khaldūn. The *rasūl* must have an authority (*sulṭānah*) more extensive than that of a governor over the governed, of a father over his sons. The 'more' naturally includes everything that pertains to the temporal authority just mentioned. But it also denotes an additional function which the Prophet shares with no one, which is unique to him ; his is 'the rule over the affairs of body and spirit. . . the administration of this world and of the hereafter'.[50] He has both a general and a comprehensive authority over all men whom he is to lead to Allāh, an authority different from that of the king. His is a holy power (*quwwah qudsīyah*) which transcends—and is dissimilar from—the power of the kings and from the authority of the sulṭāns. In short, the government of Prophecy (*ḥukm al-nubuwwah*) is different from the *ḥukm al-salāṭīn*, precisely because the former has a religious sanction and purpose—to lead man in voluntary submission to his eternal happiness—and the latter is only concerned with man's material interests in this life.[51] Roughly, it is the same distinction as that between *khilāfah* and *mulk*, leaving aside Ibn Khaldūn's important division of *mulk* into a Muslim state based on the *Sharī'ah* and political laws, and the power state primarily serving the interests of the ruler. 'Ālī 'Abd al-Rāziq distinguishes, as we saw, between *ḥukm al-nubuwwah* and *ḥukm al-salāṭīn* and significantly explains that the prophetic government was not a *dawlah siyāsīyah*, a political government.[52] What matters, in his view, is that he is the apostle of Allāh (Qur'ān, XXXIII : 40) and not a king. Both the Qur'ān and the *Sunnah* bear out his religious and spiritual pre-eminence and that Islam is a *da'wah* to Allāh aspiring to a religious unity (*waḥdah dīnīyah*) of all mankind, but not to a political unity, one world government. In order to further religion and to support his preaching (*da'wah*) the Prophet made use of means which we would call political actions in other men. 'Ālī 'Abd al-Rāziq claims that the rules of Islam have absolutely nothing in common with the method and measures of political government and civil administration.[53] The Prophet did not designate a successor ; he died after he had accomplished his mission as the apostle of Allāh.

This view is diametrically opposed to that held by the majority of Muslims, as 'Ālī 'Abd al-Rāziq himself clearly states, illustrating it from Ibn Khaldūn. In his view the Prophet did not combine prophetic with royal dignity in the accepted sense of the term. Religious propaganda is incompatible with the application of force.[54] Not a single Prophet has had recourse to the sword in order to win people to have faith in God. But what about *jihād*? It is undeniable that the Prophet engaged in *jihād*, and that *jihād* is one of the five pillars of Islam. 'Ālī 'Abd al-Rāziq, therefore, must admit that the Prophet fought in order to establish the rule of Islam, something quite different from pursuing his prophetic mission, which resulted in Muḥammad being simultaneously the apostle of Allāh and a political monarch (*malik siyāsī*).[55] He asks whether this military and political activity of the Prophet resulted from his prophetic mission or from the wider sphere of revelation covering all his activities, and concludes that the two cannot easily be separated from each other. Another view – held by the Muslims—sees in the political administration a part of his apostolate inasmuch as the duty of preaching Islam entails practical measures for the implementation of its principles. Alone among Muslim authors Ibn Khaldūn recognized this as distinguishing Islam from the other religions: in Islam alone religious and political authority are united. 'Ālī 'Abd al-Rāziq rejects this view on the grounds that if this were so we would know a good deal more about the political organization and administration of the state founded by the Prophet who acted from Divine revelation (*waḥy*).[56] He cannot answer the question why the historical sources are silent about the Prophet's government. However, since the government of the Prophet was founded on the revelation of Allāh, the wisest of rulers, it was of utmost perfection, yet inaccessible to human reason. In his view, laws must be based on verifiable factual knowledge. While it is, then, quite possible that the prophetic government was exemplary, we must, he believes, nevertheless ask why we know so little about it. It is this scientific approach to historical knowledge which apparently leads him to exclude the Prophet and his rule from the accepted canons of political government and administration.[57] That we have no detailed knowledge of the organization and administration of the time of the Prophet in contrast to the caliphate obviously confirms 'Ālī 'Abd al-Rāziq in his view amounting to religious conviction that the Prophet's mission was a purely and exclusively religious mission, a call to Allāh. The organization of the state and the foundations of government are, thus—according to a certain view—accidental conventions (*istilāḥāt āriḍah*) and artificially created institutions (*awḍā' maṣnū'ah*) which are not necessary for a simple state (*dawlah basāṭah*)—and a natural government (*ḥukūmah al-fiṭrah*).[58] Simplicity was the keynote of the Prophet's life (*yuḥibb al-basāṭah*), hence his government lacked those appearances which are today considered by political scientists, foundations (*arkān*) of political governments. Therefore, we find among the laws the Prophet laid down only simple, natural ones, such as those concerning prayer and fasting. The Prophet's government, though it may appear vague and confused, is in fact nothing but simplicity and the pure state of nature.[59] This, says he, most accords with religion, but on examination it is unsound, hence another explanation must be attempted.[60] He now works out the difference between prophetic and temporal authority from the premiss that Islam is a religious unity and that the Muslims are one community. It is for this unity that the Prophet has called.[61] He insists that there is no clear proof in the Qur'ān and in the *Ḥadīth* of the Prophet of the political character of the Islamic faith, only mere conjecture. 'But conjecture (*ẓann*) cannot replace anything of the truth.'[62] The government of the universe is a temporal concern left to our minds in complete liberty by Allāh.[63] During his whole life the Prophet never referred to anything which may be called an Islamic state or an Arab state.[64] The administration of justice, finance, military affairs, every function of state are purely political. Religion has nothing to do with them. It does not command nor forbid them, it simply leaves them to us so that we have recourse to laws of reason, to the experience of the nations and to the rules of politics with regard to them.[65] In another place, 'Ālī 'Abd al-Rāziq expresses the essential difference between the Prophet and the kings and their respective states by contrasting the *qawm* of the Prophet with the *ra'āyā* of the kings,[66] that is to say, *qawm* stands for the religious community guided by the apostle of Allāh, whereas *ra'āyah* stands for the subjects of a sovereign temporal ruler.

Still, there is the institution of *jihād* which 'Ālī 'Abd al-Rāziq considers as a war of aggression, but concedes that it may further human civilization.[67] He sums up his argument from the Qur'ān, the *Sunnah* and history in an eloquent exposition of the universality of Islam which is, to repeat, a *waḥdah dīnīyah*, a religious unity, a *waḥdat al-īmān wa'l-madhhab dīnīyah*, a unity of faith and a religious way and direction, and not a *waḥdat dawlatin wa madhāhib al-mulk*, translated freely, a political unity and temporal-royal institutions and directions. Muḥammad, he asserts, never mixed in their affairs, never deposed a governor, nominated a judge (*qāḍī*) or regulated economic affairs. What Islam teaches in principles, social relations, ethics, legal punishments and so forth is only religious law (*shar' dīnī*) directed towards Allāh and man's *religious* welfare (*maṣlaḥah*).

Neither the religious law nor the Prophet care for the *political* welfare of man (*maṣlaḥah madaniyyah*) which is entirely irrelevant. The *Sharī'ah* only united the Arabs in a religious unity, but politically, socially and economically they were different peoples.[68] He warns against the picture the historians painted of the course of Islamic history. Religion minimised Arab dissensions and differences ; it united them. But with the death of the Prophet the unity vanished, and he quotes Abū 'l-Fidā' in support.[69] Only a lay pre-eminence remained after the Prophet's death (*za'āmah lā-dīnīyah*). True, the Arab state arose on the foundations of a religious call (*da'wah*) under Abū Bakr, the first king (*malik*). It was already stated that Abū Bakr followed in his private and public life the example of the Prophet so that a religious nimbus surrounded him, but his rule nevertheless constituted a *ḥukūmah madanīyah dunyawīyah*, a political, temporal government, wherefore the Muslims rebelled against him. Their opposition had nothing to do with their religion (*dīn*) and faith (*īmān*). Abū Bakr's wars were not wars of religion but purely political wars. But since he gave his political administration a religious direction as far as possible in the way of the Prophet, the error could arise and grow among Muslims that the *khilāfah* was a religious dignity and the vicegerency of the master of the *Sharī'ah*. For political reasons this fiction was maintained in the interests of the rulers : they equated obedience to the *Imām* with obedience to Allāh, rebellion against him with rebellion against Allāh. 'Ālī 'Abd al-Rāziq considers this a crime of the caliphs against the Muslims, in the name of religion.[70]

He now launches out into a sustained attack against the caliphs who have misled the Muslims in the understanding of their religion and of the *khilāfah*. In the name of religion, they forbade them the study of and research in the political sciences until the faculty of research and all intellectual activity among the Muslims came to an end. Otherwise he could not understand why those who admired the Greek philosophers should have neglected the study of the political philosophy of Plato's *Republic* and Aristotle's *Politics*. Political science is most dangerous because it shows that there are different kinds of government, besides the absolute monarchy of the caliphs. It is perhaps surprising that 'Ālī 'Abd al-Rāziq who quoted Hobbes and John Locke should have been completely unaware of the political treatises of al-Fārābī, Ibn Sīnā and Ibn

Rushd, although admittedly these writings had little influence on constitutional thinking among the jurists and theologians of Islam and were, moreover, edited for the most part and studied in the last thirty years only.

He attempted to demolish the traditional claim that the *khilāfah* was obligatory since the Qur'ān and the *Sunnah* demanded its institution. That Rashīd Riḍā's treatise and political movement advocated its re-establishment prompted him to his searching inquiry in which he combined traditional learning with contemporary historical criticism relying on reason and experience. In this he showed considerable courage and had to pay a heavy price for his daring.

That his aim was not merely academic is clear from his eloquent concluding statements in which he vigorously denies that Islam has anything to do with the *khilāfah.* All political functions are left to us, our reason, its judgments and to political principles. 'There is nothing in religion which hinders the Muslims to compete with other nations in all the social and political sciences, to demolish the old order before which they bowed and to which they submitted. Let them build up the bases of their state (*mulk*) and the organization (*niẓām*) of their government (*ḥukūmah*) in accordance with the most modern (principles) the human intellect has devised and with the best principles of government in the experience of the nations. ...' [71]

'Alī 'Abd al-Rāziq's challenging treatise, written by a deeply religious Muslim, seems to provide the theoretical basis for the radical separation of Islam as religion from the affairs of state which are the concern of man.

IV

MUḤAMMAD AL-GHAZĀLĪ

Muḥammad al-Ghazālī, on the other hand, upholds—like Rashīd Riḍā—the religious and political unity of Islam and consequently stresses the Muslim's duty to apply the teachings of Islam to political and social life. His views are those of the Muslim Brotherhood, strongly coloured by the nationalists' uncompromising stand against Western 'colonialism' and 'imperialism' which are held responsible for the separation of religion and politics. At the same time, he sees in modern nationalism the dangerous foe of Islam.

His treatise *Min hunā na'lam*[72] was occasioned by and is intended as a counterblast against Khālid Muḥammad Khālid's *Min hunā nabda'*[73] which represents a radical application of 'Ālī 'Abd al-Rāziq's thesis. Muḥammad al-Ghazālī is not only against the actual separation of state and religion but is opposed to its acceptance in the minds of presentday Muslims who distinguish between temporal power and spiritual forces. This, he holds, is the result of Western imperialist influence out to destroy Islam by isolating it from legislation.[74] In order to be successful Islam must gain political power, like the French and Russian Revolutions, he avers. In clear opposition to 'Ālī 'Abd al-Rāziq he states: 'this happened to the great Prophet, the master of this *Sharī'ah*, for he began as a preacher, an announcer and warner, but ended as a judge and ruler (*ḥākim*) . . . his messengership turned from *da'wah* to *dawlah* . . .'[75] Like the Prophet, the *Khulafā' Rāshidūn* were religious rulers: God and His Book, not power guided them in establishing a government safeguarding Islam and applying its principles. This is good orthodox doctrine. He blames the traditional enmity of Europe towards Islam for considering Islam as a religion separate from the state.[76] He leads this enmity back to the crusaders whose spirit still animates the West today. For he qualifies East as Islamic and West as Crusading Christian (*ṣalībī*) in order to stress their alleged present enmity as the 'traditional (religious) conflict' for he is apparently convinced that the West is out to damage Islam 'by reducing its legislation and destroying its tradition'.[77] He, therefore, draws the conclusion that the West must be acting under the hidden influence of the Church. Such a view is quite understandable in the light of the record of a missionarizing and colonizing West of yesterday. But it is a little difficult to see how in our own day a largely secularized West with its lay national states should be intent on destroying Islam. Organized religion is just as much threatened in the West as it is in the East. While it is true that the separation of religion and politics goes back to the French Revolution and the ideas which influenced it, it poses a challenge to Christianity no less than to Islam though in a different way, since Christianity and classical Islam are not the same—neither in theology and structure nor in organization and practice. To my mind, the threat to classical Islam comes from a secular attitude, not from Christianity, and it is for this reason that it is so dangerous. To meet this challenge Muslims ask the fundamental question: 'What is Islam?' Broadly speaking, the answer is either that of al-Afgh̲ānī, Muḥammad 'Abduh, Rash̲īd Riḍā, Muḥammad al-G̲h̲azālī and those who think like them or of 'Ālī 'Abd al-Rāziq, K̲h̲ālid Muḥammad K̲h̲ālid and their spiritual kinsmen in Muslim lands. Their answers issue in the demand for an Islamic state based on the *S̲h̲arī'ah* on the one hand, and for a lay state with Islam as the religion of the individual citizen on the other, quite apart from opinions all the way between the two.

To return to Muḥammad al-G̲h̲azālī we note that, contrary to the view held by many Muslims that Islam is *dīn lā dawlah* (religion, not a state), he claims that Islam means 'a religious government of free men ... (who) devote themselves and their aims to the path of their religion and nation (*ummah*)'.[78] This is expressed in the title of his first chapter already: *ḥukm islāmī lā qaumī*, an Islamic, not a nationalist government; it sums up his attitude and his programme. It also highlights the real problem: the validity of the *S̲h̲arī'ah* in our time. Islam as faith faces the same challenge as other faiths. But unlike Christianity, Islam as a religious and political unity expressed in constitution and law faces an additional challenge which can only be met on the basis of a clear affirmation of faith. Hence, we have believers divided in their attitude to an Islamic or a lay state, but both equally concerned about Islam.

For Muḥammad al-G̲h̲azālī the separation of religion from the state is *bid'ah*, heresy. He is convinced that Islamic government alone answers the need of the world, for it guards revelation.[79] Religion without power would be powerless, we have here an echo of Ibn K̲h̲aldūn. The duty of *jihād* can only be performed in society organized in a state.[80] He recalls that all the texts stress the presence of spiritual as well as temporal power in the person of the ruler who combines the offices of commander, judge and *imām* in himself, and he blames cultural imperialism and the domination of Christian powers for their separation in the Muslim mind and in actual fact.[81] Since in his opinion Islamic ideals and teachings must be realized in the state a nationalist government which disregards them would be irreligious. Muslims must fight such a government and replace it by a religious one. He extols al-Afgh̲ānī, Muḥammad 'Abduh and their followers whose reforms were to a large extent thwarted by obstacles, and ridicules the imitators of the West. Nationalism is blamed for the loss of Islamic unity: 'the nationalist attitude is the most important thing we copied from the West [which he identifies with Christian imperialism !], and formed the cornerstone in establishing the modern state'.[82] It is tantamount to a return to the first *Jāhilīyah*—the heading of this chapter. He goes on to ask 'how could we abandon the Islamic for the nationalist government?' The bond of Islam is stronger than kinship based on community of blood. He blames the separation of state and religion for the loss of the Turkish Empire : nationalism inflicts but losses on Islam.[83]

Nothing less than a determined return to the purity of Islam can save the situation, for Islam is universal with Allāh as sole ruler, law-giver and judge. Islam's internationalism and religious and political unity derive from its pure monotheism. Truth, brotherliness and justice form the solid basis of world order, as taught by Islam.[84] Against Khālid Muḥammad Khālid he maintains that the Prophet was guided by God in his political and social actions, not by circumstances. His wars were not wars of conquest but of liberation of subject peoples, and Khālid Muḥammad Khālid is wrong when he claims that prophethood is superior to government ; as religious government it uses power for the good of all, not for its own sake : this is true Islam.[85] Hence he calls for repentance and a return to God and His Book and for the application of His *Sharī'ah*.[86]

A scathing attack on the European colonial powers in India, China, America, North Africa, Syria, etc., quoting G. B. Shaw and Gustave Lebon in support, is followed by praise for the virtues of Islam and its state based on the Qur'ān and the *Sunnah*. In contrast to France with its suppression of liberty in her colonies, Islam has liberated Egypt, Syria and Persia and has brought virtue and prosperity to a large part of the world. As in its glorious past so today Islam is our only salvation, he avers.[87] The example of the Qur'ān and the *Sunnah*, not Western authorities, are needed against Khālid Muḥammad Khālid's reliance on the latter. In the section on 'religious scholars and rulers' he opposes Khālid who, from the fact that throughout Muslim history religious scholars supported unjust rulers, drew the conclusion that the separation of state and religion was inevitable. In fact it was the only answer capable of freeing religion from collusion with such a government and of ridding the people of it.[88] Muḥammad al-Ghazālī retorts that the fault of people cannot be blamed on the religion they profess ; he accepts Khālid's strictures on certain 'priests' (!), i.e.

religious leaders, but insists on the unshakable authority of the Qur'ān and the *Sunnah*. Nationalism is reproached for throwing all religions into the same pot, as it were: for Muḥammad al-Ghazālī Islam is the only universal religion.[89] Nationalism, according to him, leads to the destruction of Islam. In proportion to the growth of particularist nationalisms Islam has become weaker as a general nationality among its adherents all over the world.[90] He admonishes the '*ulamā*' in Islam to try and bring the people back to God and to attack their governments if their acts should run counter to Islamic principles.[91] Since religion must be the basis of the state and Islam is the religion of the majority in Egypt, political government must be founded on Islam. This is the conclusion of his attack on Salāmah Mūsā who is—wrongly it appears—charged with advocacy of the union of all Egyptians based on the rejection of Islam and Christianity. Once again, Muḥammad al-Ghazālī returns to his attack on European imperialism in the guise of Christian missions. He claims that, while communism severs religion from every aspect of public life, imperialism separates state from religion only if the religion is Islam.[92] In his discussion of socialism—reminiscent, as his pronouncements on woman in Islam, of Rashīd Riḍā—he distinguishes between Russian irreligious socialism which he rejects, and Islamic socialism based on monotheism and the brotherhood of all men, teaching equality and justice. First, fundamental principles in conformity with the Qur'ān and the *Sunnah*, must be established and then Muslims can legislate for their realisation. An Islamic constitution is imperative, everything else must follow from it.[93] He refers to Abū 'l-A'lā Mawdūdī in Pakistan and others, e.g. to Sayyid Quṭb in Syria, who hold similar views to those held by him and his associates in Egypt. All tried to find a solution to the crisis on the basis of Islam. Islamic socialism is the remedy. These views are typical for the Muslim Brotherhood.

We have here been concerned with Islam under the aspect of the classical doctrine of the religious and political unity of Islam and its contemporary interpretation—the traditionalist view upholding it and the lay, but not the secularist, view of the separation of religion and politics. Only incidentally, the relationship between Islam and nationalism was touched upon, in connexion with the views of Muḥammad al-Ghazālī. Other writings could be adduced, but they would offer little variation. An excellent evaluation of the problem of Islam and Nationalism is provided by Ẓafar Isḥāq Anṣārī.[94] He rightly states that the views of the *'ulamā'* of al-Azhar and of the Muslim Brotherhood represent Islamic attitudes rather than those of Khālid Muḥammad Khālid or Ṭāhā Ḥusayn, and that the orthodox Muslim writers predominantly follow 'the traditional formulations of Islam . . . A more or less literal interpretation of the Qur'ān and the *Sunnah* is still regarded as valid'. The article well presents the ideas of Ḥasan al-Bannā, Sa'īd Ramaḍān and other like-minded men, including Muḥammad al-Ghazālī ; it deals with their social and political ideas as well as with their attitude to nationalism as adherents of Islam as a universal faith and way of life. Z. I. Anṣārī also clearly sees that the orthodox attitude to nationalism is part of a wider problem : their attitude 'towards the assimilation of Western ideas and institutions'.[95] Since there is naturally a good deal of common ground between the believers and secular nationalists in the necessary struggle for national liberation and independence,[96] it is obvious that a certain tension between religious universalism and political particularism is unavoidable which patriotism is to overcome. This tension underlines the complexity of the problem and increases the difficulty of defining the place of Islam in a modern national state and of working out an Islamic policy. This can be well observed in the attitude of these orthodox Muslims to their non-Muslim compatriots. Z. I. Anṣārī rightly says that 'more or less equal statutory rights' and 'just and generous treatment of non-Muslims in an Islamic state' do not by themselves constitute full integration of non-Muslim fellow-citizens into the cultural society of the majority in the common fatherland. He is fully aware of the dilemma which faces the orthodox Muslim—who, to repeat, demands an Islamic state—when he says that a 'development of a homogeneous secular nationality, which is the aim of the nationalists, does not fit into the framework of the contemporary Islamic socio-political thought'.

In conclusion, it is necessary to realize that such a fundamental problem as that posed by the existing situation in relation to the role of Islam demands an urgent solution. Its very complexity favours the taking up of radical positions. This can only increase confusion and contradiction, yet it is perhaps inevitable. It needs goodwill and patience and demands the creation of public opinion, well informed and rooted in the Islamic past no less than determined on the lasting establishment of a modern society. Willingness to take into consideration the extreme positions and to attempt a reconciliation in the interests of the entire citizenry for the good of all is essential.

The issue is undoubtedly aggravated and confused through the actual political situation and as the result of the aftermath of foreign domination. This colonialism has left its mark both positively and negatively ; but the benefits are inevitably dwarfed at this early stage of national independence and sovereignty by the disadvantages arising from its negative features. The most important of the latter is the neglect of education and the consequent backwardness coupled with a wide gulf between 'Western' and traditional education. A solution would be easier and nearer if two conditions could be found to be actively present in the building up of nation and state. The one is the internal strength flowing from a strong Islamic consciousness based on deep knowledge of Islamic law and lore, history and cultural achievement. The other concerns the attitude to the West. As long as the 'West' is identified with Christianity a peculiar theological argument clouds the discussion and blurs the cultural and political issues. For Christian missionary activity today threatens Islam much less than an exaggerated nationalism which is the natural result of post-French Revolution colonialism and imperialism which have nothing to do with Christianity. If the Christian missions have presented a challenge it derives less from the Christian message than from the 'secular' European ideas embodied in the arts and the sciences, foremost among them the principles of unhampered, rational inquiry and historical-literary criticism. To link 'colonialism' with 'Christianity,' as many Muslims still do, only blurs the issues, gets the real problem out of focus and hinders a bold coming to grips with the challenge of modern life in all its facets, political, economic, social, cultural and religious. Nobody can do without the scientific and technical achievements in our time or we would relapse into backwardness. But we have all—without exception—to pay the price : a radical rethinking leading to a new assessment of our spiritual roots and values and to a new attitude to faith and reason. We are all engaged in the same struggle and it helps no one to blame the other for our ills and shortcomings. Undoubtedly, in our inescapable self-examination we must uncover the reasons and causes of our malaise, not to absolve ourselves by accusing the others, but rather in order to lay the many ghosts we allow to haunt us and to encourage ourselves to solve our common problem in the way best suited to our specific situation and our human collective and individual advance, on the basis of historical continuity. The vital question for Islam, it would appear, is how it can better contribute to an urgently needed solution : as a religious and moral force in a modern *lay* state, or through its *Sharī'ah*—howsoever modified by believers—in an *Islamic* state.

NOTES

1. Cairo 1923, translated into French with valuable notes by Henri Laoust under the title *Le Califat dans la doctrine de Rašīd Riḍā*, Beyrouth 1938. The first figure refers to the Arabic text, the second to the French translation.
2. Cf. p. 22/37.
3. Cf. p. 66/112 ; 87 ff./146 ff.
4. Cf. p. 59 f./101.
5. Cf. p. 62 f./105 f.
6. Cf. p. 66/111.
7. Cf. *ibid.*
8. Cf. p. 77/129 ; 137 ff./231 ff. On Kemal Atatürk, cf. p. 82 f./137 f.
9. Cf. p. 90 ff./151 ff.
10. Cf. p. 58/99.
11. Cf. p. 79/133 ; 83/139 ; 85 f./143.
12. Cf. p. 70/117 f. ; 67/112. Naturally, the Muslim Brotherhood shares this view.
13. Cf. p. 76/128.
14. Cf. p. 77/130.
15. Cf. p 79/132 f. ; 65/109 and Laoust's note 36, p. 262 f.
16. Cf. p. 81 f./136 f.
17. Cf. p. 84 ff./142 ff.
18. Cf. p. 99/167 f.
19. Cf. p. 97/163.
20. Cf. Laoust's Introduction to his French translation and also his study Le Reformise orthodoxe des 'Salafiya' in : *Revue des Etudes Islamiques*, LI, 1932.
21. Cf. p. 99/166 f. and n. 41, p. 266.
22. Cf. pp. 114-116/194-198, taking issue with Lloyd George and Lord Cromer.
23. Cf. p. 119/202.
24. Cf. p. 126/213.
25. Cf. *ibid.*, p. 103/174 f. which clearly contradicts the passage quoted in the previous note. The distinction between 'general principles of spiritual guidance'—as the Catholics expect of the Pope—and 'spiritual authority' which Rashīd Riḍā denies to the caliph is ambiguous and unconvincing. It

may be due to the apologetic and polemical tendencies in relation to Christianity which are so strong with him.

26. Cf. p. 119/202, already quoted earlier (n. 23).
27. Cf. p. 122/207 f.
28. Cf. *ibid.*/208.
29. Cf. p. 90/151, and Laoust's n. 38, p. 264.
30. Cf. p. 66/111.
31. Cf. p. 92/154.
32. Cf. p. 93/156.
33. Cf. p. 123/209.
34. Cf. p. 124 f./210 ff., a quotation from Muḥammad 'Abduh.
35. Cf. again p. 126/213 and n. 25 above.
36. Cf. p. 127/214.
37. Cf. pp. 134-7/225-31.
38. Cf. p.124/210.
39. Cf. preface to his *al-Islām wa-uṣūl al-Ḥukm*[2], Cairo 1925 from which the quotations are taken. The second figure refers to the French translation by Bercher in *Revue des Études Islamiques*, 1933, pp. 357 ff. and 1934, pp. 163 ff.
40. Cf. *Aḥkām al-Sulṭānīyah*, ed. M. Enger, Bonn 1853, p. 3 and my treatment of Al-Māwardī in my book *Political Thought in Medieval Islam*, 1958 and 1962 (reprint), p. 28 in particular.
41. *Muqaddimah*, ed. Bulāq, p. 191. Cf. also my treatment, *op. cit.*, pp. 84 ff. For 'Ālī 'Abd al-Rāziq cf. p. 13/368.
42. Cf. p. 17 f./373 ff.
43. Cf. p. 25/380.
44. Cf. p. 36/389, (*Muqaddimah*, p. 180.)
45. Cf. p. 29/383.
46. Cf. p. 38/391.
47. Cf. p. 35 f. (par. 16)/389.
48. Cf. p. 27/382.
49. Cf. p. 15/370. The term *'ulu'l-'amr* is wider than '*khilafah*' and independent of it.
50. Cf. pp. 66 ff./186 ff., one of the most important sections of the treatise, based on the Qur'ān and the *Sunnah* of the Prophet.
51. Cf. p. 68 f./189.
52. Cf. p. 69/189 ff. and, also for what follows, 78 ff./198 ff.
53. Cf. p. 84/204.
54. Cf. p. 52 f./175.
55. Cf. p. 54 f./177.
56. Cf. pp. 55-59/178-81. In view of the difficulty of proving his point, 'A 'Abd al-Rāziq's argument appears somewhat laboured.
57. Cf. p. 58 f./180 f. ; also 46 f./169 for a full account.
58. Cf. p. 59 f./180 f.
59. Cf. pp. 60 ff./181 ff.
60. Cf. p. 62/184.
61. Cf. p. 70/190.

62. Cf. p. 76/196 f.
63. Cf. p. 78/198 f.
64. Cf p. 87/206.
65. Cf. p. 103/221.
66. Cf. p. 65/185.
67. Cf. p. 69/199, on the ground that 'perhaps evil is sometimes necessary for good (to come out of it)'.
68. Cf. pp. 83 ff./202 ff.
69. Cf. p. 85/205.
70. Cf. pp. 90 ff./209 ff.
71. Cf. p. 103/221.
72. Cairo, 5th edition ; English translation by Ismā'īl R. al-Fārūqī under the title *Our Beginning in Wisdom*, Washington, 1953 (American Council of Learned Societies). I have adhered to a more literal translation.
3. This treatise was also translated by the same writer in the same series under the title *From Here We Start*, Washington 1953. Arabic text used, Cairo 1950.
74. From the Preface to the second edition, p. 11/xii f.
75. Cf. p. 23/4.
76. Cf. p. 24/5 f.
77. Cf. p. 39/15.
78. Cf. p, 28/7.
79. Cf. p. 55/25.
80. Cf. p. 55 f./25 f.
81. Cf. p. 56/26.
82. Cf. p. 68/34 f.
83. Cf. p. 70/36.
84. Cf. p. 73 f./38 f.
85. Cf. p. 81/43 f.
86. Cf. p. 90/50.
87. Cf. p. 112/64.
88. Cf. pp. 120 ff./68 ff.
89. Cf. pp. 134 ff./78 ff.
90. Cf. p. 138/81.
91. Cf. p. 142/84.
92. Cf. p. 161/96.
93. Cf. pp. 224 ff./135 ff.
94. In his article 'Contemporary Islam and Nationalism : A Case Study of Egypt' in *Die Welt des Islam*, N. F. VII, 1-4, 1961, pp. 3 ff.
95. *Ibid.*, p. 18.
96. *Ibid.*, pp. 20 ff.

II

POLITICS IN ISLAM

In the classical concept Islam is a religious and political unity. The juxtaposition, even contrast or contradiction of 'religion' and 'politics', assumed in the subject of this Symposium, clearly implies that this unity can no longer be taken for granted in contemporary Islam. In order to understand why this should be so we must realize that in the Muslim national states of our time the individual owes allegiance to the fatherland (*waṭan*) first and only second to the *umma*, the universal religious community of all believers. This does not necessarily mean that there exists a conflict of loyalties; traditionalist Muslims would undoubtedly claim complete compatibility in the form of a natural dual loyalty. This is possible only, however, because the idea of *umma* has itself undergone a significant transformation in that it is understood as a purely religious and not as a political, national community as well. Even if Kemal Atatürk had not abolished the caliphate, a caliph could today only expect recognition as the *spiritual* head of all Muslims; he would certainly not receive *political* allegiance from any Muslim not of his own nation. Yet, the classical concept of Islam as a political and religious unity postulates a caliph who is both spiritual and temporal ruler of the world-wide *umma* of Islam, at least in theory. The absence of a caliph in our time only conceals the changed character of the idea of the *umma*. For the traditionalist Muslim living within a national state demands the implementation of the *Sharīᶜa* in its totality; not to re-establish the caliphate as the symbol of the world-wide *umma* of Islam, but to restore the political and religious unity of Islam within the national boundaries by recognizing the *Sharīᶜa* as the constitution and the effective law of the state. This is amply borne out by the program of the Muslim Brotherhood.

The Pan-Islamism of a Jamāl al-Dīn al-Afghānī would today be utopian, if it were possible at all. For although it was the Muslim answer to Western imperialism and Christian missionary activity, that is to say, a positive response both to a religious challenge and to political designs against the Ottoman empire as the premier Muslim power, Pan-Islamism as a political force could not be entertained in a world of independent national modern states.

Of even greater significance is the grave threat to Islam as a faith and a way of life (with or without direct participation in national politics) that stems from the very crisis of faith as such in our time the world over. We need only take our minds back to Nāmik Kemāl in 1867 and to Ziya Gökalp who died in 1924 to realize the situation which has crystallized in Turkey during that time-span and which can be characterized—though rather crudely—as the battle between Islamism and Westernism, between an Islamic state based on the *Sharīᶜa* and a modern national lay state in which Islam is ousted from public life, has no say in politics, but is given due recognition as the citizen's religion in his private life. How oversimplified this polarization is becomes clear when we remember that Islam is still today if not *the,* then at least *a* most important problem in the Turkish lay republic. For in Turkey as in all other Muslim states there exists a gulf between the masses of naive, fervent believers and the intellectual elite which governs and mans the services of a modern state. This gulf is more than a contrast between Western civilization and traditionalism in religion and all other spheres of life, largely because atheism and agnosticism as well as 'modernism' or (religious) liberalism only reflect the gradual recession of faith, at least of orthodox, traditionalist faith. In those sixty years or more a battle was begun (and transformed as it progressed) which culminated in the spiritual crisis of our time which—in our context—has forced into the open the serious question: 'What is Islam?'. Before the principles of the French Revolution and the institutions it created with the separation of religion and politics made their impact on the Muslim world such a question and its corollary 'Who is a Muslim?' would have been as unthinkable and nonsensical as to ask who and what is German, English, French or American.

It is obvious that especially in developing states of Asia and Africa it is the intellectual elite in government, administration and the army and, one would hope, in the universities and research institutes that determine the course of events and shape the future of a modern national state. What they believe and think is, therefore, of far greater significance today than the piety and devotion to traditional religion of the masses of the people. Moreover, the well planned and high-minded national education, which is the key to national unity and prosperity, concentrates in all Muslim countries on education for citizenship through a conscious attempt to mould character by teaching Islam as faith and way of life, as history, culture and civilization. Alongside this character training, national education tries to inculcate love of country and civic responsibility, and to impart vocational training on Western scientific and technological lines. Until the right teachers are trained and the necessary textbooks produced, Islamic education is largely traditional. A case in point is the teaching of Islam and of other religions in the Faculty of Theology in the University of Ankara at present on parallel lines without any attempt at integration of the two streams, the traditional Islamic and the scientific study of comparative religion, psychology and philosophy of religion. Without such integration no harmonious personality can be attained, a personality equally at home in the religion, history and civilisation of Islam as meaningful to its full human existence, and in historical and literary criticism of that same Islam compared with other religions and civilizations. While, therefore, integration is desirable, even necessary, it can at the same time present a serious challenge to faith in our time in that it treats Islam as a means to civics and good citizenship for political rather than for religious ends and thus may lead to a complete secularization of classical Islam as we know it from the past at the height of its spiritual and political power.

The impact of Western civilization on Islam appears to have changed, if not perverted, its classical meaning and image. For many a Western educated Muslim looks at Islam rather as a personal religion like Christianity in the West than as a personal and social way of life to which Western science and technology must be applied. This is so because we cannot take over the scientific method without succumbing to some extent to its underlying philosophy. This philosophy places man as a rational creature in the centre of the universe, be it a humanist or outright materialist philosophy. There does not seem to be any room left for God as the source and centre of all men and things, of all life on earth. Yet without faith in Allah no Muslim can be expected to submit voluntarily to the dictates and injunctions of His *Sharīᶜa*. This is not the old contrast between faith and works, since works without faith are useless and pointless without ethics anchored in religious faith and commandment. The intellectualism of medieval Judaism, Christianity and Islam allowed for, nay was based upon, the acceptance of the overriding authority and power of God, circumscribing and severely limiting the scope and range of man's free exercise of his reason. The religious law was accepted as obligatory because its divine source was believed and acknowledged. In the case of Islam, we naturally know that the *Sharīᶜa* in its entirety was never implemented in political, social and economic life and that only what we call personal status law (marriage, divorce, inheritance, etc.) has always been Islamic law in the form of one of the accepted orthodox schools of law, notwithstanding customary law alongside of or even ousting it in some respects. But what alone matters is that classical Islam (and it reaches in this respect right to the threshold of our age) accepted the *Sharīᶜa* as the ideal, immutable norm. Some might call this a fiction, but let us at least admit that even if fiction it outlasted the political collapse of the caliphate in 1258 and preserved the unity of the *umma*. We recall the significant shift from the *khilāfa* as the ideal Muslim polity to the *Sharīᶜa* binding the *umma*, performed by Ibn Taymīya, the source—together with Ibn Qayyim al-Jawzīya—of modern 'reformers'. The emphasis on the *Sharīᶜa* instead of on the *khilāfa* is an indispensable legacy of classical doctrine to those traditionalists who today want to build an Islamic state based on the *Sharīᶜa*, immutable or modified. What they do not seem to realize is that without faith in Allah, and in Allah as the source of the law of Islam, they cannot expect a secularised intellectual elite bent on building a modern national state (if possible on Islamic principles) to acknowledge and implement the *Sharīᶜa*.

For this reason Islam finds itself today in an unprecedented crisis and in an uneasy state of transition. This expresses itself on the theoretical side in the use of a modern terminology which claims to derive from the religious and political unity of classical Islam on the one hand and from political ideologies on the other. By coining the term 'Islamic ideology' those leading Muslim statesmen and politicians, including the spiritual leaders, the *ᶜulamā,* particularly in Pakistan, are undoubtedly motivated by a number of different standpoints and aims, but they all share in the attempt to justify their policies by calling them Islamic. Yet they differ widely in their understanding of Islam as such and of its role in a modern national state. I use the word 'claim' advisedly, because we must not be led to justify the use of the term 'ideology' on the basis of the classical concept of the *khilāfa* as the ideal unity of what we are used to understand today in the West by 'religion' and 'politics'. The French Revolution and, in the context of Islam, the Turkish Revolution in its wake changed the situation radically and irrevocably. Voices have emerged, led by ᶜAli ᶜAbd al-Rāziq,[1] which insist on the separation of religion and politics by denying the unity of both in original Islam, break with the time-honoured concept of the *khulafā rāshidūn* as the true continuators of Muḥammad's religious community *and* state, and consequently see in Islam the ultimate monotheistic revelation, superior to Judaism and Christianity, but like the latter a personal faith apart from the political organisation in a state. Though their premise may be or (so I believe) is in fact wrong the consequences they draw from it can be considered a logical application to Islam, past, present and future, of the modern situation and the relationship between religion and politics as the result of the French Revolution and the emergence of modern national states. Their premise is wrong because the prophet Muḥammad was both messenger (*rasūl*) of Allah and *malik*, temporal ruler, and bequeathed his twofold authority, spiritual and temporal, to the *khalīfa.* The Vicegerent is guided by Qurʾān and Sunna.

At the opposite end we have Rashīd Riḍā and his successors who draw from European nationalism the conclusion based on the correct premise of classical Islam and may be claimed to have fathered the present tendency expressed in the term 'Islamic ideology' as used both by the adherents of an Islamic state in the orthodox traditional sense and of a modern national state built on Islamic principles applied in a liberal sense through a fresh interpretation of Qurʾān and Sunna. In so far as both sides claim adherence to Qurʾān and Sunna they may be said to practise political theology. In reality, only the orthodox position is consistent and clear; it is a perpetuation of the medieval attitude of the *ᶜulamā* and *fuqahā* with modern means borrowed from Western political ideologies. The liberal position is more obscure

[1] Cf. my *Islam in the Modern National State,* chapters 4 and 5. Cambridge, 1965.

and—at least at a first glance—appears to graft Islamic principles derived from Qur'ān and Sunna, liberally interpreted, on to a political ideology. The inherent difficulty of the latter position (as of the orthodox one though for different reasons) becomes apparent if we examine modern Muslim attitudes to a fundamental tenet of classical Islam, namely the existence of two realms, the *dār al-Islām* and the *dār al-ḥarb,* with the intermediary stage of the *dar al-ṣulḥ*, and the institution of *jihād* (cf. my *op. cit.*, pp. 45, 58, 108, 184).

The student of Islam would do well to ponder this dilemma with its consequences for national and international policies and affairs. While it is entirely a matter for Muslims to decide, their decision must needs affect the larger international community. In our context it clearly shows the difficulties of building Islam—in whatever way it is interpreted—into contemporary politics and the danger inherent in making it an ideology, be it in the shape of a political theology patterned on that of the *ᶜulamā* of classical Islam or in rivalry with one of the ideologies of modern politics, since strictly speaking ideologies belong to the political order.

One way out may be—and I must stress that this is entirely a matter for the Muslims, the Western student of Islam should describe, but never prescribe—the accommodation of Islam in our age to other religions in the West by limiting it to the private concerns of the individual moulding his personal behaviour as a responsible citizen. This is largely the position of Indians of the Muslim religion. It is a religious attitude which is compatible with the concepts and institutions of a modern lay state and, since hardly any state is without its minorities (ethnic, linguistic or religious) today, such an attitude would remove a source of friction and a pretext for discrimination on religious grounds, provided the religions established within the national boundaries of a modern state are without exception willing to exist side by side. This would not only outlaw communalism but would ultimately lead to its disappearance as a political force and weapon. Yet speaking of Islam it may be seriously doubted whether such a personal religion would remain Islam as we know it by foregoing the discipline of the religious law and simply concentrating on the basic tenets which are, after all, today the common property of the civilised world.

Further, an Islam restricted to a personal faith might be at a disadvantage as the result of the exclusion of Islam's social teachings about brotherhood and justice, for example, from the political scene. In order to compete with political ideologies regnant in our world today the political leaders in the Muslim sector must be able to appeal to the social teachings of Islam. By stressing them—largely at the expense of the validity of the *Sharīᶜa* today—they justify their recourse to Islamic principles in place of the implementation of the *Sharīᶜā* (which originated and evolved in an entirely different political, social and economic situation centuries ago). Hence, their 'invention' of Islamic ideology as a rallying cry to give nationalism a content more enduring than mere political nationalism, yet, one is bound to fear, promoting a rapid secularisation of Islam. One Muslim nationalist leader of calibre and stature, ᶜAllāl al-Fāsī of Morocco, has seen this danger and, as far as I can see, has succeeded in blending Islam with nationalism and with Arabism. [2] How difficult it is to make of Islam an ideology which can unite the people irrespective of their personal commitment to Islam as a discipline can best be seen in the long drawn out struggle for a constitution in Pakistan. The outside observer is bound to fear for the effectiveness of Islam as a unifying, creative force in the life of Pakistan as long as parties exist which tend to monopolize Islam (or a form of Islam) and thus use a meaningful faith and way of life as a counter in the political game. Using this rather harsh language we must stress, however, that there are many earnest, devout Muslims who want to see Islam play a central role in national life, including politics, just as there are many pious Muslims who hold that at this juncture in the evolution of Pakistan as a viable state and nation Islam should be kept out of politics altogether.

Sympathy and understanding are needed to see the very real problem which Muslims are facing today with regard to the part Islam is to play in their individual and collective lives. This is the more imperative since Western domination is largely responsible for the conditions prevailing in developing Muslim countries, conditions which aggravate, though they have not created, the position of Islam today.

While the medieval *ᶜulamā* who left us treatises on constitutional theory and law had little if any influence on affairs, they evolved a political theory or better political ideas which represent an ideal far removed from political reality, but in agreement with the teachings of Islam. Again, while they were forced to compromise and to bow (sometimes too deeply) to expediency, they succeeded in preserving the unity of the *umma* in the face of political disunity and disintegration. [3] An ideal polity ruled by the divinely revealed law stands out as an ideal which could—and largely did—unite the Muslim believers, preserve Islam as a force even after the decline and fall of the caliphate, and make possible missionary activity on a large scale and pan-Islamism.

Accepting the classical distinction between *khilāfa* and *mulk,* the empirical, realistic thinker and man of affairs, Ibn Khaldūn, has not only refined the concept of the *umma* and provided a deeper understanding of their basic differences, but has (this is at least my reading of his fundamental discussion in his *Muqaddimah*), through his analysis of the *mulk* and its differentiation into an Islamic *mulk* and

---

[2] Cf. Op. cit., chap. 7.

[3] Cf. my *Political Thought in Medieval Islam*, chapter 2. Cambridge, 1962.

a mere power state, shown the way to a state based on a mixed constitution and a mixed law which could perhaps serve as a guide to a modern Muslim state. A very brief reference, in conclusion of these introductory remarks, will therefore be made to his ideas because of their possible relevance to the present-day problem of state and religion in Islam.

Khilāfa versus *mulk* was for Ibn Khaldūn not a matter of theology, but primarily of politics in two directions. In the first place, politics are or should be concerned with the Highest Good (an Aristotelian idea). Therefore, the ideal polity (*khilāfa*) produces the Good Society since its aim is the welfare of the subjects in this life and in the hereafter. (As a Muslim living in Muslim states governed by absolute rulers he deals with subjects and not with citizens.) Secondly, but of no less importance, it is the law in force in the state which determines its character. Thus, the *Sharīᶜa* of Islam guarantees the Good Society by promoting the welfare of the subjects in an Islamic state. By contrast, the *mulk* is—in so far as it is an 'Islamic' *mulk*—concerned with the welfare of the *malik* and of his subjects. 'Islamic' means that religion largely determines the attitude and actions of the ruler. If the religious *élan* becomes weaker, the *Sharīᶜa* recedes and shares with temporal laws the governance of the *mulk* until the monarch becomes an absolute ruler who makes his own laws to maintain his personal rule. Through a process of gradual transition the end result may well be the naked power state, a secular *mulk* as far as rule and law are concerned even when ruler and subjects are Muslims. We have here an empiricist Muslim's evaluation of *Realpolitik* for whom religion in relation to the state has a primarily political significance. He says in defining the *mulk*: "Politics based on reason can take two forms. In the first, care is taken of welfare in general, and of the advantage of the *sulṭān* in respect of the maintenance of his rule in particular ... Allah had dispensed with it for us in [our] religious community (*milla*) ...., because the statutes of the *Sharīᶜa* dispense with it in respect of the general and the particular welfare. The statutes of the *mulk* are included in it [the *Sharīᶜa*]. In the second form care is taken of the advantage of the ruler, and that the *mulk* should be firmly established for him by force and superior power. The general welfare of the subjects takes second place. Such a government is that of the other kings in the world, Muslim and non-Muslim, except that the Muslim kings act in accordance with the requirements of the Islamic *Sharīᶜa, as far as they can.* Hence, their laws are composed of statutes of the *Sharīᶜa*, of rules of right conduct, of regulations which are natural for association, and necessary things concerning power and *ᶜaṣabīya* ... Although the *mulk* is capable of looking after the welfare of man in this world, even this is achieved more perfectly with the aid of the laws of the *Sharīᶜa*, since the prophetic lawgiver knows best what is to man's advantage in both mundane and religious matters. Therefore, if the *mulk* is Islamic it comes second in rank after the *khilāfa*, and they are linked together. But the *mulk* is isolated if it is outside the religious community." The *khilāfa* is a *siyāsa dīnīya,* that is, an administration based on the religious law (*Sharīᶜa*). The *mulk*, on the other hand, is a *siyāsa ᶜaqlīya,* that is, an administration under the authority of a human-Muslim-sovereign (leaving aside the sheer power-state) who, from political reasoning adopts laws of different origin of which the first (in time and in importance) are laws of the *Sharīᶜa* since the Islamic polity comprises *dīn wa-dunya* (religion and this-worldly politics). The 'Islamic' *mulk* has, thus, a mixed constitution and a mixed law, it is the product of the human founder of a state under Islam, but different from the *khilāfa* ruled by the vicegerent of the prophet and administered by the divine law which the prophet promulgated (cf. my *Islam in the Modern National State,* chapter 2).

It seems to me that Ibn Khaldūn's Islamic *mulk* could serve as a pattern for Muslims who are building up a modern national state, unless they want to break with the past lying behind the period of foreign domination, leave aside tradition and enthrone the practical reason of the contemporary statesman and politician concerned no longer with *dīn*, but exclusively with *dunya.*

APPENDIX OF ADDITIONAL NOTES

p. 3: cf. also chapter IV 'The Theory of the Power-State: Ibn Khaldūn's Study of Civilization' of my *Political Thought in Medieval Islam* (*PTMI*) (3rd ed., Cambridge, 1968).

5: cf. vol. II, chapter 6.

16: of more recent books and studies on Ibn Khaldūn, the following are of special interest: Muhsin Mahdi, *Ibn Khaldûn's Philosophy of History* (London, 1957), and my review of it in *The Times Literary Supplement* of 2 May 1958, under the title 'Islamic Student of Human Civilization'; Franz Rosenthal's 'Translator's Introduction' in his English translation *Ibn Khaldûn, the Muqaddimah* (3 vols., London, 1958; 2nd ed., 1969): this book also contains an Ibn Khaldûn bibliography by Walter J. Fischel; Heinrich Simon, *Ibn Khaldûn's Wissenschaft von der menschlichen Kultur* (Leipzig, 1959), and my review of it in *BSOAS* (1961); Mohammed Talbi (Tunis), 'Ibn Ḫaldūn et le sens de l'histoire' in *Studia Islamica*, XXVI (Paris, 1967), 73–148; Svetlana Batsieva, 'Ibn Khaldun et son milieu social' in *Atti del III Congresso di Studi Arabi e Islamici* (Napoli, 1967), pp. 133–44.

30: cf. also chapter IV of *PTMI*.

36: cf. now chapter VIII of *PTMI*.

38: L. V. Berman, *Ibn Bājja and Maimonides* (Hebrew) (Jerusalem, 1959), p. 52 f., states after R. Walzer that Book X was in Arabic XI.

39: cf. A. Altmann, 'Ibn Bajja on man's ultimate felicity' in *Studies in religious philosophy and mysticism* (Ithaca, N.Y., 1969).

45: cf. also chapter VIII of *PTMI*, especially p. 163.

53: cf. *PTMI*, p. 138 f.

55: cf. *Averroes' Commentary on Plato's 'Republic'* (*ACR*) (3rd ed., Cambridge, 1969), *s.v.* education.

56: cf. also vol. II, chapter 4.

60, n. 1, l. 5: published independently as no. 1 of the University of Cambridge Oriental Publications (*Averroes' Commentary on Plato's 'Republic'*), 1956, 1966, 1969.

n. 1, l. 12: cf. also vol. II, chapter 5.

87: a fresh appraisal of Alfārābī's thought is needed through the edition of *K. al-milla* by Muhsin Mahdi (*Alfārābī's Book of Religion and related texts* (Beirut 1968)).

93: cf. now D. M. Dunlop, *Al-Fārābī Fuṣūl al-madanī* (Cambridge, 1961).

94, l. 19: cf. vol. II, chapter 8.

n. 1: critical editions are now available: *Alfārābī's Political Regime*, ed. Fauzi M. Najjar (Beirut, 1964); Muhsin Mahdi's *Al-Fārābī's Philosophy of Aristotle* (Beirut, 1961). Cf. also chapters V and VI of *PTMI*.

95: a comparison between the K. taḥṣīl and the *K. al-milla* is called for; M. Mahdi (*Alfārābī's Book of Religion*. . .) concentrates on parallels between the *K. al-milla* and the *Madīna fāḍila*, *K. al-siyāsāt* and the *Iḥṣā*.

Appendix of additional notes

99: further investigation of these passages in their context and through comparison with Alfārābī's other political writings is necessary.

103: cf. now Muhsin Mahdi, *Al-Fārābī's Philosophy of Aristotle* (Beirut, 1961).

104: published 1956, 1966, 1969.

124: published 1956, 1966, 1969.

147: these matters are fully discussed in my *Islam in the modern national state* (Cambridge, 1965).

172: cf. now E. Kedouri, *Afghani and 'Abduh. An essay on religious unbelief and political activism in modern Islam* (London, 1966); Malcolm H. Kerr, *Islamic Reform. The Political and Legal Theories of Muḥammad 'Abduh and Rashīd Riḍā* (Berkeley/Los Angeles, and Cambridge, 1966), and my review of it in *Journal of Semitic Studies* (1970); Nikkie R. Keddie, *An Islamic Response to Imperialism. Political and Religious Writings of Sayyid Jamāl al-Dīn al-Afghānī* (Berkeley/Los Angeles, 1968).

INDEX

'Abbāsids 18, 176, 192
'Abd al-Mu'min 63, 65
'Abduh, Muḥammad 172, 176, 177, 181, 199, 205 n.34
Abū Bakr 188, 192, 196
Abū 'l-Fidā' 196
Abū Walīd (grandfather of Ibn Rushd) 62
Abū Ya'qūb 63, 65
Abū Yūsuf 63, 71
Ādāb 20
'Adālah 19
'Adl 21
Afghānī, Jamāl al-Dīn al- 172, 176, 177, 199, 207
After-life—*see* Hereafter
Ahl al-ḥall wa'l- 'aqd 177, 179, 184
Alexander of Aphrodisias 38 n.12, 55, 98
Aligarh (Muslim University of) 159
Allah –*see* God
Almohads 31, 62–5 *passim*, 70–3 *passim*, 83, 107, 109
Almoravids 31, 62–5 *passim*, 70, 71, 73, 109
Alpagus 48 n.48, 120 n.5
Altmann, Alexander 215
Anawati, P. 117
Ankara University 208
Anṣārī, Ẓafar Isḥāq 202, 206 n.94f.
Anthropomorphism (*tajsim*) 71
'Aql 18, 21–*see also* Reason
Arberry, A. J. 53 n.63, 119 n.2
Aristotle 12, 22–5 *passim*, 29, 35–42 *passim*, 47, 47 nn.45,48, 48 n.48, 54–7 *passim*, 60, 61, 62, 64, 65, 66, 69, 72, 74–7 *passim*, 79–90 *passim*, 92, 94–8 *passim*, 102, 105, 107, 108, 114, 119, 120, 120 n.1, 124 n.2, 127, 129, 133, 134, 136, 137, 138 n.1, 141, 143, 196, 213
Arnold, T. W. 191
'Aṣabiyya 8, 9, 11, 12, 15, 31, 80, 186, 192, 213
Asad, Muhammad 151, 152
Ash'arites, Ash'arism 70, 71, 72
Asín, M. Palacios 35, 35 nn.1,3, 36 n.5, 38 n.13, 39, 40 n.18, 41 n.19, 43 n.25, 44 n.31, 45 n.34, 46 nn.38–40,42, 47 nn.45–7, 48 n.49, 50 n.54, 51 nn.55,56, 53 n.63, 54 nn.64,65, 55 n.67, 56 nn.71,72, 57, 57 n.75, 59 n.82, 91, 99 n.2, 138 n.1
Atatürk, Kemal 172, 179, 204 n.8, 207
Authority 17–20 *passim*, 22, 122, 185, 190, 192, 193, 195, 210
Āzād, Abū 'l-Kalām 177
Azhar, al- 167, 202

Bachya (Baḥya), b. Paqūda 131
Badâwa/Bâdiya 10, 11
Baneth, D. H. 99 n.2
Bannā, Ḥasan al- 202
Barker, Ernest 43 n.28, 47 n.48, 49 n.51, 53 n.61
Batsieva, Svetlana 215
Beatitude (blessedness)–*see* Happiness
Bedouinism 181
Bel, A. 91
Bergstraesser, G. 38 n.13, 84, 90
Berman, L. V. 215
Bonafos, Menahem b. Abraham 53 n.63
Bouthoul, G. 3 n.1
Bouyges, M. 75, 91, 98 n.2
Britain, British 149, 152, 161–*see also* India, British rule
Bryson 48 n.48

Caliph, Caliphate 182, 185, 186, 188–92 *passim*, 194, 196, 207, 209, 212
duties of 18, 19, 20, 176, 180, 183, 184, 185
election of 19
re-establishment of 175, 178, 181
—*see also Imām, Imāma*; *Khaḷlfa*; *Khilāfa*
Causality, law of 12, 13, 14, 31, 32, 125
Christensen, A. 56 n.72
Christianity 5, 67, 75, 88, 173, 178, 183, 198–201 *passim*, 203, 205 n.25, 207, 209, 210
Cicero 107 n.5
'Colonialism' 149, 155, 171, 197, 200, 203
Communism 155, 169, 201
Conversion to Islam 153
Cornford, F. M. (trans.) 59 n.81
Creation out of nothing 95 n.5, 96
Crescas, Ḥasdai 134
Cromer, Lord 204 n.22
Crusades, Crusaders 198

David 19
Dawlah siyāsīyah 193
Descartes 128
De Slane, 120 n.1, 124 n.2
Dieterici, F. (Dieterici-Brönnle) 36 n.6, 45 n.35, 52 nn.58–60, 90, 94 n.1, 104 n.5
Djihâd—*see* Jihād
Dozy, R. 91, 120 n.1
Dunlop, D. M. 35, 35 n.2, 38 n.13, 46 nn.41,42, 47 n.45, 50 n.54, 54 n.64, 93 n.3, 110 n.2, 111, 111 n.1, 114 n.1, 215

Education 89, 95, 99, 149, 150, 154, 156–8, 166–9, 177, 182, 203, 208
by persuasion of the masses 75, 95, 107, *passim*

[entry cont. p. 218]

by teaching of the elite 75, 95, 107, *passim*
Egypt 177, 180, 200, 201
Emanation, theory of 76, 85, 94, 100, 136
Ethics 159, 160—*see also* Law, revealed; Philosophy, practical
Eudaimonia **127–34**—*see also* Happiness; Philosophy
Europeanisation 177, 178, 181

Falāsifa, *Falsafa* 5, 18, 22–5 *passim*, 28, 32, 37, 38, 39 n.13, 41, 44, 46, 47 n.45, 52, 60, 61, 66–73 *passim*, 75, 76, 77, 80, 81, 84–8 *passim*, 90, 93, 96, 99 n.2, 107, 114, 116, 117, 118, 119, 128, 135, 135 n.1, 136, 137, 139, 140, 142
falsafa and *sharī'a* 67–71, 75f.
Falqera, Shēmṭoḇ 48 n.48
Faqih 84
Fārābī, Abū Naṣr al- 15, 22–5 *passim*, 28, 36, 36 n.5, 37, 37 n.10, 38 nn.12–13, 40–59 *passim*, 60, 64f., 67, 69, 75–7 *passim*, 81, 83, 84, 85–7 *passim*, 90, **93–114**, 119–20, 121 nn.4,5, 124, 128, 130, 133, 135, 138–41 *passim*, 196, 215f.
his *k. al-siyāsa*; *k. taḥṣil al-sa'āda*; *madina fāḍila*; *Talkhis nawāmis aflāṭūn*; *Fuṣūl-al-madani* 93–114 *passim*
—*see also* Ibn Bājja; Ibn Rushd; Happiness; Philosopher-king; Philosophy, political, practical, theoretical
Fāsī, 'Allāl al- 212
Festugière, A. M. J. 129
Fiqh 17, 19, 22, 62, 66, 69–73 *passim*, 102, 113, 114, 132, 143, 151, 174, 177
Fischel, Walter J. 215
France 200

Gabriel, angel 98 n.2
Gabrieli, F. 92, 93 n.3
Galen 27, 37, 37 n.8, 38 nn.12,13, 40, 46 n.42, 47 n.45, 53 n.63, 54 n.64, 79, 80, 81, 83, 84, 92, 97 n.1
Gardet, Louis 117 n.1, 120 n.5, 138 n.2, 139 n.3
Gauthier, Léon 36 n.4, 67, 68, 69, 70, 76, 88, 91
George, David Lloyd 204 n.22
Ghāniya, Banū 62
Ghazālī, Abū Ḥāmid al- (Ghazzali, Ġazali) 41, 41 n.19, 45, 47, 48 n.48, 73, 75f., 99 n.2, 107, 132, 136
Ibn Khaldūn follows 117, 117 n.4, 119
Ibn Rushd's attack on 75f.
Ghazālī, Muḥammad al- 173, 186, 197–202
Gibb, H. A. R. 3 n.2, 5 n.1, 18
Gnosticism 127
God
approach to 27, 29, 32, 44, 78, 89, 95, 131, 134, 143, 185, 193, 194, 196
authority of 185
belief in 90, 141, 159, 175, 209
of Bible and Qur'an 128
existence of 89
fear of 21, 26
knowledge of 24, 25, 28, 68, 70, 71, 73, 74, 75, 79, 128, 129, 132, 133, 134, 140, 142
love of 24, 128, 129, 131, 133, 134
return to 200
ruler of the universe 32, 46, 95 n.5, 96, 200
will of 25, 67, 72, 74, 90, 107, 142, 143
Gökalp, Ziya 207
Goldziher, I. 44 n.31, 71, 91, 113 n.2, 119 n.2
Good, highest—*see* Happiness
Government 128, 174, 183, 184, 185, 190, 193–200 *passim*, 213—*see also* Caliph, duties of; *Siyāsa*; State; *Tadbir*
of self (*mutawaḥhid*) 39–59 *passim*

Hackforth, R. 129
Ḥadâra 10
Ḥadith 17, 61, 68, 71, 195
Halakhah 69
Happiness, ultimate 22, 39, 40, 52, 54f., 67, 89, 95, 96, 99, 100, 119f., **127–34**, 138
in contemplation of *Intelligibilia* 48
is future life as speculative knowledge 45
guaranteed through prophecy 142
is highest perfection 22, 23, 97
of *mutawaḥḥid* 55
only possible in state 43, 45
possible in isolation 39f., 58f.
true 130
twofold, in this and next world 15, 95, *passim*
is union of divine and human intellect 45
—*see also* Hereafter
Hereafter (world to come) 18, 89, 96, 101, 129–32 *passim*, 137, 142, 143, 144
Hermetic ideas 127
Herzog, D. 53 n.63, 54 n.65, 59 n.82
Ḥijāz 176
Ḥikma 66, 67, 88, 103, 113, 116—*see also* Philosophy; Wisdom
meaning prudence 55
Hinduism 149, 159
Hippocrates 38 n.13
Hobbes, Thomas 196
Holy war—*see Jihād*
Horten, M. 53 n.63
Ḥunain b. Isḥāq 38 n.13, 47 n.45, 80, 83, 84, 86, 90
Ḥusayn, Ṭāhā 192, 202

Index

Ibn Abī 'Uṣaibi'a 84, 91
Ibn Al-Athīr 91
Ibn al-Ṭiqṭaqa 20, 20 n., 21, 30, 60, 79
Ibn Bājja (Avempace) 22, 23, 28, 29, **35–59**, 60, 60 n.1, 61, 64, 69, 82, 85–7 *passim*, 90, 106, 107, 130, 131
dependent on Fārābī 42, 43, 46, 49, 51f., 55–8 *passim*
influences Ibn Rushd 48, 64f., 82
his *k. tadbīru-l-mutawaḥḥid* 35–59 *passim*; *k. ittiṣālu-l-'aql bi-l-insān* 35, 40, 41, 45, 58; *r. fi-l-wadā'* 35, 41
—*see also* Happiness; *Mutawaḥḥid*; Philosophy, practical; Reality; *Tadbīr*
Ibn Dā'ūd, Abraham 134
Ibn Ghāniya 62, 63
Yaḥya b. 'Alī 62
Ibn Ḥazm 71, 72, 91, 99 n.2, 114, 191
Ibn Khaldūn (Jaldūn) **3–16**, 21, 30–3, 60, 79, 80, 87, 91, **115–25**, 186, 188, 191–4 *passim*, 199, 212–15 *passim*
on *'aṣabiyya* 9, 213
his attitude to philosophers' state 5, 115–25
on history, new science of history 4–16, 30–3 *passim*, 115
looking at human society as a whole 3–16 *passim*
on power-state 4–16 *passim*, 22
on religion and state 5, 15, 16
—*see also Mulk*; *Sharī'a*; *Siyāsa*; *'Umrān*
Ibn Miskawaih 20 n.
Ibn Qayyim al-Jawzīyah 181, 183, 209
Ibn Rushd (Averroes) 15, 22–30 *passim*, 36, 36 nn.4,5, 37, 37 n.8, 38 n.12, 41, 47 n.45, 48, 48 n.48, 50 n.53, 52–3, 53 n.62, 55 n.67, 56 nn.72–3, 58, 59 n.82, 97 n.1, 98 n.2, 99 n.2, 104 nn.1,6, 105, 105 n.4, 107–14 *passim*, 119, 119 n.2, 121, 121 n.3, 122 n.4, 124 nn.1,2, 130, 132, 133, 136, 137, 138 n.1, 141, 143, 196
his *Commentary on Plato's 'Republic'* 61–7 *passim*, 78–83 *passim*, 85, 86; *Faṣl al-maqāl* 61, 64, 68–70 *passim*, 72, 77, 82, 88; *Manāhij* 60, 64, 74; *Tahāfut al-tahāfut* 60, 69, 75–6, 79
his criticism of contemporary states 61–7
on *falsafa* and *kalām* 66f., 70, 72
and Fārābī 84–7
and Ibn Khaldūn 79, 80, 124
and Plato and Aristotle 77, 80–4
his political philosophy, **60–90**
on prophecy and *sharī 'a* 72–8
—*see also* Fārābī; Ibn Bājja; Law, revealed; *Sharī'a*; State
Ibn Sīnā (Avicenna) 39 n.13, 41, 46 n.42, 47, 48 n.48, 60 n.1, 69, 76, 77, 81, 85, 87, 119–22 *passim*, 130, 131, 136, 138–43 *passim*, 196
Ibn Tāshfīn, 'Alī b. Yūsuf 63
Yūsuf 63
Ibn Taymīyah 180, 183, 190, 209
Ibn Ṭufail 22, 28, 35, 36, 36 n.4, 41, 41 n.19, 52, 62, 66, 69
Ibn Tūmart 63, 70, 71, 73, 91
Ijmā' 17, 19, 71, 191
Ijtihād 19, 152, 168, 173–7 *passim*, 179–83 *passim*, 185, 187, 191
Ikhtiyār 54, 108
'Ilm 19, 26, 73, 74, 102, 119, 121 n.1
Iltid͟hād͟h 41, 41 n.19, 44, 44 n.32
Imām, *Imāma* 18, 19, 22, 24, 25, 56, 56 n.72, 57, 64, 65, 72, 73, 77, 84, 85, 88, 98–103 *passim*, 110, 124, 177, 183, 184, 188–91 *passim*, 196, 199—*see also* Caliph, caliphate; *Khalifa*; *Khilāfa*
Imitatio Dei 18, 24, 95
'Imperialism', 149, 154, 155, 159, 171, 172, 173, 183, 197–201 *passim*, 203, 207
India 147 ff., 177, 180, 211
British rule 149, 151
Caliphate movement 175
Congress party 159, 177
Mughal rule 149, 160
Partition 147, 159, 177
Intellect, active 43, 44, 45, 48, 50, 51 n.57, 59 n.82, 76, 98, 98 n.2, 106, 132, 137, 141, 142
Intelligibilia—see Spiritual Forms
Interest (*ribā*) 150, 161, 165, 166, 179, 181
Islam, Muslims
common ground with Greek philosophy 25ff., 80, 88, *passim*
in modern state **146–69**
religion and politics in modern **171–206**, **207–14**
restoration of 186
'secular' 158, 160
—*see also* Law, revealed; Philosophy; Reason; Revelation; *Sharī'a*

Jāḥiẓ 53 n.63, 99 n.2, 107
Jamā'a 17, 18, 19, 67, 73, 179—*see also Umma*
Jesus 191
Jihād (*Djihâd*) 9, 66, 71, 73, 83, 103, 110–13 *passim*, 193, 195, 199, 211
Jinnah, Muhammad Ali 153
Judah Halevi (Yehudah Hal-lewi) 48 n.48, 128
Judaism 5, 60, 68, 75, 88, 101, 140, 178, 209, 210
—*see also* Philosophy, Eudaimonía in Jewish and Islamic
Jumhūr 46, 75, 89

Index

Kalām (dialectic theology) 67, 72, 117 n.4, 120
Kathi—*see* Qāḍī
Keddie, Nikkie R. 216
Kedourie, E. 216
Kemāl, Nāmik 207
Kerr, Malcolm H. 216
Khālid, Khālid Muḥammad 198, 199, 200, 202
Khalīfa(*h*) 17, 18, 19, 20, 24, 26, 41, 73, 84, 103, 176, 189, 210
Khan, Ayub 147
Khan, Sayyid Ahmad 151, 159
Khilāfa(*h*) 17, 18, 20, 21, 27, 73, 137, 138, 176, 183, 184, 186, 188–93 *passim*, 196, 197, 209, 210, 212, 213, 214
Khulafā' rāshidūn 123, 139, 173, 188, 189, 190, 198, 210
Kindī, al- 84, 88, 94
Klatzkin, J. 56 n.72
Kohen (*Kohanit*) 24, 56 n.72
Koran—see Qur'an
Kraus, Paul 24 n.2, 38 n.13

Laoust, Henri 183, 204 nn.1,15,20, 205 n.29
Law, revealed 67–78, 88–90 *passim*, 116–18 *passim*, 121–4 *passim*, 127–34 *passim*, 136–8 *passim*, 143, 150–3 *passim*, 162–6 *passim*, 168, 175, 177, 178, 179, 182–6 *passim*, 188, 190, 192, 214—*see also* Religion; *Sharī'a*
  central position of 22ff., *passim*
  contrasted with *Nómos—see Nómos*
  and *falsafa* share aim 67–71
  secular—*seeNómos*
Lawgiver
  Ibn Rushd on prophetic 73ff.
  and *Imām* identical with prophet and philosopher-king 100f., 103
  —*see also* Prophet; Ruler
Lebon, Gustave 200
Leo Africanus 65
Leon, Messer 56 n.72
Lévi-Provençal, E. 91
Lloyd George—*see* George
Locke, John 196

Ma(c)chiavelli, N. 4, 7, 21
Macdonald, D. B. 117
Madīna—see State
Madkour, Ibrahim 93 n.1, 97 n.1, 107 n.5
Maghreb 60, 61, 63, 64, 88, 115 n.2, 119 n2, 124
Maimonides, Moses 23 n.1, 24, 36 n.6, 76, 90, 93, 101, 122 n.4, 128, 133, 134
Mahdi, Muhsin 215, 216
Malaya 147ff., 161–6
  University of 167, 168
Malik 20, 192, 194, 196, 210, 213
  mulūk al-tawā'if 55, 87
Mamlūks 192
Mantinus (Mantino), Jacob 56 n.72
Maqqarī, al- 91
Marrākushī, al- 71, 91
Maṣlaḥah 183, 195, 196
Massignon, L. 107 n.1.
Maudūdī, Abul A'lā 151, 201
Māwardī, al- 5, 5 n.1, 17, 18, 18 n.1, 19, 19 n., 41, 102, 191, 205 n.40
Mehren, A. 119
Menahem b. Abraham Bonafos—*see* Bonafos
Metaphysics 7, 85, 97, 128, 130, 132, 133, 138
Miracles 74, 89, 141
Morocco 212
Moses 19, 74, 133, 136, 140
Mossul 20
Mu'āwiya 63, 186, 189
Mufti 163, 166, 168
Muḥammad 9, 17, 72–5 *passim*, 77, 78, 88, 90, 98 n.2, 123, 130, 136, 139, 140–3 *passim*, 151, 153, 173, 184, 185, 188, 189, 190, 192–6 *passim*, 198, 200, 210, 214
Mujtahids 19, 174, 177, 180, 184
Mulk 20, 21, 28, 63, 123, 189, 193, 195, 197, 212, 213, 214
Munk, S. 36 n.5, 51, 53 n.63, 59 n.82, 91
Muqallids 19
Mūsā, Salāmah 201
Muslim Brotherhood (Egypt) 173, 197, 201, 202, 204 n.12, 207
Muslim League 147
Mutakallimūn 61, 66, 67, 70–4 *passim*, 120, 121
Mutawaḥḥid 45, 51, 57ff.
Mu 'tazila 18

Nāmūs, Nīmūs 79
Naql 74
Narboni, Moses 35, 49 n.51, 51, 53 n.63, 56 n.72, 59 n.82
Nationalism 146–69, 173, 174, 178, 180, 181, 189, 190, 197, 199, 200–3 *passim*, 207–10 *passim*, 212, 214
Nawābit 51, 52, 53, 53 n.63, 57 n.75
Neoplatonism, Neoplatonic ideas 127, 129, 130, 134, 137
Neopythagorean ideas 127
Nomocracy 25
Nómos 25, 61, 74, 79, 81, 85, 101, 133, 138
  and *Sharī'a* 87–90, 101, 138

Pakistan 146ff., 201, 210, 212
Panaitius 135, 139

Pan-Islamism 207, 212
Pan-Malayan Islamic Party 161
Parwez, Ghulam A. 151
Pascal 128
Perfection
  four-fold 97, 101, 107
  three-fold 18
  —*see also* Happiness
Persia 200
Philo of Alexandria 140
Philosopher-King (Plato's) 22, *passim*
  in Fārābī 100f.
  in Ibn Rushd 77
  identical with lawgiver and *imām* 22
  —*see also Imām*; Lawgiver; Rulers
Philosophy
  Eudaimonía in Jewish and Islamic **127–34**
  political **35–59, 60–92, 93** 114; aim of 45, 95, 97
  practical 22f., 47, 47 n.48
  theoretical, necessary for intellectual perfection 24–9 *passim*, 82ff., 97, 99–101, 107
  —*see also* Aristotle; Plato; Politics
Pines, S. 38 n.12
Plato 5, 12, 22–9 *passim*, 35 n.2, 36–41 *passim*, 43, 43 n.28, 44 n.30, 46–51 *passim*, 53, 53 n.63, 56, 56 nn.72,73, 57, 58, 60, 60 n.1, 61, 62, 64–7 *passim*, 69, 70, 72, 75, 77–90 *passim*, 92–7 *passim*, 99–111 *passim*, 113, 113 n.1, 114, 114 n.1, 123 n.2, 124, 124 n.1, 127–32 *passim*, 134–7 *passim*, 139, 141, 142, 143, 196
Plessner, M. 48 n.48
Plotinus 94, 95 n.6, 127, 128, 141
Politics
  Ibn Khaldūn's view on **3–16, 115–25**
  in Islam **207–14**
  orthodox theory of 17-20 *passim*
  —*see also* Islam; Religion
Pope 183, 185, 204 n.25
Porphyry 94, 127
Proclus 94, 127
Prophecy, Prophet 24, 25, 26, 51 n.57, 67, 69, 72–8, 81, 85, 88, 94, 98, 100, 101, 102, 102 n.1, 107, 108, 110, 117, 120–4 *passim*, 128, 132, 135, 138–43 *passim*, 148, 186, 191, 193, 194, 200, 213
  philosophical theory of prophecy **135–44**
  —*see also* Law, revealed; Lawgiver; Muḥammad
Pythagoras 141

Qāḍī (Kathi) 62, 84, 163, 165, 166, 195
Qibbūṣ 80
Qifṭī, al- 102
Quraish (Quraysh) 19, 176
Qur'ān (*Koran*) 17, 19, 61, 68, 71, 72, 74, 75, 77, 86, 106, 117, 120, 128, 131, 132, 141, 150, 151, 152, 155, 157, 165, 168, 173, 176, 180, 182, 187–91 *passim*, 193, 195, 197, 200, 201, 202, 205 n.50, 210, 211
Quṭb, Sayyid 201

Rahman, Abdul (Tunku) 168
Rahman, F. 135, 138, 139, 140–3 *passim*
Ra'is 42, 51 n.57
Ramaḍān, Sa'īd 202
Ramadhan 164, 166
Rāzī, Fajr al-dīn 120 n.6
Rāziq, 'Alī 'Abd-al- 173, 184, 188–97, 198, 199, 205 nn.41,56, 210
Reality 97
  is perception of Existing Things 99
  —*see also* Happiness
Reason 7, 12, 18, 19, 23, 68–72 *passim*, 90, 99 n.2, 117, 118, 120, 121 n.5, 122, 125, 130, 134, 194, 197, 203, 209
Reform 150ff., 173, 175, 177, 178, 179, 181, 199, 209, 210
Religion 15, 16, 21, 25, 31, 32, 60, 61, 64, 87, 96, 99 n.2, 102, 106, 107, 109, 141f., 148, 153
  and politics 149, 152, 159, 164, 165, 166, 169, **171–206, 207–14**
  —*see also* Law, revealed; Lawgiver; Revelation
Renan, Ernest 91
Revelation 9, 15, 17–20 *passim*, 22, 27, 53, 68, 72–8 *passim*, 88, 89, 95, 96, 98–101 *passim*, 106, 116, 117, 118, 122, 128, 133, 136–42 *passim*, 175, 186, 192, 194, 199, 210—*see also* Law, revealed; Reason; Religion
Revolution
  French 198, 203, 208, 210
  Russian 198
Reward and punishment 89, 96, 131, 142
Ribā—see Interest
Riḍā, Rashīd 172, 173, 174, 175–88, 189, 190, 191, 197, 199, 201, 204 n.25, 210
Robin, Leon 53 n.63
Rosenthal, Erwin I. J. 3, 14, 21 n.5, 23 nn.1,2, 28 nn.1–3, 29 nn.1,2, 30 n.1., 36 nn.5,6, 37 n.9, 38 n.13, 39 n.15, 40 n.16, 41 nn. 20f., 42 n.22, 47 n.45, 48 n.50, 51 n.57, 53 n.62, 56 n.72, 60 n.1, 91, 92, 93 n.1, 99 n.2, 101 n.6, 104 nn.1,5, 106 n.5, 107 n.3, 108 n.1, 114 n.2, 118 n.3, 123 n.3, 124 n.1, 135 n.1, 136 n.1, 139 n.3, 141 nn.1,2,5, 143 nn.1,2, 144 n., 210 n.1, 212 n.3
Rosenthal, Franz 84, 90, 93 n.2, 215
Rulers, duties and qualifications of 17, 19, 20, 21, 22, 24–7 *passim*, 39, 41, 42, 44, 45,

50, 50 n.53, 53, 98–103 *passim*, 107, 110–13 *passim*, 122, 124, 129, 136, 137, 138, 139, 162, 192, 199, 213—*see also* Caliph; *Imām*; *Malik*; *Ra'is*
Rushd, Banū—*see* Ibn Rushd

Sa'āda—*see* Happiness
Saif al-Dawla 112
Salafiyyah 176, 180
Shar' (*Šar'*) 18, 61, 68, 74, 79, 88, 115, 122, 123, 124, 191—*see also Sharī'a*
Shari 'a (*Šarī'a*; *Sharī'a(h)*) 5, 7, 12, 15, 18, 20, 21, 22, 24, 26, 27, 32, 41, 44, 45 n.37, 60, 61, 64, 65, 67–81 *passim*, 84–90 *passim*, 95 n.5, 96, 101, 107, 109, 122, 123, 132, 137, 138, 140, 143, 165, 171, 174, 175, 177, 181, 183, 184, 185, 187, 188, 190, 193, 195, 196, 198, 199, 200, 204, 207, 209, 211, 213, 214
  and *nómos* 87–90
Shaw, George Bernard 200
Sherwani, H. K. 93 n.1
Shittūf 80
Shūrā 174, 185
Simon, Heinrich 215
Siyāsa 20, 21, 46 n.42, 101 n.7
  'aqliya 122, 123
  dīniya 214
  madaniyya 94, 123
  shar'iyya 190
Socialism 183, 201
Social justice 178, 179, 183
Socrates 40 n.17, 141
Sophists 72
Spiritual Forms (*Intelligibilia*) 40, 41, 43, 48, 50, 54, 57, 82, 97, 99, 118
State
  ideal, based on *Sharī'a* 5, 15, 17–20 *passim*, 73–7 *passim*, 109, 150–5 *passim* (Islamic); based on philosopher-king's *nómos* in Plato's *Politeia* 22, 24, 25, 29, *passim*; *Shari 'a* superior to *nómos* for Ibn Rushd 73–6, 88–90, *passim*
  imperfect Platonic (contrasted with perfect—*fāḍila*) 49, 49 n.51, 51, 51 n.57, 86, 104–9
  madīna imāmiyya 56f., 64f.
  modern national, either Islamic or Muslim 146–69 *passim*, 171–204 *passim*, 207–14 *passim*
  power —, of Ibn Khaldūn 5–15 *passim*, 121–5 *passim*
  —*see also Khilāfa*; *Madīna*; *Mulk*; Prophecy; Religion; *Siyāsa*
Steinschneider, Moritz 36 n.5, 38 n.13, 51, 56 n.72, 92, 93 n.1
Stoics, Stoicism (the Stoa) 127, 129, 135, 137, 139, 141
Strauss, Leo 37 n.7, 48 n.48, 69, 92, 93 n.1, 139 n.3
Sufis, Sufism 39 n.13, 41 n.19, 51, 53 n.63, 107, 119, 121
Suhrawardī, al- 107 n.1
Sunna(h) 17, 71, 151, 152, 168, 176, 180, 188, 189, 191, 193, 195, 197, 200, 201, 202, 205 n.50, 210, 211
Syria 200, 201

Tabarī,al- 56 n.72
Tadbīr 46, 47, 52—*see also* Ibn Bājja; *Mutawaḥḥid*
Tafarnuj—*see* Europeanisation
Tajsīm—*see* Anthropomorphism
Talbi, Mohammed 215
Tanzīl 137
Taqlīd 185
Theocracy 20, 25
Torah 15, 72, 74, 79—*see also Sharī'a*
Turkey 169, 172, 178–82 *passim*, 189, 200, 207, 208, 210

'Ulamā 151, 165, 173, 174, 179, 180, 182, 184, 201, 202, 210, 211, 212
Umayyads 176, 192
Umma(h) 123, 138, 191, 199, 207, 209, 212—*see also Jamā 'a*
'Umrān 5, 32, 115, 116, 121, 121 n.4
University—*see* Aligarh; Ankara; Malaya

Vajda, Georges 120
Van den Bergh, S. 138 n.1
Van Vloten, G. 53 n.63
Vaux, Carra de 97 n.1

Waḥy—*see* Revelation
Walzer, R. 37 n.8, 38 nn.12,13, 84, 90, 93 nn.1,2, 135, 215
Waṭan 207
Wisdom, wise 26, 99
Women, place of, in Islam 27, 65, 66, 80, 81, 150, 157, 164, 166, 167, 179, 182, 201

Xenophon 105

Yazīd (b. Mu'āwiyah) 192

Zaghlūl Pasha 177
Zakāt 164, 166, 178
Zuhd 132, 144

CONTENTS

For the reader's information, this is the list of contents for vol. I of *Studia Semitica*—'Jewish Themes'.

INTRODUCTION *page* vii

PART I · THE HEBREW BIBLE AND ITS EXEGESIS

1 Some aspects of the Hebrew monarchy 3
(*Journal of Jewish Studies*, vol.IX, nos.1 and 2, 1958, pp.1–18)

2 Don Isaac Abravanel: financier, statesman and scholar, 1437–1937 21
(*Bulletin of the John Rylands Library*, vol.21, no.2, October 1937, pp.445–78)

3 Rashi and the English Bible 56
(*Bulletin of the John Rylands Library*, vol.24, no.1, April 1940, pp.138–67)

4 Saadya Gaon: an appreciation of his Biblical exegesis 86
(*Bulletin of the John Rylands Library*, vol.27, no.1, December 1942, pp.168–78)

5 Saadya's exegesis of the Book of Job 97
(*Saadya Studies*, ed. E.I.J. Rosenthal. Manchester University Press, 1943, pp.177–205)

6 Sebastian Muenster's knowledge and use of Jewish exegesis 127
(*Essays in Honour of Dr J.H. Hertz* [Chief Rabbi]. Edward Goldston, London, 1943, pp.351–69)

7 Edward Lively: Cambridge Hebraist 147
(*Essays and Studies Presented to S.A. Cook*, ed. D.W. Thomas. Taylor's Foreign Press, London, 1950, pp.95–112)

8 Anti-Christian polemic in medieval Bible commentaries 165
(*Journal of Jewish Studies*, vol.XI, nos.3 and 4, 1960, pp.115–35)

9 *Jüdische Antwort* 187
(*Kirche und Synagoge*, ed. K.H. Rengstorf and S. von Kortzfleisch. Ernst Klett Verlag, Stuttgart, 1968, pp.307–62)

10 The study of the Bible in medieval Judaism 244
(*The Cambridge History of the Bible*, vol.2, ed. G.W.H. Lampe. Cambridge University Press, 1969 (completed 1957), pp.252–79)

PART II · MEDIEVAL JEWISH RELIGIOUS PHILOSOPHY

11 Maimonides' conception of State and Society 275
(*Moses Maimonides*, ed. I. Epstein. The Soncino Press, London, 1935, pp.191–204)

12 Avicenna's influence on Jewish thought 290
(*Avicenna: Scientist & Philosopher*, ed. G.M. Wickens. Luzac & Co., London, 1952, pp.66–83)

13 Torah and *nómos* in medieval Jewish philosophy 309
(*Studies in Rationalism, Judaism & Universalism*, ed. R. Loewe. Routledge and Kegan Paul, London, 1966, pp.215–30)

PART III · *WISSENSCHAFT DES JUDENTUMS*

14 Ismar Elbogen and the New Jewish Learning 327
(*Year Book VIII*, The Leo Baeck Institute, Horovitz Publishing Co. Ltd., London, 1963, pp.3–28)

APPENDIX OF ADDITIONAL NOTES 353

INDEX 355